W9-BXE-551

Exit Strategy Planning

Exit Strategy Planning

Grooming Your Business for Sale or Succession

JOHN HAWKEY

GOWER

Published by
Gower Publishing Limited
Gower House
Croft Road
Aldershot
Hampshire GU11 3HR
England

Gower
Suite 420, 101 Cherry Street
Burlington, VT 05401–4405 USA

British Library Cataloguing in Publication Data
Hawkey, John
Exit strategy planning : grooming your business for sale or succession
1. Sale of small businesses 2. Business planning 3. Small business - Finance
I. Title
658'.022

Library of Congress Control Number: 2002104534

ISBN 0-566-08498-8

Typeset in 9 point Stone Serif by IML Typographers, Birkenhead, Merseyside and printed in Great Britain by MPG Books Ltd., Bodmin, Cornwall.

Contents

List of Figures

List of Abbreviations

AIM	Alternative Investment Market
BATR	business asset taper relief
BFA	British Franchise Association
BIMBO	management buy-in, buyout
BOLR	buyer of last resort
CEO	chief executive officer
CGT	capital gains tax
CVA	company voluntary arrangement
CVL	creditors' voluntary liquidation
DCF	discounted cash flow
ESP	exit strategy planning
FD	finance director
FMP	future maintainable profits
IA	indexation allowance
IBO	institutional buyout
IHT	inheritance tax
IPO	initial public offering
IR	Inland Revenue
IVA	individual voluntary arrangement
LPA	Law of Property Act
LSE	London Stock Exchange
MBI	management buy-in
MBO	management buyout
MESP	master exit strategy plan
MSP	maintainable super profit (in Appendix 2)
MSP	master succession plan (in Appendix 4)
MVL	member's voluntary liquidation
NTA	net tangible asset
OFEX	The off exchange share marketing and trading facility
p/e	price earnings
plc	public limited company
PR	public relations
PVA	partnership voluntary liquidation
SME	small to medium-sized enterprise
STEP	short-term exit plan
STMESP	short-term master exit strategy plan
SWOT	strengths, weaknesses, opportunities, threats
UKLA	United Kingdom Listing Authority
VC	venture capitalist
WIP	work in progress

Acknowledgements

I first became interested in exit strategy planning (ESP) in 1989 in Australia and started to develop a specialised ESP programme in 1991. Since that time, I have had assistance from many quarters.

In Australia I would like to thank Ross Honeyman for his ideas, especially about how ESP should be integrated with personal financial planning; Keith Pfaul and Eddie Cohen who first worked with me on introducing the programme to private business owners; the New South Wales Chamber of Commerce who supported the programme from the beginning by holding seminars on the topic for their members; people too numerous to mention from the AMP Society with whom I worked on producing an ESP programme for their self-employed agents; and Tiara Hini my secretary who spent hundreds of hours working on the consultants' manual (which is the predecessor to this book) and deciphering my handwriting.

Since returning to the UK in 1999, I have received great help in finalizing the contents of this book from various people and organizations and I would specifically like to thank the following: John Fairhurst and Sons who helped me with the taxation appendix; Malcolm Fortnum who provided an insight into the workings of MBOs in private businesses in the UK; my good friend Maurice Glover who assisted me with the material on insolvency and ceasing to trade; and my colleague Geoffrey Winnard who has assisted with various parts of the book and developed with me the capacity to provide ESP consulting across the UK.

Last, I thank my wife Gillian and my daughter Carmen who have supported me unstintingly throughout the long period of gestation of this book and my mother, Patricia Bradshaw, for assisting me with the proof reading.

John Hawkey
Millington 2002

Introduction: The Story of Bill and Carol

The story of Bill and Carol, typical private business owners, who did not plan for the disposal of their business and who paid the ultimate price for their lack of planning, demonstrates why exit strategy planning is so important.

The story of Bill and Carol

Bill and Carol started their business in Coventry in 1975. In the beginning it was run from Bill's garage where he repaired washing machines. Carol looked after the accounts side of the business.

Three children and 20 years later, they had expanded to general manufacture of 'white goods' components. The business turned over £1 million p.a., employed 15 people and made an annual profit before owners' drawings of £120,000. Their daughter was employed in the sales department, but their two sons were not in the business. Their savings were modest, as they believed that they could sell their business for a large capital sum for their retirement.

They had been conscientious, if slightly unsophisticated, managers. They had brought in consultants from time to time to advise them on their business planning but, usually, after a little while, the process was forgotten and the business plans gathered dust.

In 1997, Bill and Carol decided the time had come to sell. They were both in their late fifties and were very tired of the long hours and pressures involved in being small business owners. Turnover was beginning to drop and profitability was also falling.

Their two sons were not interested in the business and their daughter was soon to start a family and did not want to take on any further responsibilities. Their only option to dispose of the business appeared to be a trade sale, probably to a competitor within the same industry. They had never considered any other method of disposal, such as selling to their managers or employees, and had not groomed anyone within the business who could take it over. They hoped that the sale of the business would realize enough to pay off the mortgage on their commercial property, leave them enough to give something to each of their children and to retire in comfort.

'Although the accounts might not show it,' said Carol 'this is a very profitable business. We would not sell it for less than £1 million.'

In 1999 the business was put up for sale with a company broker, who expressed doubts at the £1 million asking price, but advertised it at that price nevertheless. Two long years later, when turnover had dropped to £750,000 p.a., and profit before owners' drawings was barely £50,000 the business was sold for £200,000: stock at £150,000 and goodwill of £50,000. Bill and Carol could not clear the mortgage on their commercial property so they were forced to sell it for far less than they had hoped. They did not have enough to give the children their gifts and, although they had sufficient capital to retire, their retirement was not going to be as luxurious as they had planned.

Does this sound familiar? Can we blame their problems on the downturn in manufacturing, or bad luck, or is there a more obvious and fundamental reason for the dashing of Bill and Carol's dreams?

The real reason is that Bill and Carol never planned for the day they would have to dispose of their business. They never took the necessary steps to decide how to dispose of it, or how to remove those things that depressed the business's value, or to improve the business's appeal to potential purchasers.

These were some of the things that were wrong with their business at the time of sale:

- There was no middle management in the business, so when Bill and Carol left they took all the inside knowledge of the business (including the crucial customer contact) with them and, consequently, limited the potential buyers to owner-managers like themselves, to the exclusion of pure investors.
- Their accounts had always been prepared to depress profits and taxation, and the potential purchasers could not be convinced that it was more profitable than the books indicated it to be.
- In the two years it took to sell the business Bill and Carol lost enthusiasm for their work, the business lost direction and took on a tired, depressed look. More importantly, profits also slipped.
- The timing was not right to sell the commercial property, but they had to sell and, consequently, did not get the best price.
- They had no time to persuade their children of the benefits of taking over the business and, even if they had persuaded them, there was no time to groom them for ownership.
- They had not spent enough time on their own financial planning, or considered it in an integrated way in conjunction with their disposal plans.

Why this book was written

Having read this story I hope that you will have begun to realize that, by planning for the disposal of your business in a measured, methodical way (through a process we call exit strategy planning), you can avoid the problems that beset Bill and Carol.

Whatever your reason for wishing to exit your business – whether it be for retirement, or because you wish to buy another business, or because you are considering a flotation on the Stock Exchange, or considering an offer from a management buyout team, or thinking of transferring the business to an heir – this book will show you how to go about planning for your exit, and how you can maximize your after-tax disposal price.

As we saw with Bill and Carol, failure to plan for the exit from your business can have highly damaging outcomes for you. Some of the more usual ones are listed below:

- Your choice of exit option is not the optimum one for you or your business, in so far as you do not achieve the maximum price or personal satisfaction.
- At the time of disposal your business is in a state that does not attract the best price.

- The implementation of your exit strategy is rushed and disorganized.
- You are not prepared for due diligence and are at the mercy of purchasers or investors and their advisers.
- You have failed to maximize your taxation and personal financial position.
- You are dissatisfied with the results of all the years of hard work.

When should you start to plan?

A common mistake made by many private business owners is to delay their exit planning because they believe that:

- they are too young, or
- they will not be disposing of their business for several years, or
- they are immune to personal disaster.

In this book we show you why it is never too early to start planning, particularly with regard to structural, continuity and risk management issues (because you never know what might happen to you or your partners or shareholders). More importantly perhaps, we hope that by reading this book you will discover for yourself the advantages of giving yourself time to plan for your exit so that you can reap the maximum reward from your business disposal.

How to use this book to plan your exit

This book covers the complete process of planning for your exit. It is divided into four main parts, being:

- Part 1: Laying the Foundations
- Part 2: Choosing your Exit Strategy
- Part 3: Preparing and Implementing your Plans
- Part 4: Appendices.

In Part 1 we look at why you might wish to exit your business and how this can affect the choice of exit option and the timing of your disposal. We explain to you the importance of your business structure in laying the foundations for a smooth exit and in minimizing the impact of taxation. We emphasize that it is vital to get early, expert taxation advice. Our aim is that your understanding of the basics of current taxation legislation will give you enough information to ensure you ask the right questions of your taxation advisers. We also consider the importance of ensuring that your arrangements with partners or fellow shareholders facilitate your planning so that there are no hindrances to your exit. Finally, We explain the importance of understanding the current value of your business and what it could be worth at the probable disposal date, so that you are able to put your plans into the proper context and not be deluded by unrealistic expectations.

In Part 2 we show you how to choose the optimum exit option for your business. We do this by first explaining the options to you in brief and then showing you how you can decide on a shortlist of probable exit options by working through the 'options elimination' worksheet (Figure 5.2). Once you have made your shortlist of provisional exit options (or even decided provisionally on one option only) you should then read the detailed explanation of your provisional options in Part 4. (If you wish, you do not need to read about the options that do not apply to you.) Having studied your provisional options carefully, you will be in a position to make your final choice of exit option. Finally in this part, we prepare you for the elimination of the impediments to sale in your business, those things that will reduce its value when you come to dispose of it.

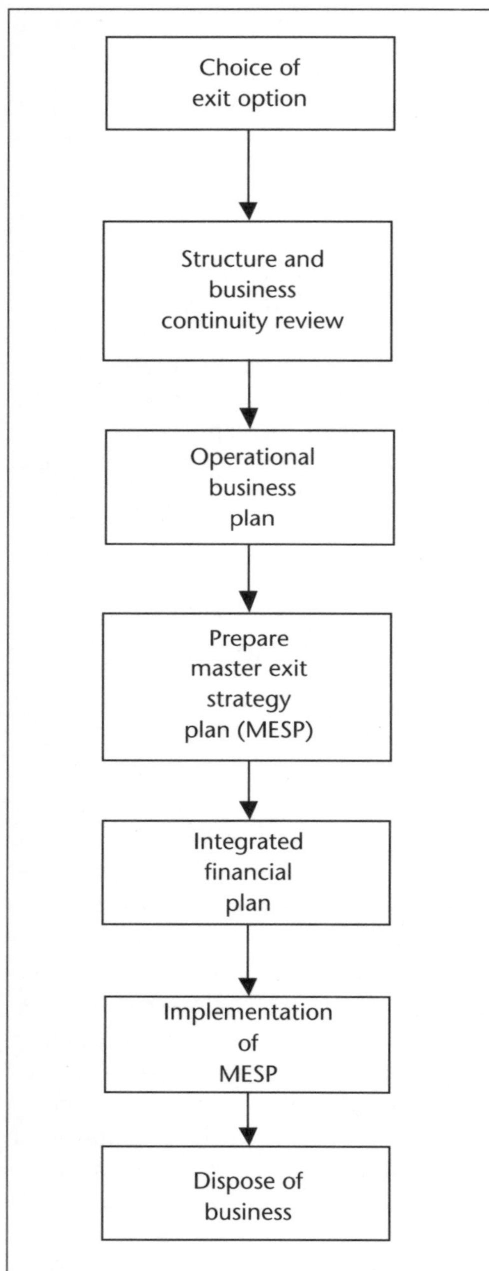

Figure I.1 Exit Strategy Planning Overview

In Part 3 we move on to the planning aspects of your exit strategy. We begin by looking at the operational aspects of your business, showing you how to grow the business and improve its value through the production of a realistic business plan. We next address short-term planning (a compromise you could consider when it is impossible for you to plan properly for your exit over a longer period). We then demonstrate how you bring together your business continuity planning and your operational business planning in a master exit strategy plan (MESP). Next, we look at some ways in which you can integrate your personal financial planning with your exit planning so that all your plans are neatly brought together should you wish to retire. Finally in this part, we show you how to implement your MESP through your chosen exit option so that you can maximize both your financial return and your personal satisfaction.

In Part 4 we take an in-depth look at the more technical aspects of exit strategy planning. First, we explain in detail the impact of taxation on business disposals and we explain in depth how you can establish a value for your business. Both these topics are vital to all business owners involved in exit strategy planning. Next we consider the special position that self-employed agents, licensees and franchisees find themselves in when trying to dispose of their businesses for value and suggest some ways you can go about this.

We then look at the major exit options available to the owners of private businesses in some detail. Once you have chosen your shortlist of provisional exit options (which we show you how to do in Part 2), we suggest that you study carefully the relevant appendices in Part 4 so that you can make your final decision about which option you think is best suited to your business. Each appendix will also show you how to undertake your exit through the option you have chosen.

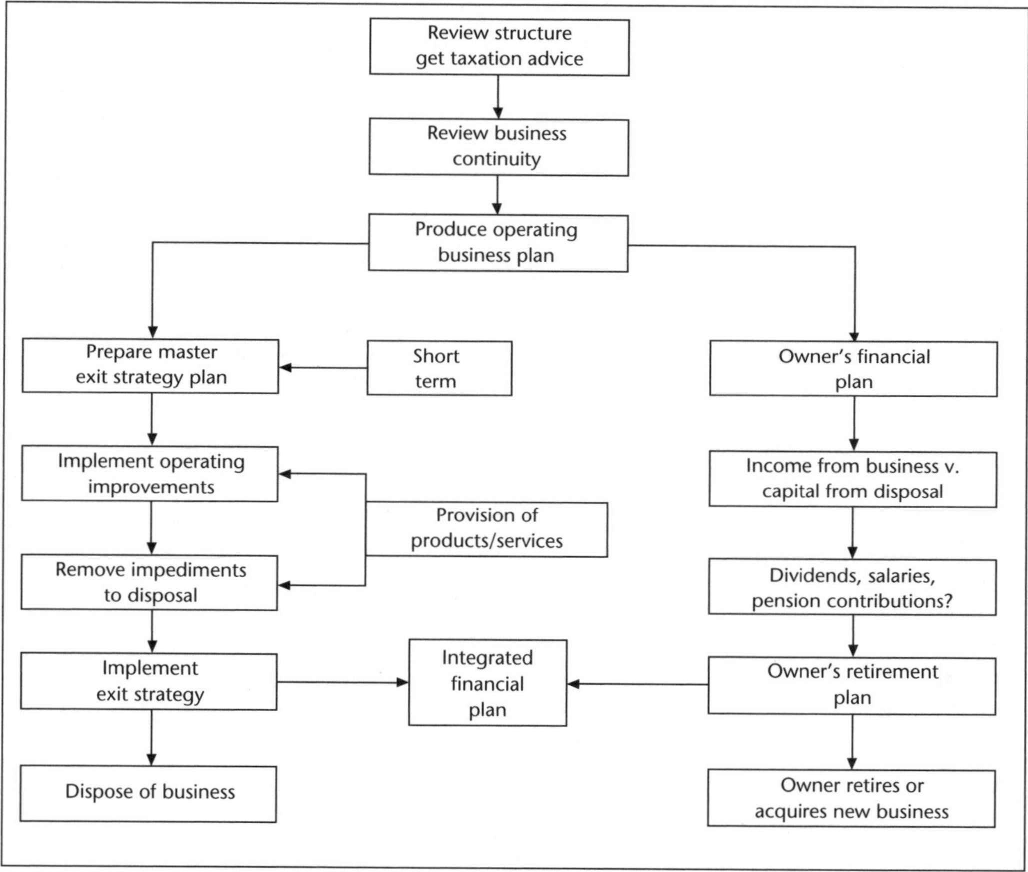

Figure I.2 Exit Strategy Planning Detailed Overview

PART 1 *Laying the Foundations*

CHAPTER 1

The Importance of Time and Timing

Why you might wish to exit

Many owners of private businesses will make the decision to exit their businesses because they have reached natural retirement age, or because they are ill, or because they have decided for personal reasons that they have just had enough. Others will make this decision because they see an opportunity to dispose of a business for a tidy profit, or because they wish to purchase another business, or because of events or influences outside their immediate control (for example, their business is failing).

The reason for wishing to exit can help to clarify at least two other aspects of your exit strategy planning. The first is the important issue of how you will exit, while the second is the sometimes vital one of when you will exit. Figure 1.1 looks at the 'Why?' decisions and how they are likely to influence your exit outcomes.

How you might exit (the choice of exit options)

The reason for your exit could influence, or limit, the choice of exit options available to you. Where you are exiting immediately because of ill health, there is little time to plan properly for an exit through a management buyout (MBO), family succession, franchising or a public flotation route and you will, probably, sell through a trade sale or a close down. If your reason for exiting is that you feel the time has come to pass the business on to an heir, obviously your exit option is limited to a family succession. If you are planning to sell because you wish to partly retire by keeping a minority equity interest and a part-time job in your old business, this will, probably limit your options to a family succession or a third party sale (and, consequently, reduce the number of potential purchasers). If you need to exit your business because it is insolvent, your exit route will be through liquidation. In all these cases the limiting of the choice of exit option could reduce the price you receive from disposal.

When you will exit

The reason for your exit (or why you need to exit) can have a direct influence on when the exit will take place. The timing of your exit could be important for at least three reasons, namely:

- the state of the economy at the time
- the time you have to plan
- the impact of taxation.

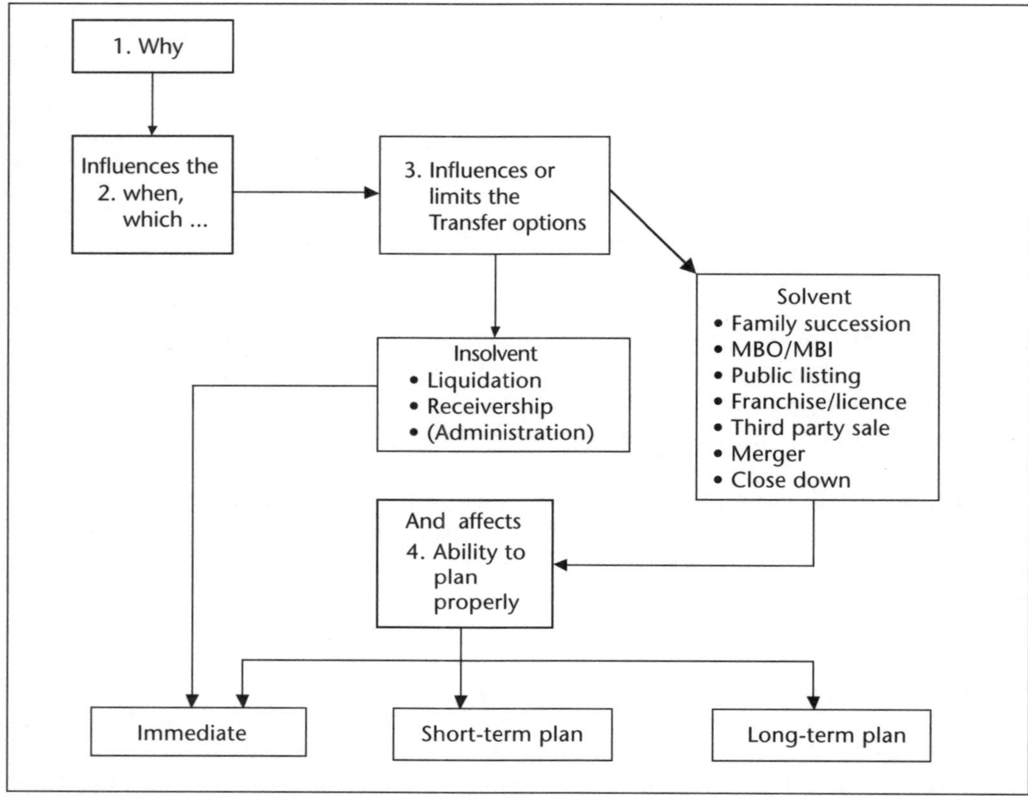

Figure 1.1 Why, When and How do I Want to Exit my Business?

THE STATE OF THE ECONOMY

The general state of the economy and the health of your own particular industry sector will have an influence on your selling price, whatever your exit option (with, perhaps, the exception of a family succession). If, for example, you are disposing of your business because of ill health, or because you are desperate to retire, you will probably want to exit immediately. In this case you will have little opportunity to pick the best time to sell (in terms of the economic cycle).

Should you have to sell because of the death of a partner or shareholder (particularly where there is no shareholders' agreement in place) you might have to act immediately with no time at all to plan. Here you will have to sell the business in whatever economic climate you find yourself.

When there is no pressure on you to dispose of your business and you set your own timetable, you should be able to choose a time to exit when the economic conditions are favourable for your industry and the economy generally.

TIME TO PLAN

The time you have to plan will have a crucial influence on the amount you can achieve through grooming your business for sale. Ideally, you should allow three to five years to implement most exit strategies (and longer for family successions), so that you are able to groom your business for disposal. However, circumstances beyond your control can sometimes dictate that you have to dispose of your business over a short period, or immediately. Where this is the case, and you do not already have an exit plan in place, you will have a very limited choice of exit option and very little time to achieve real improvements to the business structure and operations.

For all business owners, it is important to address immediately structural and continuity issues for your business. These can be considered as the beginning of your risk management planning and will give you some protection against events outside your control. If you are starting up a new business, you should ensure that you have advice on the most tax-effective business structure (with your eventual exit in mind) and, if you have partners or shareholders, you should put a shareholders' agreement in place from the beginning. By doing this when the time comes to plan your exit you will already have the foundations in place!

With the foundations in place, if events go smoothly and you are able to plan your exit over a reasonable period (and you are able to be flexible with regard to the timing of your disposal), you will be in the prime position to reap the benefits of a three- to five-year plan. If things do not go smoothly and you have a more urgent need to get out, at least you should not be inhibited from selling by your partners or shareholders and you should be able to take advantage of the tax reliefs and allowances available. You might also still be able to devote at least a year to a short-term exit plan, which will give you some opportunity to groom your business for sale and, consequently, improve your exit price.

Planning ahead

Of course, there is no such thing as a perfect business and it is unlikely in practice that all your plans will be completely fulfilled by the time you sell your equity. However, this must still be your aim. One thing is certain: you will get much closer to perfection if you plan well ahead. Finding and training the right successor takes time; grooming a business takes time; paying back debt takes time; planning to minimize your taxation bill can take time; every worthwhile accomplishment in business takes time.

There are two very important rules of exit strategy planning that you should understand from the outset, which are as follows:

1. Plan well ahead.
2. Have a sense of urgency (but be thorough) in implementing your plans.

How long do I need to plan?

You need to decide whether you will embark on a short-, medium- or a long-term exit strategy plan. A short-term plan is anything under two years, a medium-term plan is between two and four years; and a long-term plan is for more than four years. The approach to planning in each case is different and can be best approached by considering which of the steps it will be possible to take in each one.

Any *short-term exit strategy plan* is a compromise. If you are unable or unwilling to delay your disposal for at least two years you will be limited in what you can do to improve the value and saleability of your business. In the event, what can be achieved in a short-term plan will depend on such things as the state of your business operations and what its impediments to sale are.

In summary, the limitations of a short term plan are as follows:

1. Your exit options will be limited, because some options take longer to accomplish than is possible in a short-term time frame.
2. The effects of restructuring to improve your taxation position can take several years, so you might not be able to do much here. You can attempt to put shareholders'/partners' agreements in place, but this can be difficult where your co-owners have word that your are selling up shortly.
3. The extent of grooming of a successor and/or management could be very limited in the time available.
4. The ability to remove impediments to sale is limited in a short-term plan and you should refer to Chapter 6 for details of this.
5. Growth through acquisitions is possible but unlikely, whereas organic growth is virtually impossible. Success here will not only be dependent on time available; some businesses will never grow regardless of the time devoted to this task.
6. You should have ample time to undertake these preparations.
7. Integration of your plans might be difficult and will depend on how far ahead you have planned your personal finances.
8. The disposal itself should give you no problems.

(For a more detailed explanation of removal of impediments you should refer to Chapter 8 on short-term planning and Chapter 6 on impediments to sale.)

As to the *medium-term plan*, in two to four years you could achieve nearly all your exit strategy objectives, depending on the size of the business and, of course, on the extent of its problems.

Figure 1.3 on page 9 lists the important stages of planning your exit. With a medium-term plan you should note the following:

- You should have few problems with steps 1 to 3.
- Step 4, the grooming of your successor, could be a problem, depending on the age and experience of your successor. This issue could be sufficient to force you, however reluctantly, to choose a longer time frame.
- Step 5, the successful removal of your impediments to sale, will depend on what they are. (Chapter 6 will provide you with more information on this.)
- Step 6 could be partially successful, though too many people underestimate the time it takes to turn around or grow a business. (Note also the comments under 'the short-term plan' above.)
- You should have no problems with step 7.
- Your success with step 8 will depend on how long you have planned this aspect of your personal affairs, while step 9 will be fine.

A planning period of over four years (*long-term planning*) is ideal for you to achieve all your exit strategy aims and your personal estate planning objectives. This is the planning time frame we recommend you adopt if at all possible. The exception to this could be the aim to grow your business to a target size where the target turns out to be overambitious, or the business is such that it cannot grow. Similarly, working on removing impediments to sale does not guarantee that they will be removed.

THE IMPACT OF TAXATION

This is an area which has huge implications for successful exit planning and, consequently, it is covered in detail in Appendix 1. However, if the reason for your exit limits the time you have available to plan, you could fail to gain the maximum relief from taxation that is now available to individuals who dispose, or transfer, businesses or business assets.

Figure 1.2 looks at the reasons for disposal and their influence on the time available to plan.

Questions to help you to decide your timetable

Even where you have the option of a long-term exit plan, you will wish to be convinced that such a plan has advantages for you compared with a short-term plan, or no plan at all. The following summary of questions you could ask will help clarify this issue for you. (Some of the issues raised here are covered in detail in later parts of the book.)

- Check the current market conditions for business disposals in general, and for your type of business in particular. A corporate broker, an accountant or a specialist corporate adviser could be good sources of information. (What you wish to know is whether or not there is currently a demand for your type of business and whether or not prices are good.)
- Try and obtain a consensus on the current trend of the economy. (For example, are things likely to be better or worse over the next three years?)
- Check with your accountant your likely tax position (see Appendix 1, 'What about tax?').
- Review your business's operations. (Are there any obvious things in the business that currently depress its sale value or make it more difficult to sell? Can these be rectified and, if so, how long do you think it will take? You should refer to Chapter 6 'Impediments to sale' for guidance here.)
- Check whether your fellow shareholders wish to sell and the position with your shareholders'/partnership agreements. (For example, at what price will minority shareholders sell? Are they compelled to sell when you sell? What prices are you compelled to pay them if you are forced to buy them out first? Is a delay prudent, or even essential, to sort this out?)
- Check whether your management will stay on after the sale? (For example, is there anything in your management agreements that covers this?)

You should review your position having considered these issues. This will give you a good idea of the problems you are likely to have with an immediate sale. These problems then need to be compared with the likely benefits to you of delaying your sale to implement a short-term or a long-term plan. This topic is covered in more detail in Chapter 11.

Reasons	Immediate	1/2 Years	2/4 Years	+4 Years
1. Chronic ill health	✔			
2. Take advantage of positive market	✔			
3. Received good offer	✔			
4. Divorce settlement	✔			
5. New business opportunity	✔			
6. Starting new business – need capital	✔			
7. Burnt out/bored/need a change	✔	✔		
8. Want to spend more time with family	✔	✔		
9. Business going broke	✔			
10. Business not as profitable as hoped	✔	✔	✔	
11. Plan to emigrate/move area	✔	✔		
12. Told to retire (medical reasons)	✔	✔		
13. Plan to hand over family			✔	✔
14. Plan to hand over to management			✔	✔
15. Plan to retire at retirement age (?65)				✔

Figure 1.2 Reasons for Disposal and their Influence on Time Available to Plan

Positive results

We believe that by following the planning steps in this book you will achieve the following positive results:

- You will identify the best way to dispose of your business, that is, the way that will potentially maximize your exit price and achieve the maximum taxation relief and personal satisfaction.
- You will be able to draw up and implement a prioritized operational business plan that should result in dramatic improvements in performance and profitability of your business.
- You will be in a position to identify and remove those areas of operational weakness in your business that currently depress its value.
- You will be shown how to prepare a master exit strategy plan (MESP) that outlines your exit strategies in a clear, prioritized way.
- You will be able to implement your MESP, which will preserve and enhance your business's value and allow you to achieve the maximum, after-tax, price for your business when you dispose of it.

Typically, an exit plan will involve you taking all, or some of, the following steps, which will be covered in detail through this book:

1. Deciding your time frame.
2. Choosing your optimum exit option.
3. Structural planning, including taxation planning and continuity planning.
4. Grooming of management or successor.
5. Removing impediments to sale (cleaning up or grooming the business).
6. Growing the business, including acquisitions and organic growth. (You could set a specific target for growth.)
7. Finalizing disposal preparations, for example preparing a memorandum of offer, advertising for sale, and so on, and, perhaps, some of the more cosmetic cleaning up of the business's appearance.
8. Integrating your personal financial (or retirement planning) with your exit business financial planning.
9. The disposal itself.

Figure 1.3 The Steps for Implementing your MESP

CHAPTER

2 How to Plan for the Continuity of your Business

In this chapter we will consider two areas vital to exit strategy planning:

- how you should arrange your corporate structure to ensure maximum tax-effectiveness on exit, and
- how you should regulate through formal agreement your relationship with partners or shareholders to facilitate a smooth exit from your business.

The first section explains that in exit strategy planning structure is important mainly for taxation reasons and looks at some examples of why this is so. (Note also, that there can be other reasons why a complicated corporate structure is unattractive to a purchaser of a business, but here we concentrate on taxation.) The second shows that, where there is more than one owner of a business, it is essential for them to enter into an agreement that governs both their business relationships and contingencies when one or more of them exits from the business. The contents of this agreement are outlined and we explain how it can be the perfect exit plan for principals if it is properly drawn up and funded. We also look at the issues that could arise in a divorce either of the owner or minority shareholders (both family and non-family members) and what steps you might take to minimize the damage to your business in these circumstances. This part of the planning process is often called 'business continuity planning' and we will show you why it is an essential part of the your exit strategy.

Corporate structure

GETTING YOUR FOUNDATIONS IN PLACE

To plan for a successful exit you must first get your foundations in place. For most business owners, the foundations on which to build your exit strategy plans are, first, a corporate structure that is simple and tax efficient and, second, where relevant, agreements between you and your fellow shareholders or partners that facilitate a planned exit.

In an ideal world you would have addressed both these issues when you set up your business. In practice, most of you will not have addressed them because, perhaps, at that time you did not have fellow shareholders or the current capital gains tax laws were not in existence.

You should review your position immediately (particularly regarding your shareholders' agreements), and not wait until you are considering your exit, as unforeseen events can cause you severe problems at any time. You should address your corporate structure at least three years before your disposal date, which should be enough time to ensure maximum tax efficiency.

STRUCTURE AND CAPITAL GAINS TAX

Corporate structure is important mainly because of taxation. The taxation implications for business exits generally are dealt with in some detail in Appendix 1. Here we will consider only some of the early planning steps you should take to ensure you get maximum relief on exiting your business.

For capital gains tax (CGT) purposes, an important aspect of planning involves understanding the provisions concerning business asset taper relief (BATR). These include that taper relief is not available to companies; it only applies to certain kinds of assets; and its benefits increase the longer you have owned the assets.

Taper relief is not available to companies

A key provision in the CGT legislation is that taper relief is only available to individuals. For owners of companies the obvious conclusion to be drawn is that they should own their shares personally, rather than through another entity such as a holding company. Where this pertains, a company's business undertakings and assets will be disposed of through a sale of an individual's shares, rather than through the company selling its assets or a holding company selling the shares it owns in the company being disposed of.

The sale of shares instead of assets could present problems of a different kind in private business disposals, because traditionally the purchasers of private businesses prefer to buy assets rather than companies, for the obvious reason that a company can have its own undisclosed liabilities.

Another point is that many business owners consider a holding company to be a tidy way to control the affairs of a group of companies each of which might have different shareholders and in each of which the controlling shareholders might own different percentages. If the whole group is to be disposed of by the sale of the holding company's shares (which are owned by individuals) this will not, in itself, cause any loss of taper relief, but if individual companies are sold through the sale of the shares owned by the holding company this could result in the relief being lost.

Taper relief only applies to certain kinds of assets

Current business taxation legislation favours the sale of assets owned by trading, rather than investment, businesses. This can be seen in the treatment of business assets in both CGT and inheritance tax. For CGT purposes the maximum relief is given to business assets and shares in companies where the company is a qualifying company. Qualifying companies are, to put it simply, trading companies. (You can read more about this in Appendix 1.)

Problems can arise with these definitions in a business disposal where a business is deemed not to be a trading company. This can arise not only from an analysis of the main activities of the business, but also from the value of the assets on its books. If a company owns investment assets in excess of 20 per cent in value of its total asset value, the Inland Revenue is likely to deem it to be a non-trading company and its qualifying status will be lost. (These investments will usually not include the premises from which the business operates.)

This is a trap for trading companies that have, for example, invested their profits in rental properties and retained ownership in the trading company. If you are in this situation and wish to achieve maximum taper relief on disposal of your business, you should get expert taxation advice.

Taper relief's benefits increase over time

Taper relief is so named because its effect increases over time. Currently (2002), to achieve the maximum relief you must own the qualifying assets for two years. For those who owned qualifying assets when the legislation came in to force in April 1998, the two-year period will apply from 6 April 2002, resulting in an effective tax rate of 10 per cent.

The reason for establishing the most tax-effective ownership of assets as early as possible is obvious. What you need to avoid is a last minute shuffling of ownership shortly before you decide to dispose of your business. A change in ownership of shares in a family business, for example, might be necessary to reflect an earlier agreement that had not been formally documented, but this could have disastrous tax results if undertaken close to the date on which the whole business is sold. You should address these issues at least three years prior to a disposal and obtain expert taxation advice.

STRUCTURE AND INHERITANCE TAX (IHT)

In general, the relief from IHT favours trading companies in a similar way to CGT legislation. You should refer to Appendix 1 for more on this.

STRUCTURE AND INCOME AND CORPORATION TAXES

Some sole traders and partnerships believe that incorporation has taxation advantages both during the period of the ownership of their business and when they dispose of it. Whether this could be so is outside the scope of this book and we advise you to obtain expert taxation advice on this subject. The key taxation questions from an exit planning point of view (namely, personal ownership, length of ownership and the type of assets) do not usually turn on whether you trade as a company or not.

Business continuity planning

INTRODUCTION TO BUSINESS CONTINUITY PLANNING

Business continuity planning should include the formal agreements between shareholders, or partners (who we will call 'principals') entered into to regulate their rights and responsibilities and the circumstances in which they wish to sell their shares or partnership equity (which we will call 'interests'), or retire, become disabled, are declared bankrupt or die. The agreement that covers sale of interests only is sometimes known as a 'buy/sell agreement', but is one part only of a properly constituted business continuity agreement.

A comprehensive business continuity agreement should include the following:

- The transfer of interests provisions (known as 'pre-emptive rights'), which cover the rights (or options) given to the principals to buy the interests of other principals who wish to sell; and compulsory sale provisions, which cover the arrangements concerning the sale of interests in the case of certain events befalling a principal (such as death, disability, bankruptcy or reaching retirement age), and the method of valuing the interests and the ways of funding their purchase.
- Restraint of trade provisions (also known as 'restrictive covenants'), which are aimed at preventing the departing principals from competing with the business once they have left.

- With companies, 'drag along' provisions that force minority shareholders to sell their shares when the majority shareholders wish to accept a bona fide offer for their shares from a third party; and 'piggyback' provisions that ensure that minority shareholders' shares are sold if the majority shareholder wishes to sell.
- Operational matters that address the relationship and responsibilities between partners, shareholders and/or working directors.
- Other financial issues, such as retirement policy, dividend policy, and so on.

It is important to be aware that, where a business continuity agreement is being drawn up for companies, regard must be had for its compatibility with the company's Articles of Association, and that working directors will usually be parties to the agreement.

WHY BUSINESS CONTINUITY AGREEMENTS ARE OFTEN NEGLECTED

Although it is a very important part of any business planning process, private business owners often overlook or postpone the drawing up of business continuity agreements. There are many reasons for this, some of which are:

- The principals believe that their close personal relationship makes it unnecessary for them to have a formal agreement.
- Principals believe that the company's Articles of Association, or the law governing partnerships, make it unnecessary to have such an agreement.
- There is often reluctance among business owners to address the unpleasant aspects of business life, such as the departure of a principal due to untimely death or disability. It is always more exciting for business owners to plan for growth and business development.
- Business continuity agreements are complex, with many legal, valuation and taxation issues to be faced.
- For some agreements to be truly effective, funding should be put in place to cover the contingencies. Insurance is one of the more effective forms of funding in many circumstances. However, because some insurance companies promote the need for shareholders' agreements, some business owners believe that business continuity planning itself is an insurance-driven concept promoted by financial institutions for their own ends and lose sight of its intrinsic benefits.
- The agreements entail immediate expenditure, whereas their benefits are often perceived to be contingent and uncertain. When economic times are difficult, or business is tight, 'saving' money now seems to make more sense than spending it.

PROBLEMS THAT COULD OCCUR WITHOUT AN AGREEMENT

Where you do not have an agreement between business principals, the following problems could occur:

- The departing or deceased principals (or their personal representatives) may:
  - demand an unreasonable price for their interests in the business from the remaining principals, resulting in disputes and legal action
  - wish to sell their interests to potentially hostile, or totally unsuitable, third parties
  - demand immediate repayment of loans and other amounts due to them, which the other principals cannot pay immediately.

- In professional partnerships where there is no restraint of trade agreement, the goodwill value of the practice (and, therefore, the goodwill value of each partner's share of the practice) can be worthless when a key partner leaves and is able to go into competition with the practice. This can have disastrous results for partners who have purchased goodwill in the practice and hoped to retrieve this capital when they leave the partnership.
- In private companies, shareholders are often working directors who can have gained specialist knowledge while in the employ of the company. Their departure can cause considerable damage to the company unless they are prevented by agreement from competing against the company.
- Disputes, or legal action among principals, could lead to adverse publicity for the business and to creditors calling for immediate payment of accounts, or to banks discontinuing credit or calling in loans, or to employees being unsettled and even leaving, all of which could have a negative effect on the business.
- Majority shareholders may be restrained from accepting an attractive offer for all of a company's shares from a bona fide third party purchaser because minority shareholders refuse to sell, or are holding out for a higher price.
- Minority shareholders could be left stranded with a new, uncooperative (or even hostile) majority shareholder if current majority shareholders sell out.
- In a sole trader merger (see Appendix 9), a continuity agreement should constitute a complete exit strategy plan for the older owner. Also, without a formal written agreement the success of the merger and, consequently, the implementation of the exit strategy plan is extremely vulnerable to unforeseen personal mishaps to either owner.
- In the case of a divorce of a shareholder (including either the husband and wife owners or minority shareholders such as grown children in a family company) a shareholder's equity could fall into hostile hands, unless there is agreement on who is able to own shares or what they are worth. This could lead to a forced sale of the company to resolve a stalemate.

Figure 2.1 assists you in deciding whether you need a formal business continuity plan and what form it should take. Starting from the top, the figure asks you to consider the basic question of whether you have partners or fellow shareholders. If the answer is no, obviously you do not require a shareholders' agreement, but you then need to consider if you have heirs. If the answer to this is also no, you still need to consider what will happen to your business assets when you die. This prompts you to ask yourself the question: 'Do I have a will?' and, if you do not, to have one prepared immediately. If you are married, you need to consider how you have prepared for the possibility of divorce and whether you would like to put your business into trust for the benefit of a named beneficiary.

Where you have no partners or fellow shareholders, but do have an heir, you need to consider two immediate issues. First, whether you require a will to ensure your wishes are fulfilled – if you are married, for example, and wish to leave your business to your offspring and not your spouse you will need a will to ensure this happens. Second, you need to consider life or key person insurance to assist your heir when he or she takes over the business. Next you will need to consider the implications of your heir becoming divorced before he or she has inherited the business and whether it would be wise to put the business into a discretionary trust with the heir as a named beneficiary. Finally, under this option, you need to consider the taxation implications (especially inheritance tax) of all this.

Returning now to the top of the Figure 2.1, if you do have fellow shareholders or partners you require a shareholders' (or partners') agreement. If you already have one in place, you

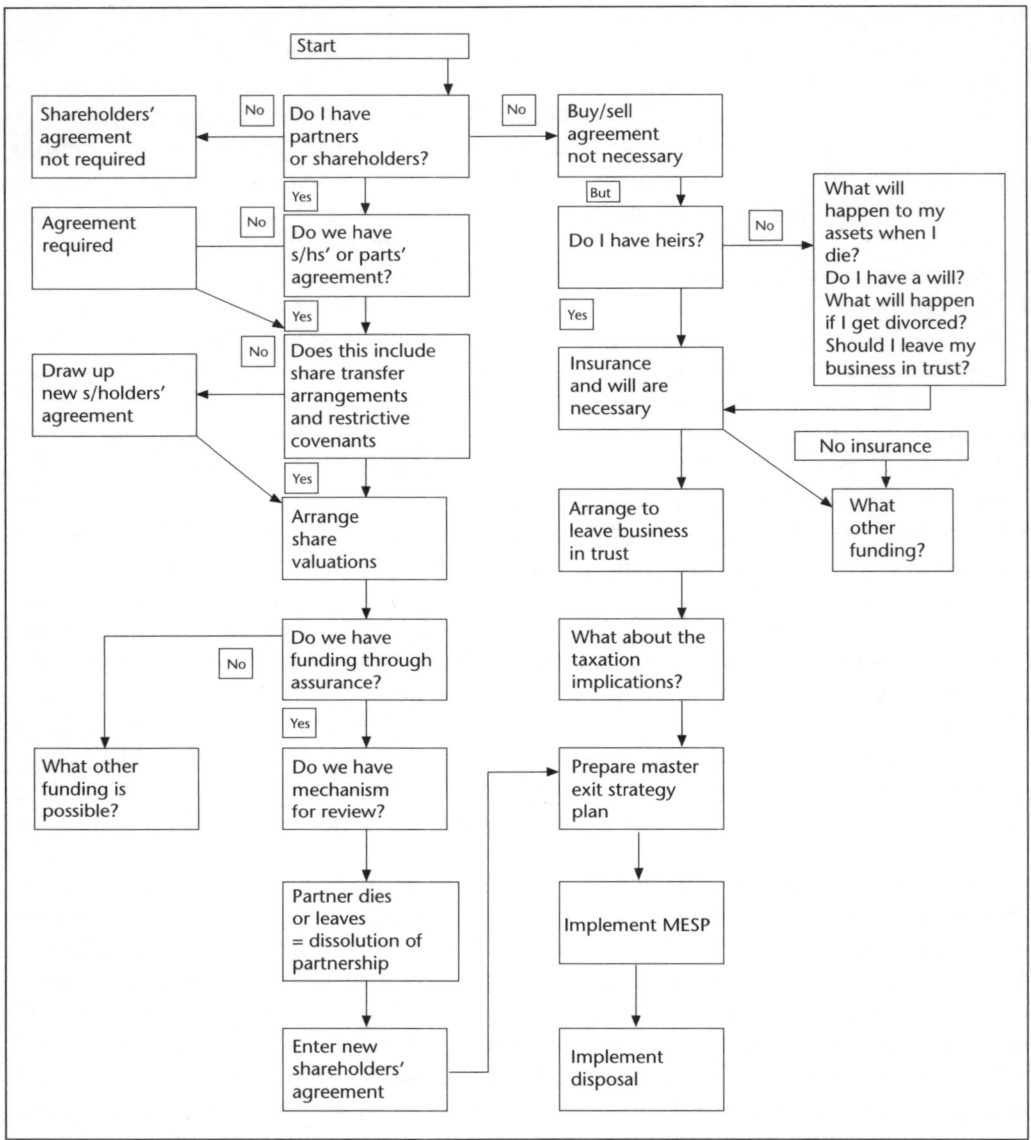

Figure 2.1 Do I Need a Business Continuity Plan?

need to check that it adequately covers the matters addressed in this chapter, especially the circumstances surrounding the transfer of interests. If so, does it also address the valuation of these interests, the funding mechanism that will facilitate the purchase and make a provision for regular review of value and that the funding is still adequate? Finally, with a partnership agreement, does it remove the problem that a partner's leaving usually gives rise to the necessity of a new agreement?

Where you have fellow shareholders or partners, but no shareholders' agreement, you need to draw one up in accordance with your requirements following the guidelines provided in this chapter.

Having covered the risks associated with your particular circumstances (including drawing up a shareholders' agreement, writing a will, taking out insurance, putting your business into trust, and so on), Figure 2.1 confirms that you are now in a position to advance your exit strategy planning by preparing an MESP, implementing this plan and disposing of your business.

BUSINESS CONTINUITY AGREEMENTS AND EXIT STRATEGY PLANNING

In the context of exit strategy planning the following matters in particular should be included in all business continuity agreements:

- sale of interests between principals
- restraint of trade (restrictive covenants)
- 'drag along' and 'piggyback' provisions.

(Operational issues, such as division of responsibilities between shareholders/directors and financial arrangements between them, are also crucial aspects of a shareholders' agreement, but are not strictly relevant to exit strategy planning and will not be covered here.)

The sale of interests between principals

This covers the obligation of principals who wish to sell their interests to first offer them to the remaining principals (who usually have the right but not the obligation to buy them) – known as 'pre-emptive rights' – and the right (or option) of the remaining principals to buy the interests of departing principals under various circumstances, or the happening of various events.

This part of the agreement will cover the following aspects:

- stipulation of the circumstances (or events) that will activate the agreement; for example, death, divorce, disability, becoming bankrupt, or retirement
- method of valuation
- what valuations of the interests are to be agreed in the different circumstances
- how to plan for funding to be available to enable remaining principals to pay for the interests in the various circumstances outlined above.

We expand on these issues below.

The buy/sell events Here the principal in question (or his or her personal representative) is compelled by agreement to offer the interests to his or her fellow principals. The event needs to be as unambiguous as possible.

The fact of death is absolute and requires no explanation in the agreement. The death of any principal will trigger the rights, obligations or options of the other shareholders. The fact of divorce is similarly clear. Explaining disability can be more difficult, as there are degrees of this condition. This can be conditional on an insurance assessors' confirmation that payment will be made on policies taken out in conjunction with the agreement (see below). Retirement can be for various reasons (for example, because of reaching normal retirement age, or through disability, or desire to retire before normal retirement age) and each type can be treated differently with regard to the valuation of the interests.

Method of valuation The valuation question must be covered for both pre-emptive rights and the events leading to the compulsory offer to sell. It is useful to decide on a general valuation method to be adopted and whether different values will apply in the different circumstances. This is considered in more detail below.

Firm agreement on valuation of interests is very important in business continuity agreements, but even those businesses that have agreements in place often fail to address valuation with any thoroughness. The reasons for reaching agreement on valuation of interests are, first, to avoid disagreement and misunderstanding among principals and, second, the recognition of potential problems in negotiating with personal representatives, executors or beneficiaries under a will. The approach should be to reach agreement in advance with as much clarity as possible, including a method of dealing with the changes in business value.

There are various methods that can be used to value the interests that will change hands under the agreement. You will understand these better if you have read Appendix 2 on valuing a business. The methods of valuation that could be included in the agreements include the following:

- A predetermined amount that might be fixed in advance, or might be adjusted in line with an inflation index. Some might consider this to be an unsatisfactory method, as values in a particular business can alter dramatically, and sometimes in the opposite direction to inflation.
- An 'industry yardstick', or a formula based on such things as a capitalization of gross turnover or gross profit (or whatever approach is accepted within the particular industry sector the business is in). This approach has the advantage of simplicity of description and is also a reliable indicator of value in very small businesses in relatively stable industries.
- Adopting a widely accepted standard method of valuation to apply to future maintainable earnings (or cash flow, or real profit), such as a price earnings (p/e) ratio. This approach assumes that the capitalization rate that has been accepted as appropriate will remain appropriate in the future, which is a reasonable assumption in times of stable inflation, but is not so reasonable in times of economic volatility (or in volatile industries) when acceptable rates of return and capitalization rates (such as a p/e ratio multiple) fluctuate widely.
- Periodic reviews of valuation (or new valuations) by agreement. The problem here can be that principals forget to, or do not bother to, complete these periodic reviews, and old values remain in the agreements.
- A valuation by the firm's accountants (or company's auditors). The problem here is, first, that not all accountants are experts in business valuations and, second, it is open to either party to disagree with the valuation and dispute it in court.
- Mutual agreement between the parties, or failing such agreement, by arbitration. Here the partners are potentially heading off to the law courts!

So which method should be adopted?

We certainly consider the mutual agreement method as a recipe for disagreement and legal dispute (and probably disaster), and suggest it should seldom be used. Similarly, leaving the valuation to a third party to decide after the event is not wise.

Incorporating a widely accepted standard method of valuation in the agreement, together with provision for periodic reviews of the capitalization rate (probably at yearly intervals) is, in our view, the most satisfactory method because, even if the reviews are overlooked, the standard method of valuation will still provide a reasonable valuation.

You should, however, obtain specialist advice on this issue to suit your particular circumstances.

Different values for different circumstances The issue to consider here is whether the agreed value of a departing principal's interests should be the same in all circumstances of departure from the business. To take extreme examples, should the agreed values be the same for when a principal dies as for when he or she decides to sell out early and leave the business to join a competitor? What value should be put on a husband's shares if he divorces his (business partner) wife and wishes to leave the family business?

It might be agreed that on the death of a principal the remaining principals could be prepared to pay full market value (including goodwill value) for the departing principal's interests, both for moral reasons and because the funds are available through an insurance policy. But the remaining principals could have quite a different attitude towards a principal who leaves early to take up a position with a competitor. In this case, an agreed value that reflects net tangible asset value only (and no goodwill value) might be considered more appropriate.

So that the agreement does not become too long-winded with many different formulas or valuation methods, it is a good idea to agree on one main method (such as a p/e ratio method) for most circumstances and to vary the multiple only for the different contingencies, and to have one other (much less generous) method for those circumstances that the business wishes to discourage (such as leaving early).

HOW TO MAKE SURE THE FUNDS ARE AVAILABLE

Central to all business continuity agreements should be a funding mechanism by which the remaining principals' financial obligations can be met. If this is not put in place, the agreement could be a huge burden on remaining principals, as lack of adequate funding could lead to the forced sale of the business, or of its key assets.

We will now look at how you can attempt to ensure that funds are available in the various circumstances that trigger the rights, or options to buy.

- *Death of a principal.* The obvious funding mechanism here is life insurance, where each principal's death is insured with the other principals as the named beneficiaries, or the principals are insured by the company, which will buy back the deceased principal's shares. Term insurance up to retirement age could be considered as an economical way of covering this. Other funding methods could be savings plans, pension funds or sinking funds. The problem with this approach is that it is difficult to plan with any precision, as there is no knowing when a death will occur. Failing this, the remaining shareholders will have to use their own funds (and, perhaps, pay in instalments) or resort to borrowing. Of all these possible funding options, insurance is the most satisfactory from the remaining principals' (or the company's) point of view, assuming always that the principals are considered an acceptable risk by insurers, and subject to premium costs.
- *Disablement of a principal.* The result of disablement could be that the principal is unable to continue to work. Here suitable and adequate disability insurance could meet the costs of acquiring the departing principal's interests. You should note that premiums are usually

high for this type of cover. Inability to obtain this sort of cover could lead to an agreement that provides for payment over extended terms.

- *Normal retirement (that is, at retirement age).* Pension or savings plans can be used if sufficient time is available before retirement age and adequate forward planning has taken place. Otherwise, arrangements similar to early retirement (but, perhaps, more favourable to the retiree) can be entered into. Again this is a matter of policy for the principals to decide having received competent advice.
- *Early retirement.* Where there is early retirement not brought on by ill health or injury or death, insurance does not provide remaining principals with cover, so it is generally difficult to fund for this eventuality. Also, it is not usually in the interests of the business to encourage early retirement among principals, as we have discussed above. For these reasons, shareholders' agreements often state that early retirees will not receive full consideration for their interests on retirement.
- *Divorce.* Similar to early retirement, divorce can occur at any time. In a family partnership or company, should either of the divorcing parties wish to sell their interests it will be difficult to have insurance in place to fund the purchase. Whether a court would uphold an agreement that places a valuation of less than a fair market value in these circumstances is a moot point.

  The important point with divorce is to ensure that there is a mechanism in place in the agreement that facilitates the transfer of the dissident principal's interests to the remaining principals for fair value without necessitating the sale of the business, if this is what the remaining shareholders wish. This is particularly important in the light of the courts attitude to family businesses being part of divorce assets. (Refer *White* v. *White*, in which the court decided that this was the case.) Prior to *White* v. *White* family business assets were not usually considered to be part of the assets divisible for divorce settlements and, consequently, it was not necessary to sell businesses for this purpose. It now appears, following *White* v. *White*, that in many cases business assets will be considered as divorce assets, and to meet their obligations business owners could be forced to sell the family business.

Restraint of trade (restrictive covenants)

This part of the agreement aims to restrict competition from principals who leave the business. For it to have a chance of being upheld in court the restrictions need to be reasonable, which often mean they have to be specific, restraining competition in the same type of business or industry in a strictly defined geographic area.

The basic rule of English law is that all restraints of trade are void unless they can be justified as being reasonable. Another fundamental principal of the law is that you cannot prevent someone from earning a living. A restraint must afford the party who has sought it no more than adequate protection for the interest he or she is entitled to protect. In practice it is harder to try to prevent an employee form working for a competitor than preventing a principal (or key manager) from using the information gathered while in your business to compete against you, or to entice away your customers or employees.

Where restraint of trade could be vital is in the area of professional partnership competition. Without such an agreement, the value of goodwill for the whole practice could be in doubt and, therefore, so could the value of individual partners' equity. This could be particularly damaging to newer partners who, because they do not have the direct personal contact with a large number of clients (and, therefore, in whom the goodwill does not personally reside), would be in a precarious position should the partnership break up.

Restraint of trade is a difficult area of the law and you should take expert legal advice when drafting your agreements.

'Drag along' and 'piggyback' provisions

The idea of these provisions is, first, to compel minority shareholders to sell their interests when the majority shareholders wish to sell theirs and, second, to compel the majority shareholders to arrange for the purchase of the minority shareholders' interests if the majority is selling out to a bona fide third party.

Drag along provisions are particularly useful for dominant shareholders who have brought minority shareholders into a business, or have issued shares of the same class as their own to employees, but who still wish to be in control of their own destiny, particularly with regard to their exit. The ability to be able to sell all the shares in a private company is important because purchasers seldom wish to acquire less than 100 per cent of the shares in such companies.

It is usual for the drag along provisions to be couched in terms that compel minority shareholders to sell their shares in the company to a third party when the majority shareholders have accepted a bona fide arms-length offer from that party for their shares. This ensures that minority shareholders are unable to thwart your exit strategy plans.

The piggyback provisions guard against minority shareholders being left with outside (and perhaps unsympathetic) majority partners and should also ensure that a 'minority discount' is not applied to the minority shares when they are sold.

Legal advice

There are many complicated legal issues involved in business continuity agreements and it is important that you obtain legal advice before finalizing any agreement with your shareholders or partners.

If you are a company shareholder, you must also check that your proposed agreement is compatible with your company's Articles of Association and to do this probably requires help from your legal advisers. You can amend your Articles if necessary to allow you to include certain provisions in the agreement, or you may need to include certain provisions in the Articles themselves. The latter course may not be appropriate as the Articles are a public document.

Figure 2.2 summarizes what should be included in a business continuity agreement.

A NOTE ON WILLS AND TRUSTS

It goes without saying that business owners should support their intentions for the disposal of their businesses with a will. If, for example, it is your exit plan to leave your business to your children and not your spouse, you should have a current will to this effect.

One way of countering problem ownerships that could arise from a potential divorce among your heirs, who you wish to become shareholders in your company during your lifetime, is to place the shares in trust for them (rather than making them shareholders in their own right) until their marriages have proved to be stable. If the trust is discretionary, in the event of a divorce their spouses might find it difficult to have any claim on their interests in the company.

a) Introduction

- ☐ Neither the standard Articles of Association of a company nor the Partnership Act adequately cover the arrangements between principals in businesses and firms with regard to their rights and responsibilities, issues connected with disposal of their equity and the sale of the business.
- ☐ In partnerships particularly, the lack of a formal written agreement on restraint of trade can lead to premature dissolution of the partnership and loss of partner's goodwill value.

b) A business continuity (or shareholders') agreement would usually cover the following:

1. Capital structure of the business, initial capital contribution and working capital contributions.
2. Course of action in case of disagreement between principals on major matters, including agreement to wind up and method of winding up.
3. Appointment of directors, directors' responsibilities and emoluments, dividend policy, termination provisions.
4. Sale of equity between principals. This is a key issue in business continuity agreements and would usually cover the following points:
   - ☐ The rights and options of principals to buy each other's shares and interests ('equity') in the organization. (These arrangements are usually known as 'pre-emptive rights'.)
   - ☐ Events or circumstances which give rise to rights (or options) to the purchase of equity, e.g. death, divorce, disability, bankruptcy, retirement, etc.
   - ☐ Methods of valuation of equity to be adopted under the various circumstances, or events.
   - ☐ Provision of funding for each circumstance.
   - ☐ Terms of payment where funding is not available in whole or in part.
5. Restraint of trade between principals (restrictive covenants):
   - ☐ In companies, certain fiduciary duties apply to directors both current and past, which could be binding despite the absence of an agreement on restraint of trade. This would not apply to shareholders who are not working in the business.
   - ☐ In partnerships, in the absence of agreement for restraint of trade (or non-competition) there is no legal restraint on individuals competing against their old practice or former partners. This can have devastating effects on the goodwill value of a professional practice that is a partnership.
   - ☐ Generally, restraint on principals must be reasonable to be upheld by the courts. The chances of enforcement could be improved where there has been a payment for equity.
   - ☐ Note: restraint of trade for employees is always difficult to enforce.
6. Sale of business to third parties. Majority shareholders will usually require that minority shareholders agree to sell their equity in certain circumstances, such as when majority shareholders wish to accept a bona fide third party offer for their equity. (These arrangements are known as 'drag along' provisions.) Minority shareholders will seek provisions that compel the majority, where they wish to sell, to either buy the minority's shares at the same price as they are selling for, or to procure that the purchaser buys the minority's shares on the same terms. (These arrangements are known as 'piggyback provisions'.)
7. Rights and responsibilities between principals. Business continuity agreements usually contain provisions that clarify the tasks and responsibilities of partners or working shareholders/directors in the operations of the business. These would include simple job

descriptions, allowable business expenses, dividend (or profits distribution) policy, limitations on spending without Board approval, signatories on cheques and so on.

8. Other issues. The agreement could also address circumstances that could cause disruption to the business and especially to the exit strategy planning process. Examples of these are as follows:

- ☐ Professional negligence by principals.
- ☐ Liabilities as a result of a principal being a director or officer of another company.
- ☐ Death or disability of key employees.
- ☐ Death of principals who have outstanding capital loan accounts.
- ☐ Infidelity of officers and employees.

Figure 2.2 Contents of a Business Continuity (or Shareholders') Agreement

CONTINUITY PLANNING'S PLACE IN EXIT STRATEGY PLANNING

Where there are co-owners in a business, business continuity planning is a vital part of your overall exit strategy plans. In particular you should consider the following advantages in business continuity planning:

- For outgoing shareholders, exit strategy planning's aim should be to establish a market for their interests and to optimize their exit price. Where an outgoing shareholder retires, a well-drafted business continuity agreement can achieve this by confirming the buyers (that is, the remaining principals), establishing the price (through the agreed methods of valuation of interests) and providing the buyers with the means by which the price can be paid (through insurance, and so on). Furthermore, in certain circumstances, a business continuity agreement could be the only way a disabled principal has of disposing of his or her interests at a reasonable price. In other words, a carefully structured business continuity plan could be the only exit strategy plan available to an outgoing principal; but it could be the perfect plan!
- From the remaining principals' point of view, a business continuity agreement could ensure that the business remains in their hands, provides a mechanism for establishing an agreed selling price and, hopefully, the means to pay for their acquisition.

The reasons for having a business continuity plan are reiterated in Figure 2.3.

The advantages of arrangements that facilitate an exit strategy and provide peace of mind should be obvious to business owners. Some of the reasons given for having business continuity agreements, in which adequate financial provision has been made, are as follows:

- ☐ It ensures that the business need not be wound up upon the death, disablement, bankruptcy, early retirement, or normal retirement of one of the principals.
- ☐ It ensures the continuation of the business without prolonged interruption or loss of momentum, enabling surviving principals to assume control of the business as a going concern with equipment, employees, customers, goodwill, etc. intact.
- ☐ In the event of death, the deceased principal's estate can be settled promptly and efficiently with no undue delays caused by difficulties encountered in the disposal of an interest in the business.
- ☐ The outgoing principal or his or her estate is free from the fear of being completely dependent upon the fortunes and skills of the surviving principals.
- ☐ It overcomes the emotional and practical problems associated with negotiations having to be entered into with, for example, the widow or widower (or personal representative) of a deceased principal at the time when she or he will be most distraught.
- ☐ In the event of death, the deceased principal's estate can be relieved of the worries and responsibilities in connection with the business, more so if the agreement enables the estate to obtain a release from personal guarantees.
- ☐ It allows for the principal to plan with the knowledge that he or she can expect to receive a just and fair price for his or her interest in the business.
- ☐ By ensuring its continuation, a business can engender confidence in its employees, creditors and bankers.
- ☐ It could motivate principals to be loyal and work harder knowing that the business equity will remain in their ownership.
- ☐ It ensures a guaranteed market for the outgoing or deceased principal's interest in the business at a pre-agreed price.
- ☐ By clearly defining rights and obligations of all parties to the arrangement it assists in the elimination of any potential friction between the parties.

Figure 2.3 Why have a Business Continuity Agreement?

CHAPTER 3 *Establishing the Value of your Business*

In this chapter we consider why business valuation is important to exit strategy planning. We discuss:

- the relationship between value and the timing of your exit
- some of the misconceptions business owners have about business values and how this can lead to unrealistic expectations and plans
- some of the definitions and principles of valuation, before explaining a simple business valuation method
- the value of goodwill
- the fact that an understanding of future value can help you calculate the cost/benefits of an exit strategy plan
- the importance of taxation planning and whether time or value is more important to you
- why some businesses sell for more than their valuations.

More information on how to value a private business is given in Appendix 2.

Valuation and timing

When you are considering an exit from your business timing is always a key issue. Should you exit now or at some time in the future? When is the optimum time in the future to exit? Central to this decision could be what net price you can expect from a disposal of your business now compared to, say, in three years time. The questions you need to ask yourself about value (and assuming for the moment that price and value are the same thing) are as follows:

1 What is the value of my business now?
2 What could my business be worth in, say, three years time?
3 What are the taxation implications of a disposal at either time?

Where it is obvious that a delay in your exit will result in significant increases in business value, a decision to delay will make good business sense. However, where you are certain (as you can be) of the current value of your business but uncertain about its future value, or even have reason to believe that its value might decline, the arguments for selling immediately could be compelling.

Besides gross value, you also need to also consider taxation. The impact of taxation on the proceeds of your sale can be affected by the length of time you have owned business assets and by the nature of your business. So you need to consider whether a delay in your sale to improve value, either by improving profitability or minimizing tax, will increase your net return.

Another factor to consider in future value is whether the choice of a particular disposal option will determine the disposal price you are likely to achieve. For example, are you likely to achieve a better price though an MBO than you are through a trade sale?

ESTABLISHING FUTURE VALUE

The future value of your business will be based on projected profits (or cash flows) and assumptions about asset values at the designated time. The profitability, in turn, could rely on the improvements you can make to the business, for example, by removing impediments to sale (see Chapter 6) or implementing a successful marketing campaign, or other operational plans. But, even assuming that the projected profits are achieved, the future value of the business will be affected by such external factors as interest rates and the state of the economy at the time in question.

Working within these limitations, you can estimate the future value of your business by establishing a basis by which its value will be arrived at (for example, a price earnings ratio method) and accepting that the same multiple will be used now and in the future, regardless of the external factors such as interest rates. Although such an approach will have its detractors and is not perfect, it is probably as good a way as any to estimate future value.

ART OR SCIENCE; PRICE OR VALUE?

Business valuation is an art and not a science. Opinions as to the current value of a business can vary greatly even between so-called experts, not only because they might be using different valuation methods (see Appendix 2), but because they could be using different fundamentals within the same valuation method.

A business valuation is an estimation by a valuer of what a business is worth on the day the valuation is made. What is meant by worth in this context is what the valuer believes the price of the business would have been (or what someone would have paid for the business) on the day the valuation was prepared, under the circumstances assumed to have been prevailing (for example, a fire sale or a going concern). A valuation is not a price. A price arises when a sale transaction is completed, when it confirms or otherwise the valuation estimate. As they say: a business is only worth what someone will pay for it!

Misconceptions about value

Most private business owners overvalue their businesses, giving rise to one of the major impediments to sale in business disposals. Overvaluation can come about through use of incorrect valuation methods, or inappropriate multiples, or because of confusion about terminology such as gross and net profit, or real profit or maintainable profit (which are explained in Appendix 2). Misunderstandings also arise because business owners find it difficult to be objective, or to put themselves in the shoes of potential purchasers. Their opinions about value are influenced by non-economic, subjective considerations, such as how hard they have worked to build up the business, or how well they think it will perform in the future.

These misconceptions lead to the overpricing of businesses by their owners, and to unrealistic expectations and ultimate disappointment and frustration. It can also lead to difficulties in circumstances where owners themselves might set the price of the business, for example, in a family succession, and especially if the heir needs third party financing to complete the purchase.

Unrealistic price expectations can also derail the planning process at a very early stage. For example, the choice of an exit option will sometimes rely on a minimum value for the business, examples being a public listing or an institution-backed management buyout. Unrealistic expectations about value can also adversely influence personal financial planning. For example, an owner can base all his or her retirement finances on an expectation of a business sale's price that, in reality, can never be achieved. So, before you begin the process of considering the best exit option for your business, it is necessary to establish with some certainty what your business might be worth.

Before looking at a simple way in which you can form a reasoned opinion as to the value of your business, we would like to establish some basic valuation definitions and principles that should help you to better understand the valuation techniques explained later.

Some basic definitions

GOING CONCERN VALUE

This is the value placed on a business (or its assets) when it is still trading (and generating income), compared with when it has stopped trading. The total going concern value of a business could include an element of goodwill value, which is considered below.

The phrase can also be applied to assets only and explains the notion that when all the assets are together at the place of business they will be worth more than if they were sold individually and having, typically, been taken from the place of business (usually after the business has ceased to trade).

FIRE SALE VALUE

This usually refers to the value of business assets sold under conditions of distress (often off-site and sometimes at auction). The assets are often sold individually rather than together as a business unit. This circumstance is the opposite of going concern.

GOODWILL VALUE

Goodwill value can be a difficult concept to understand. It has been variously described as follows:

- The benefit and advantage of a good name, reputation and connection of a business . . . the attractive force that brings in custom ... the one thing which distinguishes an old established business from the new one.
- The difference between the total value of a business and the value of its identifiable assets.
- Goodwill comprises the future benefits from unidentifiable assets which, because of their nature, are not normally recorded individually in the accounts.

(We consider goodwill in more detail in Appendix 2.)

TOTAL NET VALUE

Total net value of a business is made up of:

- the value of the tangible assets, plus
- the value of intangible assets, including goodwill, less
- the value of any liabilities.

MARKET VALUE

Market value can be described as the price that a willing arm's-length buyer will pay for a business sold by a willing, but not anxious seller on the open market. Once such a transaction has taken place, the price paid becomes the market value of a business at the time of sale, regardless of any theoretical valuation that might have been placed on the business previously. A valuation for sale purposes of a business that is currently trading could be described as being on the basis of 'a fair market value as a going concern'. A business could sometimes achieve a value well in excess of its fair market valuation where a buyer, who might have particular opportunities to develop the business's profits through amalgamation and/or cost cutting, pays more than market value. More often, businesses achieve less than their market valuation on sale.

Valuing your business: a simple approach

(The explanation given here is a simplified one and for a more detailed explanation of this and other methods you should refer to Appendix 2.)

Although there are many methods of business valuation, the one that is almost universally accepted in private business is the capitalization of future maintainable profits (FMP) through the price earnings ratio method. To value your business through the p/e ratio method you should take the following steps:

- Step 1: establish the FMP of your business.
- Step 2: decide on an appropriate capitalisation rate, or p/e ratio.
- Step 3: calculate the value of the business by multiplying the FMP by the p/e ratio to arrive at total value.
- Step 4: add the value of 'surplus assets' to total business value to arrive at total value. For example:
  - The business's FMP are £175,000.
  - You believe the appropriate p/e multiple is 6.
  - The total business value would be £1,050,000 (and there are no surplus assets).

Valuing the goodwill of your business

To calculate the goodwill value of your business you deduct the value of tangible assets from the total business value. The resultant value is, strictly speaking, the value of all intangible assets, identifiable and unidentifiable , but in most private businesses this will be the same as goodwill value. However, if you have any identifiable intangible assets (such as brand names), you need to deduct their value from the total value. For example:

Total value	£1,050,000
Deduct:	
Tangible assets	£ 850,000
Other intangible assets (e.g. brand names)	£ 50,000
Goodwill value	£ 150,000

The future value of your business

Once you have established a method of valuing your business that you believe is appropriate (for example, by capitalizing future maintainable profits by the appropriate multiple, as above) you can estimate its likely future value by reference to its estimated future profits. (Your business plan should include profit and loss projections for the next three years.) As an example only, you could take the following steps:

- Projected profits for the next three years are £200,000 in 2003, £220,000 in 2004 and £250,000 in 2005.
- If these are achieved, in 2005 the average of the past three years' profits would have been £223,333. We will assume this profit is maintainable and you could decide that this is an appropriate figure for FMP.
- Using the same p/e ratio of 6, you can estimate the value of the business in 2005 to be £223,333 × 6 = £1,340,000.
- This represents an increase in value of your business over three years of £290,000.

The aim of exit strategy planning is to maximize your business disposal price. One of the obvious ways by which you can increase this price is to improve profitability by improving the business's operations. The more you are able to do to improve business operations and profitability during the planning process the greater should be the increase in your ultimate disposal price.

Costs compared with benefit

Exit strategy planning will cost you time and money. You will spend your own time on planning and improving your business, and money on expert advice and assistance. It is important for you to be sure that you are receiving a greater benefit than the costs involved. In brief, you should believe that the costs you are going to incur in undertaking an exit strategy plan are less than the potential increase in value of your business as a result of the planning. This can be done as follows:

- Establish the current value of your business.
- Decide when you plan to exit your business.
- Establish what operational issues you will be undertaking to improve your business (including removal of impediments to sale).
- Produce profit and loss projections up to the date of your exit.
- Estimate the value of your business at the time of your proposed exit based on your projections.

- Estimate the total cost of implementing your exit strategy plan by aggregating your extra time costs and third party costs payable to experts and consultants.
- Compare your estimated costs with the estimated increase in value of your business once you have implemented your exit strategy plan.

The impact of taxation on your net return

Up until now we have compared current and future gross values only. But, the crucial figure you need to know when comparing the cost with the benefit of embarking on an exit strategy plan is the after-tax one.

It is possible that, even if the expected future value of your business on exit is no greater than the current gross value of your business, you could still be better off in net after taxation terms if you delay your sale to implement tax-saving measures to take full advantage of the taxation reliefs and allowances that may be available to you in future.

(You should refer to Appendix 1 for more information on business taxation.)

Time target or value target?

Your exit strategy plan should either have a time target or a value target. In other words, you could set your exit plan on the basis that you wish to sell in, say, five years, or you could set the plan on the basis that you wish to sell when the business is worth, say, £1 million (which could, of course, take you less than five years to achieve). Using an appropriate valuation method, you can now set your value target based on achieving maintainable profitability targets. Having established these parameters you can now work towards your goal.

Why theory and practice differ

Businesses will often change hands for more or less than their valuation estimates. In theory the value of a business lies in its ability to earn a profit (or generate cash flows) for its owner. If it does not earn a profit, valuation theory suggests that it is unlikely to command a purchase price in excess of the value of its assets, that is, it will have no goodwill value.

In practice, however, money is paid for goodwill in private businesses where the business makes no profit over and above a living salary or wage for its owners (what is known as 'super profits' – see Appendix 2). In very small businesses this could occur where the purchaser wishes to 'buy a living', or buy a living coupled with something to do. This can also occur where the purchaser believes that the opportunities within the business are such that it will earn super profits in future years under his or her guidance. In this case the purchaser is paying a premium for his or her own future efforts, rather than for the uniqueness of the business or the past efforts of the vendor.

Other reasons why businesses could change hands at values in excess of their 'true market value' are as follows:

- Purchasers may pay for goodwill that is not ultimately transferred to them and, hence, has no value to them. This can occur, for example, where there is no restraint of trade clause in the sale agreement and the vendor subsequently entices the business's customers away.

- Purchasers may pay goodwill value for businesses whose profits are not maintainable. For example, the business may have had a few years in which it made exceptional profits, but these are not repeated because of the loss of a major client, or increased competition, or difficult trading conditions caused by legislative changes.
- Purchasers lack understanding of financial accounts and the basic principles of valuation. For example, many valuation methods for very small businesses ignore 'real', or 'super' profits completely and base their values on profits from which owner-related salaries and expenses, necessary to the production of the business's profits, have not been deducted.

This examination of why theory and practice differ in business valuations serves to underline that business valuation is an inexact science and to reinforce the old cliché that a business is only worth what someone is prepared to pay for it.

Summary: the importance of valuation in exit strategy planning

From reading this chapter you will have gathered that establishing the current and future value of your business is the starting point of exit strategy planning. Current value establishes the framework of your plans and, perhaps, when you should start to plan, while future value gives you a target to work to and a basis for calculating the cost/benefit of the planning process itself. Finally, you will have realized that all disposal values should be considered on an after-taxation basis and that it is vitally important for you to seek expert taxation advice at an early stage of the exit planning process so that you can minimize the impact of taxation on your disposal proceeds.

PART 2 *Choosing your Exit Strategy*

CHAPTER

4 What Are the Exit Options for your Business?

Choosing the optimum exit option for your business is a vital part of exit strategy planning. In this chapter we:

- examine briefly the various exit options available to the owner of a private business so that you are able to form some initial views on the options that could be relevant to your business
- show you what to look for in your business to establish, in principle, whether it is suitable for the option being considered
- look briefly at some of the market and investor requirements for a business to qualify for various options.

Do you know how to exit your business?

Many private business owners are not aware of the various ways in which they can dispose of their businesses. Those with families will have considered family succession planning, even if they are unsure of exactly how to do it. Others will think that their only option is to sell to a third party, in what is often called a 'trade sale'. Some will be aware of the opportunities afforded through a management buyout and, perhaps, a few of you will have considered a flotation, or even franchising.

This chapter gives an outline of the many options that could be available to you to dispose of your business so that you can maximize your sale price and your personal satisfaction. After studying this and the following chapter it will be easier for you to make a preliminary shortlist of the disposal options best suited to your business. In the appendices that follow a more detailed account of each exit strategy option is given. You should study the specific appendices that cover the options on your shortlist and this should enable you to make a final decision. Before making your final decision you might wish to get further advice on your choice of option from an appropriate professional adviser.

Choice of option could be crucial

Importantly the choice of the correct option could make the difference between disposing of the business for a fair price and not being able to dispose of it at all. With the choice of the right option you could be creating a market for your equity that did not exist previously. An example of this could be to groom a manager to buy your business and to assist him or her with the purchase funding, where no other party is interested in purchasing it.

What are the exit options?

There are at least eight main ways in which you can dispose of your business. There are also various variations on the main ways. One example of a variation is where in a trade sale you sell part only of your shares rather than all of them. Another is where in a management buy-out an outside chief executive officer (CEO) is brought in to assist the internal management, making it partly a buyout and partly a buy-in.

The main exit options available to a private business are as follows:

1. Transferring it to a family member (known as a family succession).
2. Sale to internal management or employees (known as a management buy out or 'MBO').
3. Sale to outside management (known as a management buy-in, or ' MBI').
4. A public listing (or flotation) on the stock exchange.
5. Franchising your business operations (and, as an optional second stage, selling the franchisor business).
6. Sale to a third party (also known as a 'trade sale').
7. Merger of sole traders, or smaller businesses in the same industry.
8. Ceasing to trade and ultimate liquidation, or close down.

Many of the variations on the basic exit methods mentioned above are packaged and promoted by financiers or business consulting firms, but the differences are usually only in the way transactions are structured: the principles of the exit process remain the same.

The exit options explained in brief

To make even an initial shortlist of optimum exit options it helps if you understand how they work. Below we provide a brief review of the options from the aspect of how they might suit you and your business. Fuller explanations of the processes involved in each option and of how you would implement an exit strategy utilizing each option are given in the relevant appendices.

FAMILY SUCCESSION

A family succession involves passing on your business to a family member, such as a child. Most private business owners with children, or who have a close relationship with a younger relative, usually are favourably inclined to this exit choice where it is practicable. Unfortunately, even those with close relatives such as children, often find that their heirs are not interested in, or capable of, taking over the running of the family business. For these people, and for those without a family heir, the family succession option is, obviously, not applicable.

Although desirable from the point of view of personal satisfaction for the owner, family succession can be the most difficult exit strategy of all. The greatest problems are that family and business goals and cultures often clash, objectivity is often absent and emotion rather than business practicality takes over.

We cover this option more fully in Appendix 4, and if you are considering family succession as a disposal option you should read this appendix carefully.

MANAGEMENT (AND/OR EMPLOYEE) BUYOUTS

What is an MBO?

Contrary to common belief, exit through an MBO is available to any private business and not just the larger ones; nor are venture capitalists (VCs), or corporate finance specialists, or bankers necessary to organize them. An MBO is simply a business sale where the buyers are the management and/or employees of the business. It is true, of course, that financiers do get involved in most MBOs by arranging the financing and taking an equity stake in the business, but this is not a prerequisite for an MBO.

An MBO is also a widely used exit strategy by public companies wishing to dispose of subsidiaries that are considered not to be core group operations.

Could an MBO be suitable for your business?

You will need to distinguish initially between an MBO that is not funded by institutional investors and those that are. The main difference is one of size of the transaction: VCs are unlikely to be interested in a deal in which they are investing less than £500,000. Otherwise, the general prerequisites of MBOs are the same.

If you have suitably talented management in your business that you believe would be interested in an MBO, you should seriously consider an MBO, because your management and employees (who we will collectively call 'management') could be the perfect buyers of your business. There are many reasons why this could be the case, namely:

1. Management should be aware of the potential of the business and, because they understand its operations better than any outside buyer, they should have sensible ideas of how to achieve this potential.
2. Management is familiar with the business clients, suppliers, financiers and employees.
3. As an owner, you know your managers and their capabilities intimately and, hopefully, you trust them.
4. With a sale to a group of people you know well you are more likely to be able to structure the sale to suit your retirement planning needs (including your possible future involvement in the business) than in other disposal options.
5. There is a great deal of personal satisfaction in seeing people you have taught, worked with, know and like, purchase your business.
6. Management is often driven by personal and emotional reasons to buy your business, making them keener to buy than most outside buyers and, perhaps, to pay you more for it.

MBO requirements

We have looked at the potential advantages to you and your management of an MBO, but you now need to look at aspects of your business and its management that need to be in place before an MBO is likely to be successful. There are two aspects that need to be present, namely a strong cash flow and management expertise.

Cash flow Employed managers are not usually wealthy and, consequently, they will need to borrow a large portion of the purchase price if they are to undertake a successful buyout. This will result in a substantial interest bill and the business will need to have a steady, positive cash flow to meet its repayments schedule. The business will, of course, have other needs for cash, not least being reasonable salaries for the managers themselves. If the managers are put under too much financial pressure the business itself could be in danger of collapse. If you as vendor are part of the financing arrangements through providing vendor finance, this will, of course, put your own position in danger also.

Management expertise It is usual for an MBO to be a team effort, with line managers, a CEO and financiers making up the team. At the head of the team should be an effective, experienced CEO who has the right leadership qualities and good relations with the rest of the team. The management team should include members who have a wide range of business skills. Where the MBO is being financed from outside, the managers must have the confidence of the financiers and the ability to 'talk their language'.

Generally speaking the management should have the following attributes:

- experience in the essential operational functions of the business
- strong financial management skills
- involvement in the day-to-day running of the business in a hands-on way
- the ability to produce well thought out strategic and business plans, with accurate financial forecasts.

Where outside management is brought into the team, the transaction becomes a management buy-in, which we discuss next.

MANAGEMENT BUY-INS

An MBI is an MBO in which outside management (usually an individual with particular talents) puts a team together to purchase a business from a private business owner or a public company. Where an individual is brought in by the financiers to bolster a management team that has perceived management weaknesses, this is a hybrid transaction called a MBI/MBO or 'BIMBO'. A further variation on this is where an institution initiates and drives the buyout (called an 'IBO').

As a business owner if you feel that your business is suitable for a management buyout but that there are weaknesses in the current management team, you could try to find a suitable outside party as the potential CEO to lead a buyout team. On the other hand, potential CEOs from outside the business could recognize an opportunity in your business and themselves initiate a buy-in.

(For a more detailed description on the MBO process you should refer to Appendix 5.)

PUBLIC LISTING, OR FLOTATION

Most private businesses do not make enough profit (nor have the profit potential) and are not big enough in terms of capital to be attractive to investors, or to qualify for the minimum requirements of either the London Stock Exchange's (LSE) Main or Alternative boards. But although this appears to rule out the listing option for most private companies, the rules are not hard and fast.

In certain phases of the economic cycle investor requirements are more biased towards entrepreneurial enterprises, and profit potential could be enough to attract investor support for a flotation. Also, the LSE rules for the Alternative Investment Market (AIM) are not as strict as for the main board, and alternative opportunities with less structured rules, such as OFEX, exist for smaller companies.

A flotation of your company is best considered as a multistaged exit strategy, that is an initial sale of your equity to the public followed by the opportunity to sell further tranches of equity into a much more liquid market and at, hopefully, ever-increasing prices. A flotation can be a high reward strategy and if you have a profitable business with strong growth potential you should give it serious consideration.

To be listed on the LSE, either on the AIM or the Main Board, or on OFEX, a company needs to meet certain minimum requirements. These are detailed in Appendix 6, which you should study in detail if you believe a listing might be a viable exit option for your business.

FRANCHISING

Like a flotation, franchising your business could be a multistaged exit strategy. The first stage would be to establish a franchise business by selling off part of your current business operations. Next you could sell further franchise outlets and eventually you could dispose of the franchisor business itself.

If you are thinking about franchising your business as an exit option, you should check initially whether your business might be suitable. The following characteristics are usually necessary for a business to be successfully franchised:

- It must have a strong brand recognition, or be able to build one.
- It must have a unique or new way of conducting business (that is, a unique operating system), or an aspect of its business that is unique, such as a formula.
- The business system must be relatively simple and be able to be taught to others, so that suitable franchisees can be found.
- It must be able to duplicate its operations outside its current geographical areas of operations.
- There must be sufficient gross margin in the business for the franchisee to pay the franchise fees and still make a reasonable net profit.
- The business must have financial and operational systems in place that can keep track of the franchisees operations and ensure that the franchisor gets paid.

From your personal point of you as an owner (or franchisor), you must be capable of managing a group of independently minded business people who will make up your franchisees.

(A fuller explanation of franchising is given in Appendix 7.)

TRADE SALES

A sale to a third party on the open market (known as a 'trade sale') is the method of disposal most private business owners think of when they consider disposing of their businesses, and it is still the way most private businesses are sold. Most businesses in most industry sectors are suitable for a trade sale and there are usually no special attributes you or your business need if you are to dispose of it through this route. The key question that an owner should ask when considering a trade sale is the following: 'Is this the best way for me to maximize my financial return (and, perhaps, my personal satisfaction) when exiting my business, or should I be thinking of different options?' An understanding of the other options (which are described in some detail in the appendices) will obviously help you to answer this question with any authority. If, having studied the appendices, you still believe that a trade sale is the optimum exit option for your business, then all you need to understand are the procedures and the pitfalls of this disposal route, which are covered in detail in Appendix 8.

As most businesses are suitable for a trade sale, the issues that need considering are often more to do with your own financial position than the position of your business. Some of these issues are discussed below.

Selling the business yourself

You can sell your business through an agent or company broker, or you could decide to handle the sale yourself. If you decide to handle the sale yourself, you should address the following questions:

- Am I able to establish a fair market price for my business?
- Am I able to find someone who wishes to buy my business?
- Am I able to negotiate the best price on my own?
- How do I best structure the sale transaction?
- Am I in a position to provide some of the funding?
- How do I arrange a suitable handover and how long should this be for?
- If I want to continue to be involved in the business after sale (perhaps as a consultant), how do I go about this?

Funding

It is sometimes difficult for purchasers of a small business to borrow money to finance a purchase (particularly where goodwill value is a major part of the price), unless they can provide security outside the business, such as a house that is not already heavily mortgaged.

One way of overcoming this difficulty would be to provide vendor finance, so you need to consider if you are prepared, in principle, to do so. To help your deliberations, you should ask yourself the following questions:

- How badly do I need the sale to go through at the price I am asking?
- Do I need all the cash proceeds of the sale now and how urgently do I need them?
- How confident am I of the financial viability of the business in the purchaser's hands? (*Note*: your old business is likely to be the security provided for the purchaser's borrowings.)

Retentions

In a trade sale of a small business it is not unusual for a purchaser to keep back a specified portion of the purchase price (especially where the price consists mainly of goodwill) until it is proved that the business can retain its customers or clients, (that is, its turnover or sales levels). The withheld portion (or retention) will usually be held in trust until the trial period has expired. When the performance conditions are met the retention is paid to the vendor. You need to consider whether this is likely to happen in your business and whether you can cope with this if it does.

Earn outs

This refers to the circumstance where a portion of the ultimate purchase consideration is based on a multiple of future earnings of the business sold. This is not uncommon practice where a large amount of the purchase price is goodwill (for example, in many service industries where there are few hard assets in the business). Total ownership of the business will pass on completion and the payment of the first tranche of capital, and the final payment will be conditional on trading results. The main difference between a retention and an earn out is that in the former the amount held back is specified, while in the latter it will vary depending on the extent of the profit achieved.

You will need to consider whether either a retention or an earn out is likely to be asked for by the purchaser and what your reaction will be if it is. Your response is likely to turn on your immediate need for the entire sale proceeds.

(All these issues are covered in more detail in Appendix 8.)

SOLE TRADER MERGERS

The mergers we are considering here are those between smaller private businesses and professional practices who are, typically, sole traders. This exit option allows a retiring business owner to plan an exit strategy at an early stage through an arrangement with another owner, who is keen to expand his business. For the retiring owner this can be a relatively low-risk option and allows some latitude in working out your retirement at a reduced level of intensity in the newly merged business.

The sole trader merger can be a three-staged exit strategy. Stage 1 involves the merger of two businesses (with perhaps an initial purchase of equity). Stage 2 involves the buy out of the older owner' s interest (or the balance of his interests) in the merged business by the younger owner, while stage 3 could involve the retiring owner working out a retirement period as an employee.

To consider exiting through this method you would be, typically, a sole trader and you would need to find a younger sole trader in the same industry with a similar working philosophy as yourself.

(This exit option is dealt with in more detail in Appendix 9.)

CEASING TO TRADE

If 'going concern' status is not maintained, most businesses will lose a large part of their value. Experience shows that assets such as plant and equipment, or stock, which are sold in auctions (or in fire sales) seldom fetch their so-called 'market value' and often sell for less than their written-down value. Even real property can fail to reach market value when there is a forced sale. Just as damaging will be the fact that a business, which is not a going concern, will usually have no goodwill value.

To close down your business and attempt to sell off its assets is, therefore, usually the worst of all exit options for you. However, there are circumstances where the value of the business as a going concern is no greater than the value of its assets and, indeed, when the value of the assets could exceed the going concern business value. It is in these circumstances that an orderly disposal of a solvent company's assets (followed by liquidation of the company) could make financial sense and we discuss these circumstances in some detail in Appendix 10.

Sometimes, the close down of your business will be not of your choosing. If you are forced through insolvency to liquidate your company, then planning an exit is out of your hands. A detailed examination of this area of business life is outside the scope of this book, although we deal briefly with some aspects of insolvency in Appendix 10.

How to choose the right option?

In summary, the steps you should follow in choosing the exit strategy that is best for you and your business are as follows:

1. You should analyse the reasons why and when you wish to quit.
2. You should consider which option is the one you would prefer for personal as well as business reasons.
3. You should understand your disposal choices in general terms from reading this chapter.
4. You should then read Chapter 5 and make a shortlist of what appear to be the best options by going through the options elimination worksheet in Figure 5.2.
5. You should study your choices more closely in the appropriate appendices at the back of this book.
6. You can now make your final choice or, if you feel it is necessary, you could obtain professional advice to help you make your final choice.

Conclusion: choosing the best option

Now that you have had an opportunity to consider these options in brief, we show you in the next chapter how to approach the choice of the best probable exit options for your business.

CHAPTER

5 How to Choose the Best Exit Strategy

In this chapter we begin the process of showing you how to choose the best exit strategy for your business. We do this by:

- getting you to think about which option is likely to yield the greatest purchase price and give you the greatest personal satisfaction
- taking you through an options elimination worksheet, which will help you eliminate those options that are not relevant to your business, leaving you with a shortlist from which to make your final choice.

Establishing the alternatives: an overview

The first step in exit strategy planning involves choosing the best exit option, that is, the option that will maximize the value of an owners' equity and be the most favourable from a financial and personal satisfaction point of view. One way to start choosing your optimum exit strategy is by undertaking the following steps:

1. Establish your own personal preferences and needs.
2. Eliminate those exit options that do not apply to your business.

This could leave you with a choice of one or more options from which to make your final choice.

But, before you make your final choice, you should also consider the following:

- Which of the shortlisted options is likely to result in the maximum price for you?
- What is the likely impact of taxation on you personally (and any other partners or shareholders in the business) if you adopt this route?
- How long will you need to plan properly for an exit using this option and what is the possible current and future state of economy generally and your industry in particular?
- What are the likely costs of proceeding with any particular strategy (or option) compared with the potential increase in the disposal price?
- What will be the impact on your customers, financiers, suppliers and employees?
- Are you personally suited to the option chosen (for example will you make a good CEO of a public company, or a suitable franchisor of a franchise group)?

These issues are considered in more detail below.

	1 Can I achieve maximum value?	2 What is the risk factor in disposal?	3 Can I retain control after sale?	4 Will this be good for my personal financial planning?	5 Will I be assured payment?	6 Will I have deal flexibility?	7 What will my personal satisaction be?
1. Family succession	Yes	Moderate	Probably	Yes	No	Yes	Very high
2. Employees or managers (MBO/MBI)	Yes	Moderate	No (Unless on terms)	Yes	Depends on terms	Yes	Moderate/ to high
3. Sole trader merger	Yes	Moderate	Some	Yes	Yes	Yes	Moderate
4. Third party sale	Depends on timing	Low	No	Depends on timing	Depends on terms	Probably not	Moderate/ to low
5. Public listing	Yes	High	Yes	Yes	Yes for initial offering	No	High
6. Franchising	Yes	Moderate	Yes; of franchisor business	Yes	No	Yes	High
7. Managed close down	No	Low	No	Probably not	Yes	No	Low
8. Liquidation – fire sale	Definitely not	Low	No	No	Yes	No	Very low

Figure 5.1 Exit Options Assessment

Owner's personal preferences and needs

Where an owner has children (or other family members who could take over the business), it is usual for him or her to wish to pass on the business to a family member. The second preferred option for most owners is to sell to co-owners, or to management and employees. There are, of course other exit options to consider. In Figure 5.1 we look at the advantages and disadvantages of each option from the owner's personal point of view.

Figure 5.1 considers the options in terms of:

- Value: whether the option chosen will achieve the maximum value to the owner.
- Risk: the degree of risk involved in the chosen transaction.
- Control: the amount of control the owner has, both over the transaction and the management of the business after the sale.
- Personal financial planning: does the transaction assist in the personal financial planning of the owner, or can it be structured to assist these plans?
- Assuring payment: the likelihood of the seller being paid the total purchase price.
- Deal flexibility: the amount of flexibility that the transaction provides to the owner, including payment terms and working in the business after sale.
- Personal satisfaction: how much satisfaction (other than financial) is the owner likely to derive from the transaction?

Figure 5.1 could appear to favour certain methods over others in a subjective way, but these priorities may not reflect your views. The vital thing for you is whether your preferred option is practical and relevant to your business and your circumstances.

Elimination of exit options

The options elimination worksheet (Figure 5.2) will help you in the initial process of sifting out those options that are unsuitable or impractical for your particular business. Once you have eliminated the unsuitable options it will be easier for you to decide on the best option from the remaining ones.

Remember, you are not necessarily choosing the best option for current economic circumstances or for your business's current situation, but what is possible in future with planning. This is why the possible future state of the economy and your industry at the proposed disposal date could be important.

Options elimination: how to use the worksheet

The worksheet lists from left to right the various exit options available to private business owners in what could be considered as their order of preference. We suggest that you work through the worksheet from the top left-hand corner considering each question until you come to a negative and then moving on to the right to the next option until you arrive at an option that seems possible for your business.

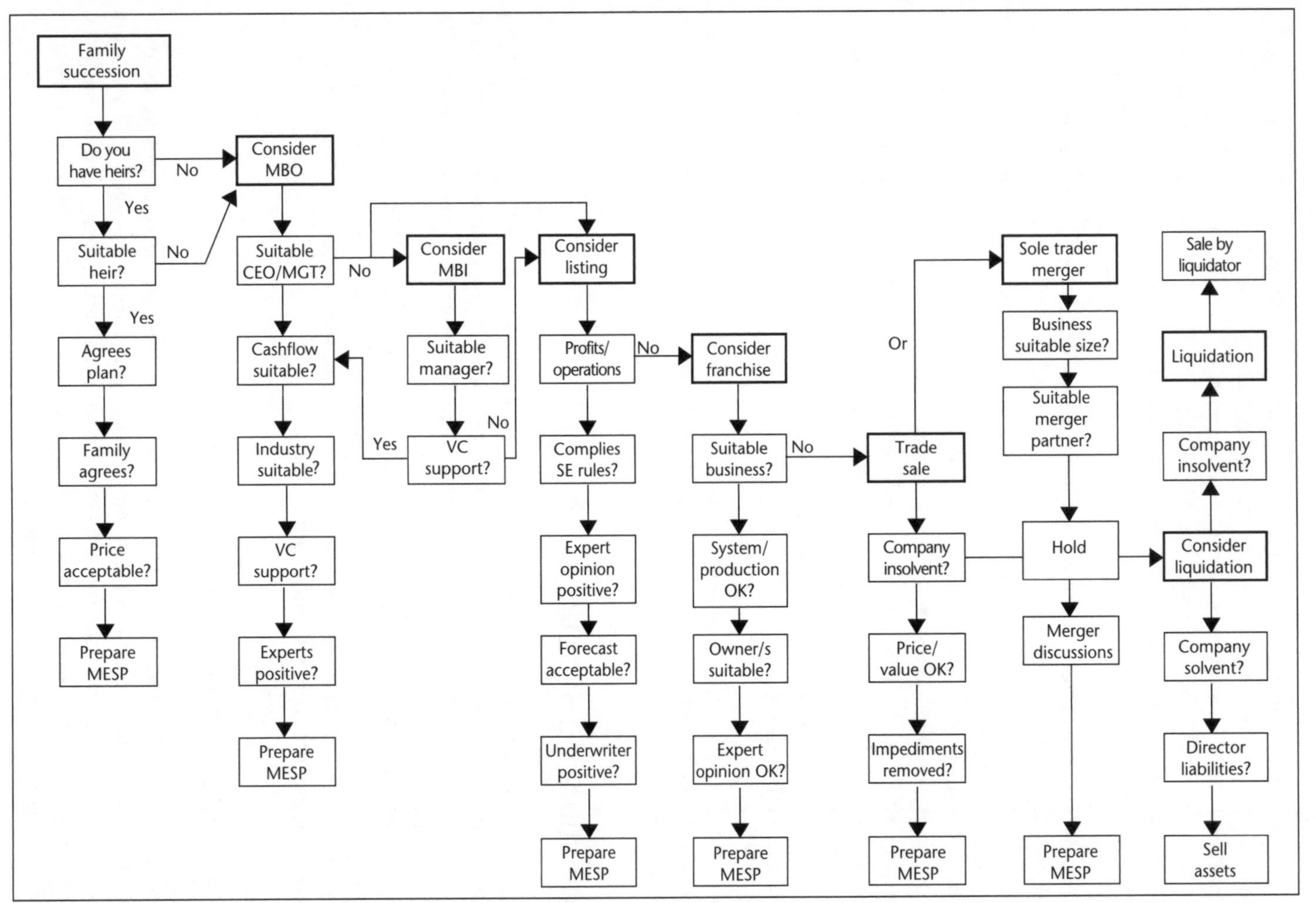

Figure 5.2 Options Elimination Worksheet

FAMILY SUCCESSION

If you have heir/s you should explore this option first (Figure 5.3). The crucial question will be how suitable they are. If the answer to either of these questions is negative you cannot proceed with this option and you will need to consider your next option, that is, an MBO.

Should you believe that there is an heir available who is suitable, you can then proceed to the next stage of elimination: that is, does the heir agree with your plan? You continue with the elimination process until you come up with a 'NO' answer, which forces you to move right to the next option. (You should read Appendix 4 if you feel that Family Succession could be suitable for your business.)

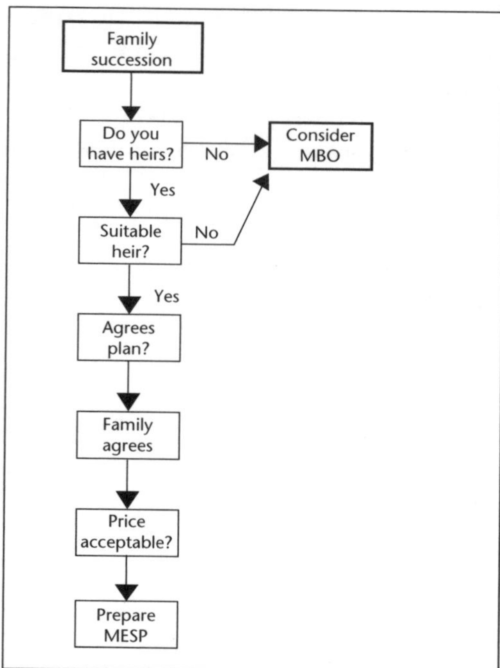

Figure 5.3 Options Elimination Worksheet: Family Succession

MANAGEMENT BUYOUTS

The first question here is whether a suitable leader exists in the business around whom an MBO team can be built (Figure 5.4). (If not can management expertise be brought in from outside?) Second, is there a suitable management team? If the answer to both is 'YES', you need then to address the suitability of the business itself for an MBO. The major areas to consider are whether the business cash flow can service the debt involved in financing the buyout (which is usually based on borrowed money) and whether a suitable investor or lender can be found to finance the buyout.

Should there be no suitable leaders or managers in the business, the next step is to see whether suitable management can be brought in and trained, or alternatively whether outside management is interested in purchasing the business. This is known as a management buy-in.

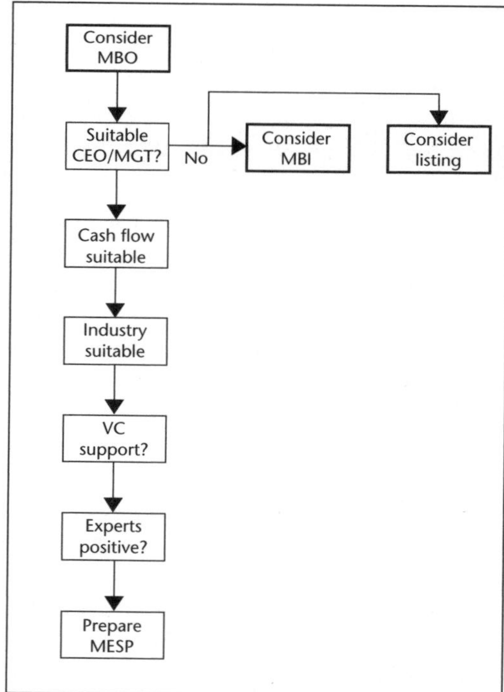

Figure 5.4 Options Elimination Worksheet: Management Buyout

MANAGEMENT BUY-INS

If you decide that a suitable leader and/or management from outside are available you would then proceed to examine the business cash flow and likelihood of venture capital investment support. (You should refer to Appendix 5 for more information on MBOs and MBIs.)

Should neither an MBO nor an MBI be practical for you, you would now move on to consider the next option, which is public listing, or flotation.

PUBLIC LISTING (OR FLOTATION)

Although we suggest here that a public listing is considered after the family succession and MBO options, if your business is suitable for a flotation listing this should probably be your first option (Figure 5.5). A public listing can represent a bonanza to the private business owner, not least because it provides flexibility in disposal, being the first stage in potentially a multi-stage disposal plan.

There are two major hurdles in considering your business suitability for listing, namely:

1. Compliance with the relevant Stock Exchange Listing Rules (which usually involve turnover and net asset value tests).
2. Garnering investment support.

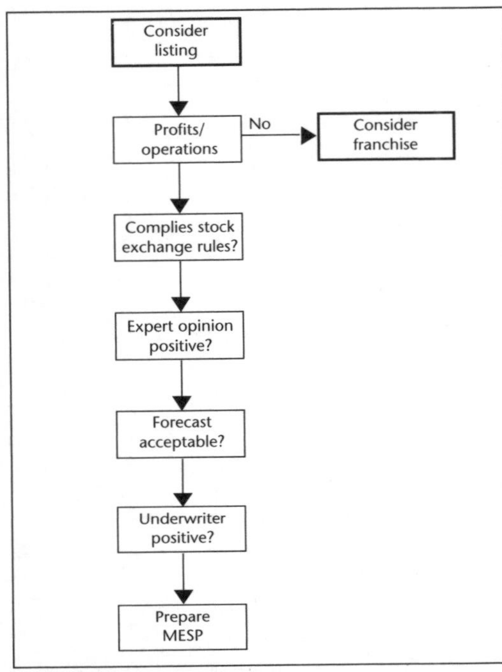

Figure 5.5 Options Elimination Worksheet: Listing

A sponsoring broker would give you preliminary advice on the second issue. If the preliminary advice is positive, you should then consider this option very seriously and commission a formal report on the suitability of your business for a public listing. (You should also refer to Appendix 6.)

If the public listing option is not suitable, or not practical, for most businesses there are still two positive disposal options remaining, namely, franchising and a trade sale.

If you are a sole trader (or run a very small business) there could also be a sole trader merger option; while the least positive option of ceasing to trade through an orderly disposal of assets could also be a possibility.

FRANCHISING

To establish whether your business is suitable for franchising you need to ascertain whether the business has a system that can be taught or transferred to third parties who would be prepared to pay for the rights to use it (Figure 5.6). This means that the system itself would have to be either new, or packaged in a new way, or that the products or services are new, or presented in a new way. Obviously, your business will have to be working well and trading profitably.

You should read Appendix 7 to establish whether your business might be suitable for franchising and you might need to consult an experienced, reputable franchising expert for advice on these points.

The next question to consider is whether you, as the potential franchisor, have the ability to provide back-up services to franchisees, and are also a suitable person to deal with and motivate franchisees on a day-to-day basis. And, of course, suitable franchisees must be available in the geographic areas in which you wish to open the franchise businesses.

If these appear positive, perhaps you could ask the expert to provide you with a report on your business's overall suitability for franchising. If this is also positive, franchising could be your best exit option.

If you feel franchising is not right for your business, you should now move onto the next option, which is a trade sale.

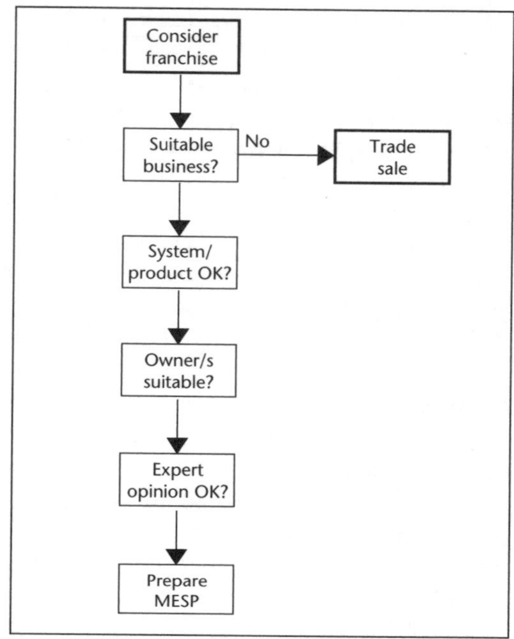

Figure 5.6 Options Elimination Worksheet: Franchise

TRADE SALE (OR SALE TO A THIRD PARTY)

A trade sale is the most utilized of all exit options available to private businesses (Figure 5.7). [*Note*: It must be emphasized that the choice of a disposal option is both a personal one and a business one, and depends on your particular circumstances. You might prefer, for example, to go down the route of a trade sale as your first choice even if a flotation or an MBO are realistic options for your business. Similarly, even if you have suitable heirs, the value or financial structure of your business may make the family succession option impossible to achieve. Also, other factors such as your health might mean that a short-term sale is the only practical option for you – see Chapter 8.]

You should now go through the trade sale elimination process. First, does your business have 'going concern' status and value (as opposed to a fire sale value)? Or if it is not currently a solvent going concern, can it be recapitalized and then improved so that by time of sale it will be?

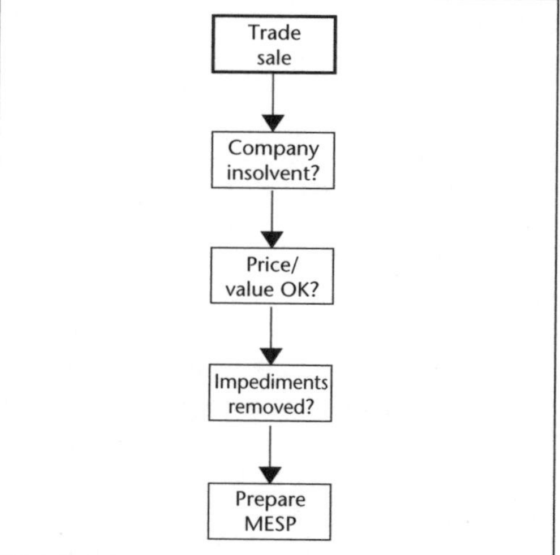

Figure 5.7 Options Elimination Worksheet: Trade Sale

SOLE TRADER MERGER

Businesses merge all the time, but most of these mergers are often not part of an exit strategy. What we are considering here is the choice of a merger as a deliberate exit strategy for sole traders, or owners of very small companies (Figure 5.8). As a sole trader of a small business, in practice your choices of exit options will be a family succession, a trade sale, a sole trader merger, or ceasing to trade.

The first point is that, obviously, you need to be a sole trader to qualify for this particular exit option. The next consideration is to decide whether you can find a suitable business with which to merge, and whether the owner of that business is of like mind to you in terms of wanting to merge and in general business philosophy. If you think all this is possible it would be worthwhile to undertake some informal research and discussions with potential partners to progress the matter before setting out formally to plan your exit through this route. (You should refer to Appendix 9 for more information of this exit route.)

If having worked through this and the other options you decide none are suitable, you are left with the option, if your business is solvent, of a managed close down or, if your company is insolvent, a liquidation.

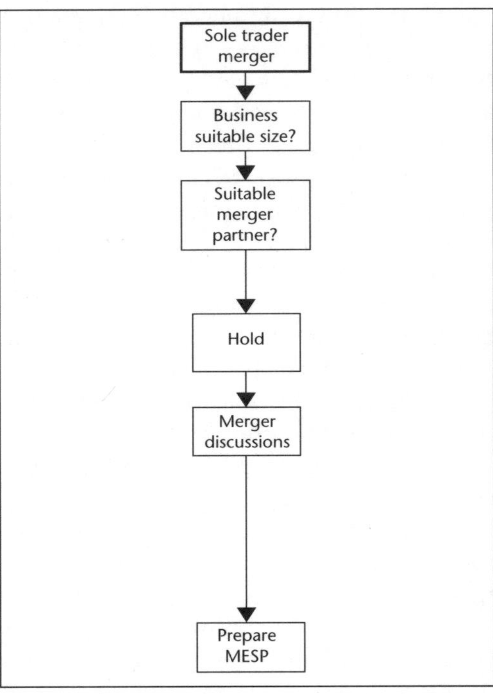

Figure 5.8 Options Elimination Worksheet: Sole Trader Merger

CEASING TO TRADE (OR LIQUIDATION)

The last, and usually the least preferred option for business owners, is to cease trading (Figure 5.9). The first question to ask if you trade as a company is whether or not your company is solvent. Where the company is insolvent, the directors will probably have to wind it up. The liquidator will then be in charge of the company's affairs and will act in the best interest of creditors. If the company is solvent you could choose a managed close down with an orderly sale of assets as an exit option. For example, where the business is of the type that loses all value when the current owner leaves or dies (because all the business 'know how' is in the owner's head) a close down might be the only practical way to exit.

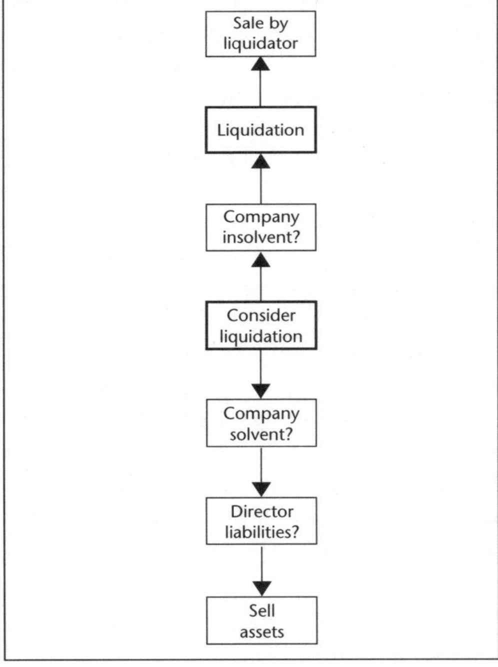

Figure 5.9 Options Elimination Worksheet: Ceasing to Trade

(Appendix 10 examines other examples of when a managed close down could be advantageous and you should refer to it if you are considering this option.)

Other considerations

The worksheet is a useful way to begin to understand the exit options that could be open to you. We do not pretend that it is the only way, or that it is a substitute for expert advice and deep consideration. When you have worked through the elimination worksheet, read the following chapters in this book and studied the relevant appendices, you will, at least, have a framework to identify the best disposal option for your business with some certainty.

The other considerations that will be important to all owners will be related to taxation, costs, timing and whether you can put your business in shape to meet the requirements of the exit option you have chosen.

Appendix 1 covers the likely impact of taxation on your disposal proceeds in some depth. This will alert you to the issues involved in selling your business and enable you to ask the relevant questions of your advisers.

The costs of exiting your business will vary greatly depending on the route you choose and how much professional assistance you require. For example, should you decide to go down the trade sale route and handle the sale yourself this will be far, far cheaper than floating your company on the Main Board of the London Stock Exchange. But the real issue is the total net sale proceeds to you from either route; the net benefit rather than the gross cost. Again, you will have a better idea of this once you have read this book and taken the appropriate advice.

The timing of any business sale is always a difficult issue. It is impossible to be sure of economic cycles and the changes in the financial desirability of industry sectors. Our approach in this book is to advise you to groom your business for disposal through a managed exit strategy with a target date in mind, but to be prepared to postpone the sale if there is an economic downturn at the time you plan to sell. Your exit planning should have made big improvements in your company's operations and profits and, hence, its profitability, so that you will be reaping current rewards anyway. You will also be in a good position to wait a while until the market improves.

The final question is whether you can put your business into the state it needs to be to take advantage of the option you have chosen. For example, will you be able to grow the business (both organically and, if necessary, by acquisition) to reach the minimum size requirement to attract institutional support for either an MBO or a flotation? Or, in a trade sale, will your business be ready for sale? These questions could be a matter of giving yourself enough time to plan whether you are able to remove the business's impediments to sale, or perhaps it depends on the projected and actual state of the economy with regard to business values in your sector.

The final choice of option

You, as the business owner, should be the best person to know your own personality and the potential of your business, and how these can be best presented to whatever parties you need to support you in your plans and ultimately pay you a reasonable price for your equity. This knowledge, coupled with a thorough understanding of each exit option, will enable you to reach a measured decision, either on your own, or in collaboration with professional advisers, on what option is the one that will maximize your exit outcomes.

CHAPTER

6 Impediments to Sale

In this chapter we will look at operational and structural aspects of your business to identify those things that could make it difficult to sell, or which will depress its sale price. We call these things 'impediments to sale'.

These can be considered in two ways, namely:

- their probable affect on the value of your business and,
- by the length of time it takes for them to be removed.

Discovering your impediments too late

One of the biggest drawbacks of unplanned disposals is that owners often find out about their business's sale impediments during the process of the disposal itself, either when they have the business valued, or during the due diligence process. This can result in a greatly reduced disposal price, or even in the sale falling through. Even worse, if you as the seller have left an unplanned sale until late in life, it may be too late for you to fix the problems and put the business up for sale again, and could result in it being closed down.

Unsaleable businesses

An important fact about business life that might come as a surprise to those unfamiliar with business disposals is that unlike real property, which will eventually sell if you reduce the price sufficiently, some businesses are totally unsaleable regardless of their price. This is usually because the business is losing money, or because its assets, operations or structure make it unattractive to potential buyers.

Through the exit strategy planning process impediments to sale can be identified at an early stage and removed (or corrected) over a period of time, hopefully well before the need to sell arises. As an owner, your objective should be to sell a profitable and vibrant business at the optimum market price. The worst outcome for you will be to try to sell a tired, disorganized business that is shrinking instead of growing steadily, and end up having to close it down. Allowing yourself enough time to plan for your exit is vital if you are to achieve your goals.

What value is affected?

The aspects of value most affected by impediments to sale in a business are going concern value and goodwill value. These concepts were discussed in Chapter 3. The value of real property, for example, can be totally unaffected by lack of profitability of the business it houses. Some hard assets, such as motor vehicles are, likewise, little affected by weakness in the business that owns them. But, if a business is unprofitable, both the going concern value of its core assets and its goodwill value (in the sense that the business can command a premium over its net asset value) can be greatly depressed or non-existent.

Categorization of major impediments to sale

One way of looking at impediments to sale is to consider them in categories of importance. For example, impediments could be listed in the following categories:

- those impediments that will make a business difficult to sell and/or have a large negative impact on its value
- those impediments that will have a moderate impact on value
- those impediments that are largely cosmetic, but can still reduce value.

(There are also other impediments or difficulties that owners face when trying to sell a business, which are not easy to categorize. We will consider these separately below under 'Other impediments to sale'.)

The above categories are by no means mutually exclusive and any individual impediment might be more or less important to your particular business, which would influence the category in which it was placed as far as your business is concerned. However, a grouping of the more usual impediments in this way will indicate which are potentially the most damaging and the order of importance of the task of removing them. Finally, all businesses are different in their way, and we cannot include in these lists all impediments to sale that could exist in every business in the UK!

CATEGORY 1: IMPEDIMENTS THAT MAKE YOUR BUSINESSES DIFFICULT TO SELL AND/OR HAVE A LARGE IMPACT ON VALUE

These impediments include the following:

Unrealistically high sale price

The biggest reason for private businesses failing to sell is owners who overprice their businesses and who will not negotiate the price downwards to a reasonable market price. If owners insist on offering businesses at unrealistically high prices and are serious about selling them, they will have to reduce the price to achieve a sale. This price reduction is often implemented in stages over a long period, which gives the worst possible signal to potential buyers and puts an unbearable strain on the business and its owners, and sometimes on its employees. The sensible approach is to ensure that the business is offered for a reasonable price from the outset. By reasonable price we mean one based on a realistic valuation using acceptable valuation methods. The price at which the business is offered need not be the same as the valuation nor the lowest price that you will take, but it must be within a reasonable negotiating distance of your lowest price and should be based on a realistic valuation.

Some partners/shareholders not wishing to sell

Although it appears obvious that all owners should agree to sell before the business is offered for sale, and that they should all be working in unison once the business is put on the market, many businesses are put up for disposal where some of the owners are lukewarm, at best, about the idea of selling. Often, the result is that these owners refuse to negotiate, or are so difficult in their negotiations that the sale falls through.

Another reason for this problem could be that there is no shareholder/partnership agreement (see Chapter 2) in place that smoothes the way for an exit by establishing that all principals will accept certain paths of action where disposal is concerned. The lack of such an agreement can seldom be rectified late in the disposal process and is a perfect example of the need to plan ahead for your exit and the problems that can beset you if you do not. One way of getting rid of this problem, when there is no shareholders' agreement in place, could be to buy out the minority shareholders well before you plan to sell.

The business is losing money

Where a business is losing money it will not usually command a goodwill value, and even if it is sold as a going concern it will not usually command a going concern premium. (Exceptions to this rule are start-up, or early-stage businesses that have not reached their profit potential, or where a business has an intangible asset of value that is deemed technically to be goodwill.) At best, from your point of view as the seller, someone will buy the business as a going concern, paying more for the assets than they would realize at auction. At worst, the business will fail to attract a buyer and will be broken up, with its assets sold at auction at fire sale prices. (If you have a company that is losing money to the extent that it is insolvent, the directors will probably have to wind it up immediately.) It is a distressing fact of business life that fire sales are a fairly common occurrence, especially in the case of smaller businesses that are losing money. Here, the realization price of assets will often fall below their balance sheet values, resulting in the phenomenon of 'negative goodwill'.

Gross margins are too low

A business can be profitable with very low gross margins (supermarkets are a good example). But outside businesses with dominant market share and huge sales, low margin businesses are usually very risky, and investors know it. Institutional investors are very wary of businesses with low gross margins relative to their sector because they fear they are particularly vulnerable to change, not only in market conditions but also in management and ownership. The important point to understand is that if two businesses have the same net profit but one is achieving it from a lower gross sales figure, it will usually be more valuable than the one that is achieving it from a higher sales figure. As a generalization, this will be because the one with the lower sales is perceived to be less risky and will, therefore, command a higher multiple applied to its profits to arrive at its value. You will need to analyse your business product by product and division by division to eradicate low gross margin areas, either by working on the cost of goods side or, perhaps, by removing some product lines or activities.

Goodwill cannot be transferred

This problem arises, first, when all the technical skills and/or managerial knowledge necessary to run the business are in the minds of the vendors and there is no remaining management able to assist the buyers, or no time for the vendors to conduct a proper handover. The other typical loss of goodwill arises when at least one of the former owners plans to go into competition with the business being sold and is not bound by a restraint of trade provision in the sales contract. This can come about, for example, when the majority of partners decide to sell a business following a partnership dispute in which a dissident partner has been dismissed.

Reliance on a few major customers, or on key short-term contracts for the majority of its business, which puts the maintainability of current profits (and the business's value) in doubt

In the case of reliance on too few customers, purchasers will be particularly concerned that the departure of the vendor will weaken the relationship with these key customers. In the case of key contracts being short term, the purchasers will be concerned that they will be lost completely, particularly when the vendor leaves after sale. It is surprising, but true, that so many businesses will trade for years with a few customers or clients only and make no effort to expand their customer base. These businesses can be very profitable in the hands of the current owners, who are usually unpleasantly surprised by the difficulty of realizing a reasonable price on disposal. Technically speaking, the values of these businesses are depressed because the p/e ratio applied to their profits is very low to compensate for the risks involved in maintaining profits.

Low market share

This is an issue for bigger private businesses trying to attract institutional investors or overseas buyers. Research has shown that the businesses with the biggest market share make the biggest profits and, if you are in this league or hoping to move into it, you must increase your share of the market in your industry, sector or niche. The amount of time you have given yourself to plan your exit will determine to some extent whether you can achieve an enhanced market share through organic growth or acquisition.

Lack of agreements with principals, suppliers and employees

When a business's operations are reliant on agency agreements, it is vital that these agreements are current and in writing. Without this a business could be valueless. Value will also be affected to a lesser extent by lack of current agreements with key suppliers and key employees, and it is important that you have locked in key employees as much as you can. Note, however, a related problem where the potential purchaser might not wish to keep people with whom you have employment agreements.

Value of assets more than value of the business

This problem arises when the total value of the business calculated by conventional methods (such as capitalization of maintainable earnings or discounted cash flow) is less than the market value of the business's assets as a going concern, or as shown on the company's balance sheet. This can arise for several reasons, such as:

1. The business owns valuable assets that are not necessary for the production of its income: for example, the freehold of commercial premises in which the business operates. Here the simple solution is to sell the property in a separate transaction. In other cases that might involve, for example, plant and equipment, some work might need to be done to establish which assets are non-essential before they are sold separately.

2. Stock accumulation. Where a business has accumulated stock levels that distort the business's balance sheet value compared with its total market value arrived at through conventional methods of valuation, a sale price based on conventional valuation will realize less than the business assets are worth. The simple answer could be to try and sell off excess stock separately but this could have adverse taxation implications depending on how the stock has been treated for tax purposes in previous accounting years. In all cases of excess assets, the key issue is whether the assets are necessary for the production of the business's income. If they are not, steps must be taken to remedy the situation through selling the excess assets separately, or the business could be unsaleable at a reasonable market price. If all the assets are necessary for income production, but market value is still less than asset value, then the business's real value will be as calculated through normal methods and unless profits are improved there will be no goodwill; or even negative goodwill (that is, where total business value as a going concern is worth less than asset value).

Size of the business

This is a difficult and often contradictory point. Sometimes in small businesses without asset backing, the bigger the business the less its relative value is likely to be. This arises because small business purchasers often have difficulty raising large amounts of capital. So it may be better to divide your business into two smaller businesses when you wish to sell, rather than trying to sell a large one. (If your business undertakes activities that are quite different, you could also find that splitting them will make it easier for you to get a sale: see below.) Conversely, there is evidence to suggest that in larger private businesses the bigger the profit the higher the multiple used to value it will be and, therefore, the higher its value will be relative to a business with smaller profits. This is particularly so if a business is being floated on the Stock Exchange, or where institutional investors are involved as purchasers, in, for example, an MBO. Where being too small is an impediment to sale, growth through acquisition is often necessary.

A history of a large turnover of key staff

The seriousness of this impediment could rely on the type of exit option and the type of buyer. It will be least serious in a trade sale where the purchasers intend to merge your operation with their own and already employ the staff necessary to undertake all the key functions in your business. But it could be a fatal impediment where an institution is thinking of backing an MBO and will be relying entirely on your staff to run the business. Why staff leave any particular business can be a complex issue but, if this is a problem in your business, you should examine all the circumstances involved and try to put permanent solutions in place.

CATEGORY 2: MODERATE IMPACT ON VALUE

The impediments to sale considered here are those that will depress sale prices, but are not usually critical to the chances of a sale being completed. The degree of negativity will rely on how severe the problem is in each case.

Business is too diversified

When a business carries on two or more completely different and incompatible activities, these businesses have usually evolved due to the special interests or skills of the owner or because of historical reasons. The answer to the problem is usually to separate the businesses and sell the parts in stages, or separately.

Poor accounting methods that produce unreliable or inadequate reports, and/or accounting records in which personal and business expenses are confused

If this problem is not rectified, potential buyers will have no confidence in the performance of the business. Some owners and their accountants try to rectify these problems by producing true accounts in the year immediately prior to sale, or by providing corrected accounts to potential buyers with what they believe are appropriate adjustments or 'add-backs'. Neither of these solutions is adequate. The answer is to introduce accurate, professional accounting methods at least three years prior to the planned disposal and to publish accurate accounting information during this time. This provides not only a reliable record of performance, but also establishes a true pattern of performance. You should also tidy up your balance sheet over this period by selling off slow-moving or obsolete stock, writing off bad and doubtful debts, and selling excess assets. Finally, you should ensure that your statutory accounts are up to date.

Profits are depressed because of excessive spending on non-essential items

The issue here is not that the owner's personal expenses have depressed profits, but that profits are depressed by expenditure, such as marketing expenses, that is not necessary for the production of current profits but has longer-term benefits to the business. The solution to this is to revert to a normal spending pattern (or to treat this expenditure in the accounts in a way that is more positive for current profit) for at least three years. (Note also the reverse approach where a business in the period immediately before sale stops spending on things that are essential to maintain profits in the longer term, and thus boosts current profits.)

Owners staying on too long

This can result in:

- trading results becoming poor
- employees lacking motivation
- brand and customer loyalty being eroded, and so on.

This is one of those impediments that is difficult to fix once it has occurred: a perfect example of prevention being better than cure. The answer is to plan for an exit in advance to ensure you do not get into this state. If you are already in this position all you can do is postpone your disposal while you rejuvenate the business either through your own efforts or through bringing in and training fresh management.

Unstable management and employees, who might decide to leave when informed of the proposed sale

If you have identified this as a possible problem, the answer is to allow yourself enough time to replace the people concerned.

Lack of suitably trained management and staff

This is a different problem to the one where goodwill cannot be transferred; rather it impacts on current trading efficiency and profitability. Recognition of the problem and time to fix it are all that is required.

Business premises

Business premises can be the cause of several problems, such as being located in a remote area that might not suit the purchaser, or having unfavourable lease conditions, or environmental or health and safety problems. Again, these impediments are difficult to fix if left to the last minute. An exit strategy plan that recognizes the need to address premises problems and has enough time to do so, should suffice.

Obsolete technology

This can go to the heart of a business and make it worthless. In other cases it is a serious problem, but one that can be fixed with planning. Alternatively, it could be a fairly minor issue of updating office computer equipment – see below.

Organizational structure

This can cover many areas, but of particular interest to buyers is the personnel structure with regard to how responsibilities have been allocated between owners, managers and staff. Part of this should be covered in your review of management's ability to assist the new owners, but issues of management to staff ratios, employee contracts and costs could be equally important. Other issues such as the need for branches and how they are managed could also be reviewed. In brief, buyers wish to purchase a business in which these reviews and the necessary clean-ups have been completed prior to sale rather than after it.

There is no business plan

This is an impediment to your exit strategy planning for several reasons. First, purchasers are likely to consider that your business is unprofessionally and badly run if it does not have a business plan. Next, they will have no confidence in your predictions of a profitable future unless it is backed up with well-considered projections. Remember, that purchasers are buying the future and not the past, and will be more interested in probable future profitability and how this will be achieved rather than your previous trading performance. Finally, where the raising of finance is an issue (for example, if you wish to make an acquisition to beef up your critical mass prior to a public listing, or where venture capital support is required for an MBO), not having a professionally prepared business plan will almost certainly scupper the project before it starts.

CATEGORY 3: COSMETIC PROBLEMS

The impediments in this category are ones that can be fairly quickly remedied within the time frame of a short-term plan. (Short-term planning is covered in Chapter 8.) Although not very serious in themselves these impediments can still have a dramatic impact on the disposal price. In business disposals, like most other areas of life, first impressions can be important and will sometimes influence whether a prospective buyer will continue to pursue the opportunity.

The business looks run down, untidy

This is a less important issue than the one where the owner himself or herself has run out of steam (resulting in a series of longer-term problems). This can merely be a matter of some tidying up, or applying a coat of paint to the factory.

Lack of statutory compliance in such areas as environment and health and safety

This is a very important issue, but one that you can probably remedy within a relatively short time. You should ensure that the business possesses all the appropriate licences and complies with the requisite procedures. It is worthwhile completing a formal audit to ensure complete compliance, as this will probably be required during the due diligence process. Of course, serious site contamination could be a much more serious issue and your audit will bring this to light.

Lack of adequate records

These are usually such things as records of suppliers, customers or subcontractors that have not been properly maintained. It should be a relatively easy matter to ensure that these are collated and presented in a business-like way. Also, it is necessary to ensure that all intangible and intellectual property has been properly valued and ownership properly documented.

Out-of-date computer equipment

There is a temptation, when a business is being sold, to leave updating of office equipment and the like to the purchasers. This could be mistake as it adds to the look and feel of a rundown business in decline. It could be preferable to update these before sale as part of the cosmetic clean-up.

Other impediments to sale

Here we look at attitudes and circumstances that make it difficult for a vendor to exit his or her business, or to receive the maximum after taxation return on sale, rather than matters that reduce the value of the business itself.

THE WRONG APPROACH

We discussed above the misconceptions vendors often have about the value of their businesses. Another major difficulty vendors have is that they do not understand what purchasers or investors are looking for in a business. For example:

- As we have said, purchasers are interested in the future and not in the past. You may have achieved great things with your business and it may have taken up the best years of your life, but purchasers are only interested in what profits it will make for them in the future.
- It is important to try to understand the different motivations of, say, an institutional investor in an MBO and private buyers in a trade sale. The most obvious one will be that the institutional investor will be looking for a reasonably quick exit (perhaps through a public listing or a secondary buyout), while private buyers might be looking at a long-term business to work in until they retire and then transfer to an heir.

NEGATIVE CIRCUMSTANCES

Circumstances or events can also impede the disposal of a business. These include the following.

Owner not able to pay borrowings in full on sale

A business disposal may be driven by the desire to clear debts and relieve personal pressures. If the disposal is not planned and is relying on an unrealistic disposal price, the final offers may be insufficient to meet the owner's expectations and, consequently, the business may have to be withdrawn from the market.

Owner not able to realize sufficient net capital from sale to retire in comfort

A business sale could be an important part of a retirement plan, which relies on a certain level of proceeds from the sale itself. If the selling price falls short, the whole retirement plan might need to be abandoned for the time being. (Note the net price could fall short through lack of taxation planning – see below.)

Unwillingness by vendor to provide vendor finance

Lack of finance is a big barrier in the disposal of smaller private companies, and to achieve the asking price vendors might need to provide help to the purchaser through provision of vendor finance on terms. But, the consequences of such a loan need to be considered in advance in the light of the vendor's financial planning so that there is the ability to be flexible if the need arises.

Unwillingness of seller to provide business information to potential buyers

It is not unusual for sellers to be reluctant to provide what they consider to be confidential business information to potential buyers. The problem is particularly acute when the potential buyer is a competitor. The seller wants a commitment before he or she will provide the information, while the buyer will not commit without the information. To counter this problem there needs to be a well thought out, progressive handover of information (depending on the buyer's response and interest) with supporting undertakings of confidentiality. As a seller, you should be aware that you will have to provide virtually all information about your business during the initial negotiating process, and you will need to provide everything during due diligence. Selling a business is often a painful experience with no guarantee of success, which is why it requires careful planning.

STRUCTURAL ISSUES

To ensure that you receive the maximum after-taxation amount from the disposal of your business requires careful tax planning. A major impediment to minimizing taxation could be the way you have structured your companies (for example, with a holding company owning, and subsequently selling, operating companies). You need to obtain advice on this at the earliest possible stage because some solutions need several years to expire before they are fully successful. (You should refer to Appendix 1 for further information about this subject.)

Another problem that could hinder a sale is lack of suitable shareholders' agreements. This is another impediment that should be addressed immediately, because the events it protects you against could happen at any time, and not only when you would usually begin planning to dispose of your business. (You should refer to Chapter 2 for more information on business continuity planning.)

COMPANY LIABILITIES

Because taper relief from capital gains tax is available to individuals only, more individual shareholders will now wish to sell their company shares (instead of companies selling their assets), which will transfer a company's liabilities as well as its assets to the purchasers. This will put added importance on vendor indemnities and warranties, and it emphasizes the need to ensure all company 'skeletons' are laid to rest before you sell! Specifically, you should complete any company litigation that is outstanding.

Figure 6.1 summarizes the common impediments to sale.

The main impediments to disposal of a business at its optimum net sales price are as follows:

a) Personal and general reasons

1. Owners have set an unrealistic sales price.
2. Owners do not understand the needs or motivation of purchasers.
3. Some owners are unwilling, or reluctant to sell (untidy share register, or lack of shareholders' agreement).
4. Timing is wrong: economy is depressed, equity values are low, finance is hard to raise.
5. Lack of taxation planning.

b) Operational issues

1. Business is losing money; inconsistent trading performance.
2. Gross margins in the business are too low.
3. Business has too low a share of its market, or niche.
4. Goodwill cannot be transferred: owner is the business; lack of management support for incoming owners.
5. Lack of a business plan.
6. Lack of suitably trained staff and management.
7. Reliance on too few customers or clients.
8. Lack of suitable employee and management agreements.
9. Supplier, agency or other agreements lapsed, or not in writing.
10. Obsolete or redundant plant and equipment.
11. Out-of-date, lapsed and uncommercial agreements with principals, suppliers, and so on.
12. Lack of compliance with trading regulations, licenses and so on.
13. Too high value of assets compared with total business value.
14. Inadequate private company accounting methods: profits depressed because of personal expenses, cash sales not recorded, statutory accounts not up to date and so on.
15. Non-synergistic business divisions or activities.
16. Premises:
    - ☐ Lack of compliance with environmental, health and safety and other regulations.
    - ☐ Premises are located in a remote or unsuitable area.
    - ☐ Lease conditions, which are not compatible with the potential purchaser's needs.
17. Owner has stayed on too long – business has suffered accordingly: looks and feels run down.
18. Lack of marketing and sales and employee records.

Figure 6.1 Common Impediments to Sale

Identifying impediments

Identifying impediments is the first step to fixing them. Some impediments are obvious: for example, you either have a shareholders' agreement that addresses all the important exit issues, or you do not. Some impediments in your business will become obvious once you have read this chapter. You could also be aware of other impediments in your business that have not been mentioned here and that are likely to prevent a sale or reduce your hoped-for sale price. If you are unsure, you might wish to consult with your business advisers for some objective advice.

Removing impediments

Broadly speaking, your plan of action in rectifying sales impediments can be divided into three groups (though it should be borne in mind that since no two businesses are the same these can only be generalizations) as follows:

- those that will take three to five years to fix
- those that will take one to three years to fix
- those that can be fixed within a year of sale.

LONG-TERM ACTION: THREE TO FIVE YEARS

The impediments dealt with below are structural, or imbedded within the operating culture of the business, and they will take a long time to rectify. They should be addressed at least three years before you plan to sell. In some cases you will take longer to solve the problems. Probably the best way of addressing the impediments in this category is to accept that they should be tackled immediately, whenever you plan to sell. These impediments include the following:

- Lack of taxation planning: you should ensure that your corporate structure does not impede your ability to minimize the impact of taxation on your disposal proceeds. You should obtain expert taxation advice as soon as possible.
- Lack of a shareholders' or partners' agreement: this could inhibit your ability to dispose of your business. You should obtain expert advice on this immediately.
- Business is losing money: it is vital to tackle this problem immediately, regardless of when you plan to sell. But, losing money is only the effect and you must identify the causes for the losses (which could be any of hundreds of reasons) and address those.
- Goodwill cannot be transferred because knowledge and/or skill are all in owner's head. The answer is to have suitably trained management in place. This could take some considerable time.
- Reliance on a few major customers or on short-term contracts: in the case of reliance on too few customers, it will be a long-term project to broaden the customer base. With short-term contracts, it could be possible to rectify this situation relatively quickly.
- Obsolete technology: the process of upgrading and updating your business should start immediately.
- In family succession the training of the successor should begin as early as possible, but at least five years before disposal, while overcoming the potential lack of funding should

begin at least three years prior to the planned disposal, depending on the type of funding package that is needed.
- Repayment of borrowings; planning to be liquid on retirement should begin as early as possible.
- Stock accumulation: depending on the extent of the problem, the task of selling off stock might need to start at least five years prior to your planned sale.
- Poor accounting methods: it is advisable to begin the process of presenting accounts that reflect the true trading position of the company as soon as possible.
- Business premises: if the problem is leased premises that are unfavourably situated or unsuitable in any other way, early action will need to be taken depending on the amount of notice required to quit.
- Large turnover of key staff: this can be a complex issue and you need to undertake a broad review. Some of the issues you could consider include the following:
  - Examine your pay structure compared with your industry as a whole.
  - Do your competitors have employee share acquisition schemes in place?
  - How does your in-house pension scheme compare with those of your competitors?
  - How good is your working environment?
  - Do key employees have a clear understanding of their promotion prospects?
  - Do you communicate with key employees about such things as the business strategy?

MEDIUM-TERM ACTION: LESS THAN THREE YEARS

Typically, the impediments listed below can be rectified within three years of your planned disposal. But, generalizations could be dangerous here and the time required to fix the particular problems in your business could take considerably longer. These impediments include the following:

- Business is too diversified: you could consider solving this through a separate sale of the smaller divisions first.
- Excess assets: with excess stock, we have suggested that, depending on the amount, you might need to begin the sell-off five years before your intended sale. If your excess assets are property or plant, the sell-off has to be timed to fit in with your use while you are still the owner of the business.
- Depressed profits through expenditure on non-essentials: a more realistic approach to expenditure and to the method of accounting for accruals adopted by the business should begin within three years of your planned sale to allow these changes to be properly reflected in the business's books.
- Agreements with principals, suppliers and key employees: work should begin on these issues two to three years prior to your sale.
- You have stayed on too long and business is suffering as a result: if you really wish to get a better price than you are likely to get with an immediate sale, you will need to put another two to three years into the business with a renewed attitude (and, probably new management) to rejuvenate it.
- Management and key employees who are likely to quit when you sell: allow yourself two to three years to replace these people.
- Training management and key staff to improve productivity: this could be related to the issue above and will also require a couple of years to complete.

- Simplifying or cleaning up the management/personnel structure: again, this could be tied up with the items above. The time you will need to fix this will depend on the depth of the problem.

SHORT-TERM ACTION: MATTERS TO BE ADDRESSED WITHIN A YEAR OF SALE

These matters should be addressed within a year of your sale:

- Establishing a realistic valuation of the business: if you have planned properly for your sale, you will have timed your exit to coincide with achieving a certain value for your business, or to coincide with a timescale. We have said that unrealistic values are the biggest destroyer of disposal plans, so it is important that, before you take the final plunge of putting your business on the market, you establish a realistic market value based on sound economic principals. This will give you a reference point to establish your asking price. This valuation can be established any time in the year before sale.
- Preparing a business plan: although this is a major impediment to sale it is one that can be rectified quickly and easily by preparing a plan in the year before you plan to sell. It is important that your business plan is a full strategic and operational plan and not just a financial forecast. It is worth considering getting professional advice on its production.
- All partners/shareholders willing to sell: you should get agreement from all partners/shareholders to sell, and to the price that is being asked and the one that will be accepted, well before you take formal steps to sell. If these issues are covered in a formal way in your shareholders' agreements you should confirm that you have the shareholders' goodwill and co-operation in the sale process.
- Business looks run down, untidy, and so on: here the action need only be completed immediately before sale, so work backwards from your selling date to decide how long it will take to complete.
- Lack of operational records: these need to be completed to show to potential purchasers and can be completed at any time in the months prior to sale.
- Out-of-date computers, and so on: this can be tackled in the months preceding sale.

There are other things you should do in the year before sale, which do not involve the removal of impediments as such, but are part of preparing your business for the sale process. These include:

- advising suppliers, customers and bankers of your plans
- advising and preparing staff for the sale
- advising all principals and agents of the sale
- attending to your personal financial plans, if you are retiring.

General ideas on removing sale impediments

Although the programme for removing impediments will de different for each business, it will help you if you follow the general guidelines below:

- Start early: all business problems take longer to fix than is first thought.
- Be realistic: can you fix the problems yourself or do you need outside help? (In some cases you might be the reason the problems exist in the first place. If so, are you really the right person to fix them?)
- If you have used advisers to identify the problems, are these advisers the best people to fix the problems?
- Are your current legal and taxation advisers sufficiently expert to be advising you on some of the more technical issues? Do you need a second opinion?
- Always keep your goals in mind: the long-term rewards of removing your sale impediments justify a great deal of effort and some expense.

PART 3 *Preparing and Implementing your Plans*

CHAPTER

7 Business Planning: The Essential Elements

Most small business owners seem to hate planning, yet planning is as important as any other function in your business. A business plan is the compass by which you steer your business and it is the operational foundation of your master exit strategy plan. In this chapter we will look at:

- how you should approach the task of putting together your business plan by starting with a strategic thinking session and then moving on to writing the plan itself
- how the business plan leads in to the master exit strategy plan
- why plans sometimes fail
- how you should monitor the implementation of the plan.

What is a business plan?

A business plan is many things. It is the map of a business's future. It establishes business goals. It sets the tramlines on which to steer the business on a successful path. It looks at where the business is now and where it wants to be in the future. It deals with what the business will do to achieve its goals and how it will do it. It provides a logical course and a framework for guiding the business forward and, importantly, checking on, or monitoring, its progress.

A business plan has both an internal use and an external use. The internal use is to assist the business in its operations, while the usual external use is to tell outsiders about the business (for such things as raising money from banks and investors).

In exit strategy planning a business plan is the foundation on which an exit strategy plan is built.

The purpose of business planning

A business plan can be said to have four main purposes, namely:

1. In operational terms, a business plan commits to writing those ideas that are sometimes only in the business owner's head. By forcing you to commit your ideas to paper it clarifies and focuses your ideas for the business's future operations and sets out the ways in which you will implement them.
2. A business plan is an essential tool in any business start-up or refinancing need, either through loans or by bringing in equity partners. Both banks and investors usually insist on business plans before making a decision to lend money to a business.

3. Where you are intending to bring investors into any venture involving the growth, restructuring or disposal of your business (including, for example, a management buyout), a well-prepared business plan is essential, especially if you wish to attract the interest of institutional or professional investors.
4. Most importantly, operational business planning is an important step in your total business planning process. It formalizes your continuity planning, it defines your operational planning and it is the starting point of an MESP, whose implementation should give you the best chance of optimizing your price and satisfaction when you dispose of your business.

How to write your own business plan

There is nothing mysterious or difficult about writing a business plan, so why do so many owners fail to write one? Business owners give many reasons for their failure, but the usual one is that they are too busy. We wonder whether they are too busy putting out fires caused by not having a business plan in the first place? Below we will provide you with the basics of a business plan, which should enable you to write one in a few hours.

We will approach the writing of a business plan in two stages, namely:

- holding a strategic planning meeting to formulate your ideas
- writing the plan.

The strategy session

Where a firm is very small and the owner makes most decisions, a business plan will be produced by only one (or perhaps two) people. Preparation of your plan should follow the steps described below in the strategy planning session, but will not be through the same formal meeting process.

In the case of a larger private business, it is important that the key managers in the business (including those in sales, production, finance and marketing) are involved in preparing the plan. It is very useful to bring these managers together in the strategy session as a first stage in preparing the plan.

SETTING UP THE MEETING

The strategy session with all key managers should take place in a location that is conducive to free discussion and which has a creative atmosphere. It is probably worth leaving the business premises and going to a conference room, or similar environment.

The length of the session should be a minimum of one day and, ideally, over a weekend when minds can concentrate on the planning process with minimum distractions from everyday work.

The session must be structured and preplanned, with agendas provided to all participants. (You should refer to the sample agenda, Figure 7.1.)

Date:

Location:

Facilitator:

Secretary:

Day One

Time	*Topic*	*Responsibility*
08.00	Opening comments	CEO
	Review agenda	Facilitator
	Review procedures for session	
	Review roles of facilitator and secretary	
08.30	Review participants' comments on mission statements	Facilitator
08.30–10.00	SWOT analysis, Part 1 Round table discussion aimed at identifying and documenting all of the company's strengths, opportunities, weaknesses and threats	Facilitator and group
10.00–10.15	Coffee Break	
10.15–12.30	SWOT analysis, Part 2 Continuance of SWOT analysis	Facilitator and group
12.30–1.30	Lunch	
1.30–2.30	Develop or redefine mission statement for organization	Facilitator and group
2.30–3.15	Analysis and identification of key results areas	Facilitator and group
3.15–3.30	Coffee Break	
3.30–5.00	Establish strategic objectives Within each key results area establish a small number of strategic objectives	Facilitator and group

Day Two

Time	*Topic*	*Responsibility*
08.00	Opening comments	CEO
08.15	Review of yesterday's proceedings	Facilitator
08.15–10.00	Establishing tactical objectives to address SWOTs, Part 1	Facilitator and group
10.00–10.15	Coffee Break	
10.15–12.30	Establishing tactical objectives to address SWOTs, Part 2	Facilitator and group

12.30–1.30	Lunch	
1.30–2.00	Integration of financial budgeting process into the strategy plan	Facilitator and group
2.00–3.45	Prioritizing objectives, assignment of responsibilities, and establishment of target dates	Facilitator and group
3.45–4.00	Coffee Break	
4.00–4.30	Discussion of business plan Co-ordinating and monitoring (including discussion of business plan format and appointment of business plan co-ordinator who will handle monitoring)	Facilitator and group
4.30–4.45	Agreement on timing of written report and method of communicating the plan to all employees of the organization	Facilitator and group
4.45–5.00	Closing comments	CEO/Chairperson

Figure 7.1 Strategic Planning Agenda

The following approach to strategic planning sessions has proved to be successful:

1. Appoint a facilitator who is independent of the company and who has experience with strategic planning.
2. Ask each participant to write, in advance of the meeting, in two short sentences their views on the following:
   (a) 'Where does the company wish to be in five years?'
   (b) 'How will it get there?'
   Agree in advance that everyone's ideas will be given a fair hearing and that no idea will be dismissed out of hand.
3. Appoint a secretary who is able to note all key matters raised and record a précis of the discussion.
4. Ensure that your conference room has the appropriate equipment for professional presentations.
5. Ensure that your agenda is followed.

THE STRATEGY MEETING

The participants' comments

To open the proceedings, the facilitator should read the two-sentence comments of the participants, which should also be distributed to each participant.

Mission statement

Now address the question of establishing the business's mission statement. The idea is to arrive at a common philosophy or statement for which there is complete agreement among all leading figures in the business. The participants' views of where the company should aim to be in five years could help in establishing a mission statement.

After this discussion, write the agreed mission statement on the board.

SWOT analysis

The meeting is now ready to address the most important part of the planning process, which is the analysis of the business's strengths, weaknesses, opportunities and threats (SWOT) analysis.

There are many ways of addressing this analysis, but one useful way is to write an objective on a chart and then for the facilitator to ask participants to identify the business's strengths, weaknesses, opportunities or threats in achieving this objective. Continue this process until all the company's major objectives have been covered.

Typically, major objectives would include the following:

1. To increase sales.
2. To improve the company's financial condition.
3. To beat the competition.
4. To improve efficiency, productivity and service.
5. To keep up to date with trends in the industry.
6. To improve products and services.
7. To improve labour relations and training; Human resources.
8. To improve distribution and supplier relationships.
9. To improve public relations, advertising and promotions.
10. To address property issues, such as location, capacity, layout, parking and so on.
11. To address partnership or director relationships.
12. To implement a successful exit strategy.

Key objectives

The next step is to identify and prioritize the company's key objectives from the major objectives discussed already. Examples of these could be increasing revenues, or cutting operating costs. Having done this, the meeting should look at how these key objectives will be achieved.

'Things to do'

You achieve your key objectives through various actions or strategies, which can be listed as 'things to do'. The establishment of actions is assisted by the SWOT analysis you have already undertaken.

For example, if your key objective is to increase sales, you might decide to take some of the following actions:

1. If you are a manufacturer, produce new products; if you are a professional firm, develop and market a new service. (Both of these are taking advantage of an opportunity.)
2. Penetrate a particular market with a marketing plan. (This could be building on one of the business's strengths.)
3. Retrain sales staff or replace weak sales staff (minimize a weakness).
4. Change your advertising plans (take advantage of an opportunity).
5. Change the salaries for the sales people from fixed salary to variable plus commission-based remuneration (minimize a weakness).

Continue with this approach to establish your actions or 'things to do' for each key objective.

Prioritizing your 'things to do'

You should now list your actions or 'things to do' in order of priority. You should also assign responsibility for their implementation with target dates. Here you must act reasonably, remembering that those to whom you have assigned tasks probably already have full-time workloads.

(*Note*: an alternative way of approaching the SWOT analysis, which includes objectives, implementation and monitoring, is the SOSTAC planning system. A summary of the SOSTAC system is given in Figure 7.2.)

This system is similar to a SWOT analysis, but unlike a SWOT analysis, which is concerned with developing plans up to the stage of implementation of the 'things to do', the SOSTAC system includes implementation and monitoring of the plan's progress.

The letters stand for the following:

S = situation analysis (where is the business now?)
O = objectives (where does the business wish to get to?)
S = strategy (what steps will we take to get to our objectives?)
T = tactics (what are the detailed 'things to do' to achieve our strategy?)
A = action (implementation of 'things to do')
C = control (the monitoring and reviewing of actions)

Figure 7.2 The 'SOSTAC' Planning System

The SOSTAC system is an excellent framework in which to produce, implement and monitor an operational business plan, and could be the framework used for your MESP, which we discuss later in this book.

Writing the business plan

You are now ready to write the plan.

In the case of a larger company (where you should have held a strategy planning session, as described above) you should now appoint an overall co-ordinator, who will be in charge of writing the plan. The co-ordinator will bring together the various parts of the strategy into one comprehensive plan and monitor the implementation process. He or she will either begin their work immediately after the strategic planning session, or after the facilitator has prepared his or her report following the session.

In the case of smaller businesses, the owners (with their managers, where appropriate) need to follow the steps described above to prepare a SWOT analysis and resultant prioritized 'things to do' list, but probably in a less formal way than described. Sole traders should follow the same steps, using this structure as a discipline to bring out, and put into writing, all the ideas and information that is stored in their heads.

THE SUMMARY CONTENTS OF A BUSINESS PLAN

A business plan need not be in any set form, but usually it contains the following elements:

- an executive summary or overview
- an index
- some background and historical information of the business
- the products or services sold (including pricing policy)
- production and supply
- plant, machinery and equipment
- the market and marketing strategies, including customers and competition
- management and key personnel's background and experience
- premises: freehold or leasehold details
- strengths, weaknesses, opportunities and threats analysis and outcomes
- objectives (both short-term and long-term), including an exit strategy
- actions, or strategies, to achieve the goals
- financial information and projections, including cash flow
- appendices, including technical information, brochures, and so on.

CONTENTS OF A BUSINESS PLAN IN MORE DETAIL

We provide below more details of the usual contents of a business plan, some of which will already be clear to you from the description of the strategy planning session above.

Executive summary

The executive summary is a brief overview of the plan as a whole. The purpose of the summary is to give the reader an overview of the business, the aims of the plan and how the plan will be implemented. The summary should also include a mission statement.

Index

The index should show at a glance what the plan incorporates.

Background and historic information

This section should include:

- the history of the business
- the owners/ shareholders' background
- the financial history of the business.

Overall, the plan should explain how the business started, how it developed and how it has reached its present position.

The products or services

This section should describe what the business does. It should explain its products and services, their special features and how they might differ from the competition. Technical matters should be included in the appendices.

Products and supply

Here you should describe what and how you make or manufacture your products or deliver your services.

Plant, machinery and equipment

This should include a description of the assets, their value and life expectancy and finance outstanding.

The market and marketing strategies

Included here should be aspects of the market size, market share, list of customers and information on competitors. The strategy section should describe how the business intends to market its goods and services.

Management and key personnel

The business plan must provide a background of key personnel's and management's ability and experience. A brief résumé should be included for each working shareholder/partner.

Premises

If freehold, details of the value, mortgage outstanding, name of lender and monthly repayments are usually included. If leasehold, details of the lease should be included.

SWOT analysis and outcomes

This is a summary of your SWOT analysis, highlighting your strengths, weaknesses, opportunities and threats.

Objectives

From the SWOT analysis a set of objectives should be established. These should be divided into short-, medium- and long-term objectives, which are further prioritized in each section. It is important that your objectives are reasonable in terms of your own resources and your industry. (See Chapter 11.)

Actions, or strategies for implementation of the objectives (including future disposal)

This is the heart of the operational business plan, the 'things to do' to achieve your objectives. You should include what you believe is the most suitable strategy for your business disposal.

Financials

This section should include historic financial information and projected profit and loss accounts, balance sheets and cash flows. The historic information should go back three to five years (if you have been trading this long), while projections should normally also be for three years. If you were using the plan for an MBO, you would be wise to provide financials for five years.

Appendices

Commonly included in the appendices will be the following information:

- curriculum vitae of key individuals in the organization
- detailed historical financial information
- key assumptions used to produce the financial information
- brochures and other business literature
- technical specifications on products.

PUTTING THE PLAN INTO DIAGRAM FORM

You now need to convert the business plan into diagram form, which is the format we will use for the MESP.

The steps involved in converting business plans and MESPs to a diagrammatic form are as follows:

- Each activity should be given a starting date and estimated duration for completion.
- Each activity should then be put in the order of its starting date and a prioritized list produced.
- The list should include details of who will be undertaking the task and when it will be completed.
- The list should show the estimated finishing date.
- The list should be depicted as a prioritized diagram, by using a computer or drawing it manually.

Examples of the MESP in diagrammatic form are shown in each of the exit options in the appendices to this book.

CONCLUSIONS OF YOUR BUSINESS PLAN

In normal circumstances, having produced the business plan you should be able to come to one of four conclusions, namely:

1. The business is sound and its objectives (including exit strategy) are realistic, achievable and can be implemented.
2. There are aspects of the enterprise that need further attention, but overall the business is sound.
3. There are serious problems with the enterprise which need drastic remedial action.
4. The current business has fatal flaws and should be closed down.

In exit strategy planning, your business plan will alert you to the amount of work you need to undertake to put the business in an optimum position for its disposal.

Some thoughts on your business plan

WHO SHOULD WRITE THE BUSINESS PLAN?

The accepted wisdom is that the business plan is the owner's plan and should be compiled by him or her with the help of key managers. Advisers can provide the structure of the plan and assistance with its production, but the actual plan itself, particularly with regard to the fulfilment of the owner's personal aspirations and desires, should be written by the business owner.

WHAT MAKES AN EFFECTIVE BUSINESS PLAN?

To be effective, the business plan must meet the following conditions:

- The business planning process and the implementation of the plan must have the commitment and involvement of the business's management and decision-makers.
- The planning process and resulting objectives and strategies must address all the significant factors that affect the firm's long- and short-term performance.
- The business plan, by definition, addresses the future, particularly the influence of trends and developments in its marketplace and operational environment; but it must do so in the context of its past performance.
- The strategy and the plan's implementation must be prioritized to provide a clear sense of direction to the business's management and staff regarding their future performance.
- The decision-makers who are responsible for implementing the plan must remain actively involved in the plan's development over the long term.
- The plan must be flexible to be able to deal with unforeseen developments.
- Above all, a business plan must be clear and simple, comprehensive, well presented and with realistic objectives.
- A business plan must be actively implemented and not quietly put away in the bottom drawer.

Why business plans sometimes fail

Even when you have written your plan, it is worthless unless it works for you. Unfortunately, a large percentage of plans do not work. The main reasons for their failure could be attributed to the following facts:

- They are constructed around incorrectly defined strategies.
- They do not have detailed objectives with clear 'things to do' to achieve those objectives.
- They do not state their goals in quantifiable terms, or show how they can be realized in small, achievable steps.
- They are not realistic.
- Most important of all, they are not carried out.

The business plan's implementation

Preparing a business plan is only part of the battle, and some would say it is only a very small part! Implementation of the plan and a system by which your progress is compared with your objectives is really the important part. Implementation of the plan is the process of doing those things you have written in the 'things to do' section of your plan. This is an obvious point and no more than common sense when put this way, but it is a sad fact that a large percentage of the plans prepared are never implemented.

When you set out to implement your plan, you should realize that it is the outcomes of your actions that are important. These outcomes are usually measured in financial terms of cash flow or profit and loss, and the simple way to monitor how you are progressing with your plan is to compare your actual financial results with your planned or projected results. This should be done on a regular basis, with a report prepared that compares these two results and highlights the differences.

Where a business is reasonably mature, the easy part of the financial projections is calculating expenses (as you are able to work from previous accounts), whereas the difficult part is getting the sales projections right. With newer businesses, both income and expense projections can be difficult. One of the real benefits of monitoring your progress (by comparing actual results with planned results every year) is that you will be able to produce new plans and financial projections that are much more accurate and, therefore, more meaningful every time you do them.

By regular monitoring of planned versus actual results you learn more about your business and you become more able to predict where it is going. This skill becomes particularly important when you wish to plan an exit based on the time it will take you to reach a predetermined market value for your business.

In Chapter 11 we discuss the implementation of plans in more detail.

CHAPTER

8 Short-Term Exit Strategy Planning

When deciding to dispose of your business you will, broadly, have three options, namely to exit immediately, to exit after a short-term plan, or to exit after a proper, long-term plan. These options will either be forced on you by circumstances, or you will have made a deliberate choice to take a particular course.

In this chapter we will:

- remind you of the questions you should ask yourself to decide if it is in your interest to delay your sale in favour implementing an exit plan
- review how you can go about making a final decision on this important issue, including showing you how your business's impediments to sale could themselves influence your decision
- consider the steps involved in producing a short-term exit strategy plan, including drawing up a short-term master exit strategy plan
- look at how to implement your plan, with particular emphasis on those things you can do to improve the business in the short term to increase your disposal price.

Selling without planning first

If you have not planned for your business exit and still wish to maximize your exit price, there are only two circumstances in which it would be wise to consider a disposal without embarking first on an adequate exit plan, namely:

- when you have no choice
- when you have no need to plan.

YOU HAVE NO CHOICE

You will have no choice but to sell immediately when your company is insolvent, or when personal reasons (such as ill health) so dictate. Where you are a sole trader or a partnership facing bankruptcy, you will have the difficult decision to make of how much longer you should continue to trade if you have no prospects of your situation improving.

The relationship between why you wish (or need) to dispose of your business, the likely exit options that are open to you in these various circumstances, and when you will dispose of it were discussed in Chapter 1.

YOU HAVE NO NEED TO PLAN

You will have no need to plan when your exit option is so obvious and your business in such good shape that you are able to complete preparations for disposal in a very short time without compromising on the value you will obtain for your business. These circumstances are highly unusual in most private businesses.

Immediate sale

Where your company or business is solvent but you still have to sell your business immediately, the best exit results will arise where you retain control of the disposal process and maintain your position of a willing but not anxious seller. Of course, this is not always easy. Where you have to act because of insolvency or bankruptcy, your pressures will be even more acute.

Appendix 10 considers your planning options under insolvent circumstances in some detail and you should refer to this appendix if you believe you or your company are in this position.

The compromise of a short-term plan

If you are unable to postpone your disposal, you will have to resign yourself to an unplanned exit, probably by a third party sale or a close down, through which you will be unlikely to maximize your exit price or personal satisfaction.

If you are able to postpone your disposal for at least a year, there is still only a limited amount that you can do to implement a meaningful exit strategy. Unfortunately, you are largely stuck with the consequences of your previous lack of planning. But all is not lost, because you should be able to achieve some added value through a short-term exit plan.

Ideally, for the best results you should find reasons to delay your sale long enough to implement a proper exit strategy plan over three to five years because it usually takes this sort of time to implement business continuity planning and effective operational changes (including removing impediments to sale) and to groom management or successors for a successful exit. Only in a few cases is a period of one to two years adequate to achieve all these things.

However, business life is seldom ideal and the very need that this book addresses, namely, the lack of exit strategy planning in the private business sector, means that the majority of private business owners still decide to dispose of their businesses without any planning at all. In these circumstances a short-term exit strategy plan is, at least, a compromise that is better than no plan at all!

(Chapter 1 looked in more detail at the 'Why and when do I want to dispose of my business?' questions, and how these can affect the time frame and choice of disposal.)

Should you delay your sale?

For most owners a most compelling reason for delaying a business sale would be because a delayed sale will result in a substantially better selling price. Assuming there are no reasons that make it essential that you sell your business immediately, you should weigh up the advantages and disadvantages of delaying your sale to implement a short-term exit plan (or, indeed, a long-term plan) compared with an immediate sale.

In Chapter 1 we considered the questions you should be asking yourself to assist you in coming to this decision. The main questions are as follows:

- Do all shareholders/partners wish to sell now and do they agree on the price?
- Do economic trends make it likely that the economy will be more favourable for a sale of your type of business now, or in the future?
- What is the likely impact of tax on a sale now or in the future?
- Does your business have some obvious impediments to sale that could be removed over the next 12 to 18 months?
- Are there any obvious basic operational improvements that can be made to the business in the short term, which will lead to increased profitability and an increased selling price?

Another way of looking at this is to ask yourself the following questions:

- What is my business worth now?
- What are its impediments to sale?
- Can I remove these impediments?
- How long will it take me to remove them?
- Most importantly, what will my business be worth when I have removed them?

If you decide you cannot improve the business's value or you cannot delay the sale, you will not contemplate an exit strategy plan. But if you think that you can delay the sale for at least a year, so that you can remove the more obvious things that reduce your business's value, then it makes sense for you to consider embarking on a short-term exit strategy plan.

Before making any decision you will need to consider carefully the risks involved in delaying the sale and to be sure that there are definite benefits for you and your business in a delay. There are some complex issues involved here and you will probably wish to discuss them with the appropriate advisers.

Other reasons to delay

There could be compelling personal reasons for delaying the sale. For example, if you were previously unsure whether your child had the ability to take over the business from you (although you very much favoured this option), but subsequently realized that with the proper training he or she could do so, you might be happy to delay your sale while this training took place (even though the price you obtained from the sale would not, necessarily, be increased by this delay).

Making a final decision on a short-term plan

To help you make a final decision on whether it is worthwhile to embark on a short-term plan, having considered your answers to the questions above, we suggest you take the following steps:

1. Summarize your conclusions of the benefits of the short-term programme from your point of view, including the possible increase in price you would receive as a result of successfully implementing a short-term plan.
2. If you are using advisers, discuss your conclusions with them.
3. If the conclusions appear to favour delay to implement a short-term plan, then (in association with your advisers where applicable) produce a detailed discussion paper outlining the following:
   (a) A possible exit options short list, and the preferred option.
   (b) A list of the major impediments to sale and plans to remove them, including estimated time to remove each one. Figure 6.1 in Chapter 6 will assist you in this.
   (c) A summary of major benefits of embarking on a short-term plan, including an analysis of the increase in the business's future value compared with the costs involved (in advisers' fees, and so on) of implementing the plan.
4. Review your summary conclusions and make a final decision on whether or not to go ahead.

Impediments to sale: a crucial factor

One of the ways you can decide whether a short-term plan will be practical for your business is to list its major impediments to sale and see whether you are likely to be able to remove them in the short term. Chapter 6 looked at impediments to sale in the following groupings:

- those that should take three to five years to remove
- those that should take less than three years to remove
- those that should take less than one year to remove.

Although these groupings are based on generalizations and will not hold true in all businesses, they will help you to estimate the time that it could take to remove those impediments that exist in your business. The impediment of having a history of bad profits, for example, can only be removed by a two- to three-year history of good profits and, obviously, will take at least three years to rectify. If you have these types of impediments to sale in your business, a short-term exit plan will not remove them. Conversely, for example, although expanding your customer base will usually take several years to accomplish, you might be able to do this in less time if you have previously ignored obvious customers (because of some reason such as their geographic location).

The steps involved in producing a short-term exit plan

Assuming you have decided in principle that a delay to your sale to implement a short-term plan would be to your benefit, you will now need to begin your plan. The steps involved in preparing a short-term exit plan (STEP) are as follows:

1. Produce a short written report identifying the advantages and disadvantages of a STEP, as outlined above.

2. Discuss this with your advisers and confirm your desire to delay your sale to produce a STEP.
3. Prepare in writing a summary of your plan that includes the following:
   (a) A shortlist of exit strategy options; and your first choice option.
   (b) A list of impediments to sale, and possible strategies for their removal. (See Chapter 6.)
   (c) A list of operational improvements that can be made to the business in the short term to improve its short-term profitability.
   (d) A possible timetable for implementation of the plan. (Usually, you will be planning for a disposal in 12 to 24 months under a STEP.)
4. Review your business plan and update it to include the operational issues in 3, above.
5. Produce a short-term master exit strategy plan (STMESP).

Once you have decided to go ahead with the short-term plan you should produce a STMESP. The production of a standard master exit strategy plan is covered in Chapter 9 and you should read that chapter to see how the MESP is put together.

Differences between short-term and long-term planning

You will notice that besides the time difference there are other differences in short-term planning when compared with long-term planning. The major differences are as follows:

- In short-term planning you do not have the breadth of choice of exit options, because besides a trade sale and a sole trader merger, most of them require longer-term planning.
- The operational changes to your business will be largely superficial.
- You will probably not have the time to integrate your personal financial plan with your exit plan because, to be effective, this is usually a long-term exercise.
- You are concentrating on only those changes which bring about quick results, both in the substance of the business and in the presentation of the business to potential buyers.

Implementing the STMESP

As mentioned previously, there is a limited amount that can be done to improve the operations of a business in the short term. However, you can make improvements in the following aspects of your business through implementing a STMESP:

GENERAL APPEARANCE

Most owners leave their disposal too late in terms of their own enthusiasm and drive, so that their business is run down and has a tired look. Smarten it up generally in whatever obvious ways you can.

SPECIFIC ASPECTS OF THE OPERATION

Look at some specific aspects of the operation that will improve profitability (and reported profitability), including the following.

Cash sales

Ensure that all cash sales are recorded in the accounts for the full financial year.

Gross margins

If these are below industry average, the reasons could be non-reporting of cash sales (as above), or prices are too low, or costs of goods too high. Investigate whether prices can be increased and whether goods can be purchased more cheaply.

Costs

Cost cutting is the obvious way to improve operational profitability and most business owners would have looked closely at this. However, it is worthwhile investigating this area further to see what can be done. Although cost cutting is a specialized area of operation (and you should consider getting in an expert to help you) you might find the following ideas useful if you are undertaking the cost cutting yourself:

- The major area of expense in most businesses is people, so look first at salaries and wages costs.
- Next, rental (or premises expense) is always a major expense. If you own the building, examine what rent is charged through the books and whether this is a true arms-length rental. If the premises are leased and the rental is too high (because of the cost per square metre or because there is unused space), consider whether the business can renegotiate the rental, or move to a cheaper or smaller location. Immediate rent reductions can sometimes be traded off against increasing the lease's term. This will have an immediate cost-cutting effect, although the business will, of course, have a longer-term commitment to its premises, which might be a subsequent impediment to disposal.

Asset review

Although this might seem obvious, a major impediment to the disposal of a business is often its price. When tangible assets (such as stock or plant and equipment) are a significant part of this price, it is necessary to determine whether their levels can be reduced so that the sale price can be reduced to better reflect a reasonable return on investment.

- Stock: a level of stock that is too high can often kill a sale. In an older business, stock can build up to a level disproportionate to current turnover. Compounding the problem can be the strategy of owners of writing-down stock to depress profits in their books. This can result in the actual value of stock on hand not being reflected in book value on the balance sheet. If this is the case, stock levels must be reduced, both to lower the eventual disposal price and to bring real stock levels into line with the book value of the stock. If necessary, stock can be sold off at wholesale prices to competitors or other traders. Dead stock must be sold prior to the disposal of the business. As an owner you will need to face the taxation problems that previous stock write-downs could present. Spreading the profit from the sale of written-down stock over two or more accounting periods can be a good way to absorb the possible impact of taxation. If you need to take this long to sell the stock, your exit planning will no longer be short term.

- Cash/debtors/creditors: traditionally, purchasers of private businesses have preferred to buy business assets and not company shares, and business owners have obliged with the company selling its assets. The fact that taper relief from capital gains tax is not available to companies may change this approach – see Appendix 1. Where you are selling a company's shares you must dispose of those assets that the purchaser does not want before the sale. Likewise you will need to settle outstanding liabilities where possible. This process is known as cleaning up the balance sheet. (Note that even when purchasers are not 'buying the balance sheet' they will still consider it carefully, and things like unusually high borrowings, or creditors over 90 days could influence their attitude towards the general health of business and, consequently, its attractiveness as an investment.)
- Debtors should be brought under control with a rigorous collection policy and the offering of discounts, if necessary.
- Creditors must be paid within normal trade terms to retain supplier support and the company's reputation. Ensure borrowings are reasonable and not indicative of a company under financial strain. Overdrafts should be within limits.
- A reasonable level of cash funds must be established for normal working capital requirements. Too low a level of cash could put strains on the company, while too high a level could indicate a lazy use of business resources

Accounting procedures

Reducing the value of assets is one way the business can be made more attractive in the shortterm. Another is to refrain from unprofessional private company accounting practices common to some private businesses. These include the following:

- not recording cash sales
- writing-down stock levels unnecessarily
- making larger provisions (for such things as bad debts, etc.) than are necessary
- including non-business expenses in company accounts
- charging unrealistic family wages and salaries to the business.

Some of these practices are contrary to accounting standards, while others are illegal. But, there are areas in accounting in which a certain amount of discretion can be exercised legally, such as amortization, capital allowances (depreciation), provision for bad debts, work in progress. Your accounting policies might have been overconservative in the past (to keep your tax down) and they could be altered in the period immediately before disposal to more accurately reflect current profit.

By a more formal accounting approach one is trying to ensure that accounting profits reflect the real profit of the business. It is easier to demonstrate real profits by publishing profits that are real, rather than having to rely on extensive add-backs or adjustments (of which buyers are usually extremely sceptical) after the accounts have been published and when the business is for sale.

As far as the balance sheet is concerned (and note the earlier comments about sale of the business rather than the company's shares), it could be worthwhile for you to commission valuations of the assets being sold, to justify the price being asked (especially where they have been heavily written down in the accounts). Formal valuations of intangible assets (such as goodwill or brand names), which might not be shown in the balance sheet, might also be necessary to support your asking price.

Conclusion

Short-term planning is a compromise that aims to paper over disposal problems for a private business that has not adequately planned for its exit. The longer you plan for disposal the better your results will be, but your limitations could be set by your personal and business needs. It is important that you understand that the results of short-term planning could be limited, but they should still be useful. Delaying the sale for proper planning over three to five years would be even more advantageous.

CHAPTER 9

How to Design your Master Exit Strategy Plan

In this chapter we will show you how to design a master exit strategy plan by bringing together the various decisions, plans and activities we have dealt with so far. Your decisions will include the time your have given yourself to exit and the optimum exit option you have chosen. Your plans will include your continuity and business plans and the activities will include remedying your impediments to sale. All these plans can be reduced to 'things to do' lists and we will show you how to arrange and prioritize these checklists into a time chart and then how to produce the MESP in both a narrative and a diagrammatic form, providing you with a framework that makes your MESP easy to implement and to monitor.

The perfect business

The aims of your exit strategy planning should be the following:

- To structure your business and its affairs so that you achieve the maximum taxation advantages on exit.
- To choose the best exit option for your business.
- Where you are disposing through a family succession, to choose the best successor for the business.
- To create the perfect business by the time of transfer or sale.
- To dispose of the business at the time, and in the way, you planned.

We have considered previously in this book the structuring of your business, choosing the optimum exit option and the selection of the appropriate heir. To create the perfect business you will need to have implemented your business plan and identified and remedied your business's impediments to sale, so that when the time comes to dispose of your business it should have most of the following characteristics:

- a strong management team with a range of specialist skills necessary for the continuation of the business after you have disposed of it
- a consistent and profitable trading history
- a good reputation (and, ideally, a strong position) in its industry
- no significant debt, especially debt secured by personal assets
- no long-term lease commitments, including asset and property leases (in particular, property leases should not extend beyond your proposed disposal date)
- a stable workforce, controlled employment costs and sufficient rewards in place for the retention of management and key personal

- be fully complying with all regulations and legislative requirements
- arrangements and agreements with key suppliers and subcontractors in order and in writing
- agency arrangements (where applicable) in order and in writing
- suitable insurance in place with regard to fixed assets, stock, equipment, fixtures and fittings and human resources
- modern and efficient plant and machinery (including fully computerized office equipment)
- up-to-date, professionally prepared business records, including a realistic business plan that includes financial projections for at least three years
- the appearance and 'feel' of a vibrant, go-ahead and enthusiastic organization, whose profits are improving, rather than a tired, dispirited business that is on a downward spiral. (This improving trend should be confirmed by the financial projections.)

The perfect retirement

Where you are selling your business and retiring, you should plan that on your retirement you will have sufficient wealth (with pensions and investments, and the sale proceeds of your business) to retire in comfort and security. This will be ensured if you adopt an integrated approach to your personal financial planning and your business exit strategy planning from an early stage.

We deal with the integration of your plans in more detail in Chapter 10.

Planning ahead

Of course, there is no such thing as a perfect business and it is unlikely in practice that all your plans will be completely fulfilled by the time you sell your business. However, this must still be your aim. One thing is certain: you will get much closer to perfection if you plan well ahead. There are two very important rules of exit strategy planning that you should understand from the outset, which are as follows:

1. Plan well ahead.
2. Have a sense of urgency (but be thorough) in implementing your plans.

Designing your MESP

The previous chapters in the book took you through the decisions, strategies and plans involved in exit strategy planning, what could be considered as the theory involved in this process. Now we will show you how to render this theory into a practical working document, which we call a master exit strategy plan.

In summary, the preparation of a MESP includes:

- choosing your exit option
- establishing the time frame

- collating and prioritizing the activities which you identified from your various plans
- writing a narrative
- updating or preparing financial projections
- preparing valuations
- preparing the MESP in diagrammatic form.

We will address each of these in turn.

CHOOSING YOUR EXIT OPTION

Although the timing of your exit can be dictated to you (by ill heath, for example) and the timing could influence the choice of option (see Chapter 1 on timing issues), it is more usual that you will choose the optimum exit option first and then set your timetable. The choice of your exit option is covered in detail in Chapters 4 and 5.

THE TIME FRAME

You now need to decide whether you will embark on a short-, medium- or long-term exit strategy plan and to set your target exit date. This will set the parameters of your planning and the extent to which you are able to implement operational improvements, removal of impediments to sale and personal financial planning.

The timing decision enables you to set up an initial time chart, from which you will design your master exit strategy plan. One way to set up your time chart is to start with the disposal date (Year 0) at the bottom and work upwards. (You can subdivide the years into halves if you wish: this is particularly useful in the first two years of the plan where you will have more control over the detail of when you would like to complete things by.) For example:

- Year 4: begin training of key managers; advertise for a new finance director (FD); seek initial taxation advice and restructure the group; begin debt reduction programme.
- Year 3: dispose of loss-making subsidiary; dispose of surplus machinery; approach VCs for support of MBO.
- Year 2: enter into new agency agreements with major suppliers; reduce stock levels; conduct environmental audit and mock due diligence. Review personal financial position.
- Year 1: dispose of profitable subsidiary (surplus to MBO team's requirements); further reduce stock (at loss) through private sales; finalize VC's financial support and management team's personal financial contributions.
- Year 0: dispose of business through MBO.

It is important to be flexible with regard to the timing of completion of activities and the exit itself. Business affairs never work out exactly as planned, so you need to be prepared to adapt to events outside your control, which could be either positive or negative. To allow for the unforeseen, give yourself a time band of two years around your target disposal date.

When you have listed and prioritized your activities (which we consider below) your chart could look something like Figure 9.1.

YEAR	ACTIVITY
4 (2002)	Begin training new managers Advertise for new FD Obtain CGT advice Begin debt reduction programme Update business plan
3 (2003)	Dispose of loss-making subsidiary Dispose of surplus machinery Implementation of business plan (see schedule) Approach VCs for support of MBO Discuss proposition with bank
2 (2004)	Removal of impediments to sale (see schedule) Appoint lead adviser Bring VCs and management team together New agency agreements with major suppliers Reduce stock levels Conduct environmental audit factory site Review personal financial position Undertake mock due diligence
1 (2005)	Dispose of subsidiary surplus to MBO's team's requirements Further reduce stock Finalize VC's support Firm up MBO team's individual financial investments
0 (2006/7)	Finalize agreements (see schedule) Complete disposal

Figure 9.1 The Initial Time Chart for MESP

COLLATING AND PRIORITIZING THE ACTIVITIES

You should now address the major planning areas covered in this book and compile lists of the things you need to do to prepare your business for disposal.

For example, under business continuity planning (Chapter 2) you confirm and list the steps you need to take to complete your business continuity plans, such as obtaining taxation advice and entering into shareholders' agreements, or reviewing and updating current agreements that are already in place. You should then prioritize these activities for inclusion in your time chart (for later inclusion in your MESP.)

Similarly, under business planning (Chapter 7) you should confirm the exit-strategy specific 'things to do' and add them to your time chart list.

As a further example, under impediments to sale (Chapter 6) you should take the following steps:

1. Establish what you believe are the impediments to sale in your business.
2. Decide what steps should be taken to remove these impediments; in other words, what are the solutions to these problems that you have identified in your business?
3. Add these solutions (or activities) as a schedule to your initial time chart list, once you have prioritized them by start date.

You are continuing to build the framework for your MESP, as these prioritized activities will be included in your diagrammatic MESP in due course. (*Note*: it will be necessary to set up schedules or sublists for the activities under the operational 'things to do' or removal of impediments to sale to prevent your chart from becoming too cumbersome.)

WRITING A MISSION STATEMENT AND NARRATIVE

An operational business plan should include a mission statement as a focus for the plan. To get your exit strategy into focus you should include your exit strategy philosophy in the mission statement of your business plan. (For example: 'Our mission is to be the best high-quality widget producer in the UK, ensuring at all times the highest quality of product at competitive prices, while providing a stimulating, pleasant workplace for our employees ... We plan to exit the business through an MBO to our key management.')

This mission statement can be expanded in your MESP by including a narrative along the following lines:

> I intend to dispose of my business in 2006 through a management buyout, with my sales manager leading the management team. In this period I need to remove the major impediments to disposal of my business, which I have identified so far to be the following: [Here you would list these impediments.]
>
> I intend removing these impediments by the following actions: [Here you would include the 'things to do' necessary to remove the impediments.]
>
> I will also need to consult my taxation adviser on the optimum timing of my disposal so that I can be sure of maximizing my taxation relief and will adjust my plans subject to his or her advice.
>
> I will need to groom my sales manager to take over as CEO of the business. I believe that he needs to improve his or her skills in the following areas: [list them] and to achieve this improvement I will provide the following training and assistance: [list what you will be doing].

UPDATING OR PREPARING FINANCIAL PROJECTIONS

Update your business plan, or prepare annual profit and loss forecasts and projected balance sheets for the years up until your disposal. (You will need to update these projections in the year prior to disposal, and extend them for at least three years post-disposal, when you produce an information memorandum for potential purchasers. (Information memorandums are discussed in Appendix 8.)

PREPARING VALUATIONS

If you have not already done so as part of a private (retirement) planning exercise, estimate the current value of your business and, using the financial information from your projections, estimate the value of your business on disposal, based on the assumption that your projections are achieved.

PREPARING THE MESP IN DIAGRAMMATIC FORM (MESP CHART)

You are now in a position to set up your MESP in chart form. (Examples of MESP charts are given in the appendices on each of the exit options; see for example Figure A4.1.)

The steps for completing your MESP chart are as follows:

- Set up the diagram with a disposal date and the years in between along the top. For your disposal date, rather than setting a specific date, set a band of time of about 12 months in which you plan to dispose of your business.
- For the current year and, perhaps, the next two years, it is advisable to divide the year up into quarters or halves.
- Working from your time chart insert into the diagram the various activities, or 'things to do' that you have identified by working through the steps listed above in chronological order of their approximate starting date. (These activities will come from your business continuity planning, your operational business plan, the impediments to sale analysis and the other areas that might be relevant to you, such as family succession grooming and training, and will not necessarily be the same as the examples given in Figure 9.1.)
- Estimate how long each activity is likely to take and block out the appropriate time to complete each activity. (*Note*: it will be easier to move the activities until you have them in the most logical order of priority if you put the chart on a computer spreadsheet. This will also enable you to adapt easily the chart in future if required.)
- Enter the name of the person responsible for undertaking the activity in the appropriate column.
- Label your chart 'Version 1', date it and print it out.

Summary contents of your MESP

Figure 9.2 summarizes the contents of your MESP and refers back to where in this book the various strategies, plans and issues are dealt with.

Conclusion

You now have a comprehensive MESP both in narrative and chart form, and all that remains is for you to implement it. We will look at implementation of your MESP in the final chapter of the book.

Step 1: Business continuity planning
(This deals with corporate structure, taxation and arrangements between principals {shareholders or partners}.)
This is covered in Chapter 2.
See also Figures 2.1, 2.2 and 2.3.

Step 2: Exit option and time frame
(This deals with how you go about choosing the optimum exit option and establishment of a suitable time frame for your exit.)
This is covered in Chapters 1, 4 and 5.
See also Figures 1.1, 1.2, 1.3, 5.1 and 5.2.

Step 3: Impediments to sale
(This covers the identification and removal of those things that reduce your business's value or make it impossible to sell.)
This is dealt with in Chapter 6.
See also Figure 6.1.
(*Note on due diligence:*
The due diligence process will take place in all disposal transactions. You must aim to remove the impediments that a formal due diligence – undertaken by the purchaser – will uncover, and undertake a mock due diligence well before the formal one takes place.)

Step 4: Business planning
(This covers strategic, operational and financial planning for your business.)
This is covered in Chapter 7.
See also figures 7.1 and 7.2.

Step 5: Integrated financial planning
(This covers your personal – or retirement – financial planning and how you can integrate this into your MESP.)
See Chapter 10.

Step 6: Master Exit Strategy Plan (MESP)
(This includes
- design
- implementation
- monitoring

of your MESP.)
This is covered in Chapters 9 and 11.
See also figures at end of each exit option appendix.

Step 7: Disposal
(This covers the disposal of your business through the chosen exit option.)
This is dealt with in Appendices 4, 5, 6, 7, 8, 9 and 10.

Figure 9.2 Summary Contents of MESP

CHAPTER **10** *The Integrated Financial Plan*

In this chapter we consider two main themes:

- bringing all your exit strategy plans together
- looking at the effect of your planning from a personal perspective, particularly after you have disposed of the business.

Our ultimate aim is to get you to think about exit strategy planning in an integrated way, with both your business and personal financial planning working in the same direction for maximum effect.

This chapter does not purport to give financial or taxation advice, which you should get from either your accountant or an independent financial adviser.

Bringing it all together

In this book we have taken you through an orderly process of planning for your exit. But, what about your personal financial plans? The last stage of an integrated exit strategy plan should be where you bring together your personal financial plan with your MESP; where you integrate all your financial plans in the light of the timing and implications of your planned business disposal.

Establishing your financial position

Initially you should ask yourself a series of questions to establish your personal ambitions, your current financial position and your likely post-sale financial requirements. (You will have come across some of these questions earlier in this book.) These questions include the following:

- When do I intend leaving my business?
- What do I intend to do when I leave?
- Assuming it is to retire, how much money do I need to retire (both in capital and income terms)?
- If I do not intend retiring after I sell, what do I intend to do and how much money do I need to do it?
- What is my current total worth? (This will be your private wealth plus the current estimated value of the business.)

- What is my total worth likely to be after I have disposed of the business (after implementing my exit strategy plan)?
- What is the likely impact of tax on the disposal proceeds?
- How should I handle the finances of the business between now and my retirement?
- What will happen if I lose a key manager, or if I become disabled or die before the sale of the business?
- What will happen to my shares if I get divorced, or what will happen to their shares if a family member who is a minority shareholder gets divorced?

In brief, you need to summarize your current overall financial position; estimate what it is likely to be when you dispose of the business; consider what income you are likely to need while you are still in the business (that is, in next few years leading up to sale) and after you sell; and think about risk management for your business and for you and your family.

All this will put the proposed sale of your business in the context of your overall personal and family financial circumstances. It will also force you to think about the issues that will evolve as you move from being an owner and employee of your business to being a retiree.

If you do plan to retire when you have disposed of your business, you should now be thinking about your overall financial position. As a preliminary step to getting expert taxation and financial planning advice, we suggest you take the following steps:

- Draw up a current personal assets and liabilities statement, including the current value of your equity in your business.
- Produce profit and loss and balance sheet forecasts for the business up to the date of disposal. Work out the expected future value of your business at disposal date (based on the same method as you have used to estimate the current value of the business) and add this to your personal estimated worth at the date of disposal.
- Start to think, in general terms, what you will be doing in retirement; for example, will you work part-time as a consultant, or give up work completely to play golf and write that novel?
- Decide whether, in general terms, you will be able to retire now (based on your current wealth) and/or whether you will be able to retire if your exit plans come to fruition at the time you have chosen. This will establish the need to be successful with your exit strategy or whether its success will merely be 'icing on the cake'.

If you can retire if your exit is successful, then proceed with your exit strategy plans on the basis of the timetable you have chosen. If the outcomes do not appear positive, you will need to rethink your plans.

Financial and retirement planning

Personal financial planning is outside the scope of this book and we will assume that you have made adequate plans for your financial future. Your financial advisers will have told you the advantages of early financial planning and, hopefully, you will have begun your retirement planning well before you decided on an exit strategy plan. Whatever the extent of your personal planning, now is the time to review your retirement plan with your advisers in the light of your planned exit.

Agreements, wills and risk management

Although you cannot easily catch up time and opportunities lost through lack of early financial planning, there are still some crucial issues that you can address at this stage.

The first of these is your shareholders' or partners' agreement. You would be wise, if there is an agreement in place, to review its contents in the light of your current plans. If you do not have an agreement, you should ascertain if your fellow shareholders will agree to one being drawn up in view of the exit plans for the business.

You should check your will to ensure that it reflects your current desires for the transfer or disposal of the business and update it if necessary. If you do not have a will, you should write one immediately.

If you wish to leave the business to your heirs before you die, but are concerned that their marital situation (or anything else) could present them with problems if they have current direct ownership of shares, you could consider putting their share of the business in trust, but you should first obtain appropriate professional advice.

It is not always cost-effective to take out insurance to support a shareholders' agreement if the parties are reaching the end of their business lives and are middle aged. If your agreements are not already backed by insurance, you should ascertain whether having insurance is appropriate and, if necessary, obtain quotations to check its cost-effectiveness.

The importance of key managers could be highlighted at this stage of your planning and you might think it prudent to effect key person insurance against the loss of any of them at this sensitive time. If you are of this mind you should obtain quotations to consider the cost-effectiveness of such a move.

A stable business environment

It is important to ensure that your personal financial requirements can be supported by your business up to the time of its disposal. The business must be financially strong enough to pay you an income that allows you to live comfortably without putting an undue strain on its resources and which becomes apparent during the due diligence process.

Assuming that the business has the capacity to fulfil your requirements, the next question you need to ask is what is the most tax-effective way of dealing with surplus income from the business during the period up to sale?

Income versus capital

How you treat surplus income from the business in the years leading up to its sale will be fundamentally a taxation issue. You have several choices, including the following:

- You could withdraw as much income from the business as it can bear, or you could leave the entire surplus in the business, thus building up its capital value.
- You could draw the income solely as salary, or partly as dividends or contributions to your pension scheme, or in any combination thereof.

Where you draw income, as a general rule you will pay income tax; and where you leave surpluses in the business (which should build up its capital value), you could be liable to capital gains tax when you sell. There will also be different taxation implications depending on whether the surpluses you draw are dividends, salaries or paid into your pension fund, and these will vary depending on your personal circumstances. A further complication is that extra certain income now has to be weighed against uncertain capital gain later, as the value of your business could actually go down even if you increase its cash reserves.

You need to get early professional advice on all these issues.

The transition

As you plan for exit, you need to come to grips with a fundamental change in your life. First, you need to make the business independent of you: to put this in another way, you need to become totally dispensable. The business must build up its management capabilities independent of you, so that the new owners have a management support system in place when they take over. In a family succession, the heir needs to be building up his or her management and leadership capabilities, while your role becomes increasingly less important.

There are two vital things that a small private business must do if it is to create real capital value on sale. The first is to increase its profits above the level of merely providing a living wage for its owners (that is, it must generate 'super profits') and the second is that it must make itself independent of its owners' day-to-day input (that is, it must be able to function efficiently and profitably after the owners have left).

Whether an extra person needs to be employed to replace you, or whether you need to increase the responsibilities of your existing management, will have an effect on how you go about the transition and also on the business's current profitability (and, probably, its price). You will also need to consider how you can reassure potential buyers that key management (whom they could be relying on for continuity) will remain with the business. This could be achieved through measures such as service contracts or share options and supported by key person insurance.

Your independence

While the business becomes independent of you, you must also become independent of the business. This will affect you in at least two ways, namely, financially and in the way you lead your life.

FINANCIAL INDEPENDENCE

Briefly, you must learn to live without the income and fringe benefits of being a business owner. The obvious adjustments will be to live without your salary and company cars, but there are probably all sorts of other small things you have taken for granted over the years that you now have to forego, or pay for yourself: your annual golf club subscription perhaps?

Your financial planning should have taken all this into account and if you have planned well ahead (and received a strong price for your business on exit) you should be able to take all this in your stride.

LIFESTYLE

The first thing you will have to get accustomed to is not going into the factory or office every day. You will also need to make a big adjustment in your status (perhaps the biggest one you have ever needed to make) from being a leader in your own world to being virtually a business nobody. Of course, some people cannot wait for this great day, while others dread it. Whatever your particular approach to this change, the important thing is to accept that it is going to happen, plan for it to happen and begin the process of dealing with it in your own way as soon as possible.

Life after you sell

Your ability to continue your way of life little affected by the sale of your business will depend on such things as the type of exit option you have chosen and on whether you have agreed with the purchaser to stay on after the sale.

Some exit options involve more than one stage of disposal. For example, with a flotation, franchising or a sole trader merger you will still be heavily involved with the business after you have disposed of the first part of your equity. This would also be true of a trade sale if you sell only a minority of your interest. With an MBO, or the sale of 100 per cent of your holdings in a trade sale your role in the business could come to an end immediately, unless you enter into a service contract with the purchaser to stay on in some capacity. This will depend on the purchaser's management arrangements and will, therefore, be partly outside your control.

You could have more control on your post-sale life in a family succession. Subject to the warning we have given (in Appendix 4) on the dangers of retiring owners attempting to continue to influence the affairs of the family business, you could, if you made suitable arrangements with your successor, maintain a happy blend of leisure and business involvement after you have retired, without detriment to the business and your heir. Naturally, this will depend on many factors, not least the relationship you have with your heir and the ability of the business to support your heir and you after you have sold.

The ability to negotiate a post-sale role in the business that suits you is one of the great personal advantages you have with a family succession plan and one that is unlikely in most other exit options, where your post-sale operational involvement could be limited to a hand-over period, which could vary from a few weeks to several months. In most cases, business vendors have to rely on their own resources after the sale.

For those of you who plan to purchase another business, the amount of the sale proceeds will be crucial in determining what sort of business you buy. For those of you retiring, the amount you get for your business could determine how you are able to live for the rest of your life. But for all business owners the net amount you realize for your business could well depend on when, how long and how well you have planned for your exit.

CHAPTER 11

Putting your Master Exit Strategy Plan into Action

In Chapter 9 we showed you how to design your MESP. Unfortunately, despite all the work and expense business owners put in to preparing plans, most of them are not implemented. In this chapter we will show how you can put systems in place in your business to assist you to implement your plans, so that your hard work is not wasted.

Of course, all MESPs will be different in their detail and will have different objectives and 'things to do'. We cannot address these specifics, but we will:

- give you general guidance on implementing and monitoring your MESP in a thorough, focused way
- look at how you can ensure that you are prepared for disposal as the deadline approaches
- discuss some general guidelines on the disposal process itself (including handing over to the new owners)
- give you some final thoughts on terms of payment.

Realistic plans

As we said in Chapter 7 on business planning, implementing plans should be a simple matter of doing those things that are included in the 'things to do' section of the plan. This sounds obvious and easy, but the reality of business life is that most plans are not implemented. There could be several reasons for this. One reason could be simply that that owners and managers do not undertake the tasks they have set themselves; while the second is that they sometimes fail in their tasks.

Some of this failure can be put down to incompetent or inadequate execution, but it is also true that some goals are simply not achievable, perhaps because the goals themselves were too optimistic. For example, you might set an objective to increase sales by 15 per cent for each of the next three years, but the reality of your sales resources and the state of the market might be such as to make this impossible to achieve. People with inadequate experience of the real world might have set these plans, perhaps because you have delegated the task to the wrong people.

The chances of a plan being implemented will improve if certain simple guidelines are followed at the time the plan is produced. These include the following:

- Ensure that the plans are produced with the involvement of those charged with implementing them. Do not have plans produced by theorists at staff level and expect them to be implemented by line managers.
- Ensure that, when the plans are made, thought is given to their implementation, with particular regard to the resources in the business.

- Ensure that key managers are committed to the plans and that they confirm their belief that they can be implemented.
- Ensure that the plans are realistic.

One way of checking whether your plans are achievable is for them to be benchmarked against your competition and your industry. Establish what you believe are the key drivers in your business. Now research key financial ratios and performance indicators (from the public sources of financial and company information, such as Dun and Bradstreet) to confirm that your plans are realistic in relation to your industry sector and in relation to your own resources: if these are both positive, you should be able achieve your objectives if your implementation is adequate.

Installing systems

Having set sensible, realistic objectives, you now need to ensure that implementation of your plan is undertaken by competent managers and to install systems that ensure continuous monitoring and review of the plan's progress. The following should assist you in these tasks:

- Ensure that your plan is both in writing and in a chart format. The chart should provide an overview that is easy to follow and to monitor. (See the appendices.) Bigger businesses might feel the need to utilize computer software programmes to monitor their plans' implementation, particularly specific plans such as a marketing plan.
- The responsibility for implementing the plan is not usually an issue in smaller businesses, as the owner directly oversees the task. With bigger businesses it is important that managers to whom implementation has been delegated have a clear understanding of completion dates and the power to achieve what is asked of them.
- Install systems that ensure implementation and monitoring of the plan is properly managed. You should allocate the task of monitoring to a committee or a senior manager (if you are not going to do it yourself).
- Set down agreed dates to meet the committee, or senior management to review progress. These meetings could be of two kinds:
  - A formal check of progress, held every two to three months, when you should compare actual results with planned results and make any necessary changes to the timetable and the goals.
  - A thorough review, held every 12 months, when you should challenge the assumptions of the whole plan in the light of current business circumstances, and rewrite the plan if necessary.

Having the right attitude

Besides setting up the right systems, having the right attitude will also assist in successful implementation of your MESP. You could be assisted in this by the following guidelines:

- You should start to implement your plan as early as possible, because improvements to a business always take longer to bring about than you think and the unforeseen can always happen.
- You must be flexible and prepared to change your plan regularly as circumstances dictate but, where possible, changes should be made within the overall structure of your plan, subject to the 12-month review.
- Be determined and persistent in implementing your plans, and maintain focus on the end result, which is to exit your business for the best price and with the maximum personal satisfaction.
- Ensure you have a mechanism in place that enables you to review the increases in your business's value (a simple relationship between profitability and value will suffice). This could help in keeping you positive and focused about implementing your plans.
- In a family succession, you should involve your successor in the implementation of the plan at all times. Communication at an early stage solves many issues, and prevents small problems from becoming big ones. You should take the same approach, albeit to a lesser extent, with an owner-managed MBO.

Being prepared for disposal

If you have followed the planning steps in this book, you should be confident that most of the operational business improvements and the removal of impediments to sale in your business have been completed well before you become involved in the actual disposal process. Conversely, if you have not planned early, you could be cleaning up your business at the same time as you are selling it.

The following checklist will serve as a reminder of the various things that you will need to have covered as you approach actual disposal itself.

- Taxation implications of disposal: see Appendix 1.
- Business continuity agreements: see Chapter 2.
- Valuation targets: see Chapter 3.
- Operational business planning: see Chapter 7.
- Removal of impediments to sale: see Chapter 6.
- Successor grooming: see Appendix 4.
- Personal financial planning: see Chapter 10.
- Owner's due diligence: see Appendices 5 and 8.
- Preparation for handover: see 'The handover process' below.

Once you have completed these steps and signed off your sale agreement you will be ready to hand over the business to the new owners, where this is applicable.

The handover process

THE PRINCIPLE OF HANDING OVER

Although the basic objective of a handover is similar for most disposals, namely, the seller familiarizing the buyer with the operational issues involved in running the company, there are differences depending on the exit route you have taken. In some exit options, such as a flotation, or franchising there will not be a handover at all because you will remain in control of the business. In other cases, the handover itself will vary with the length and nature of due diligence, the provisions dealing with the handover in the sale agreement, the size of the business, the time available and the inclination of the seller to undertake a handover process.

For example, in a family succession a handover could be indistinguishable from the training and grooming of the successor, and will be for a long period and largely before the sales contract has been signed, whereas in a trade sale the handover period will be shorter and mainly after completion of the sale. The handover to internal management in a planned MBO will usually be longer and more extensive than in a venture-capitalist backed MBI. In a merger the handover could almost be continuous as both sides develop methods of working together over a long period. Finally, a public listing should require no formal handover at all, as the owners of the company that has listed will remain in control after the flotation. These differences aside, the general principles of a handover to new owners are as follows:

- In all disposals (except where management is remaining) there needs to be a formal handover of the business by seller to buyer.
- The handover is usually in two parts: the process before completion of the sale, and that after the sale. Although some people might consider this to be a continuous process, there is a different emphasis in the two processes.
- A handover involves both a handing over of information and tuition in how things are done. The first is factual, while the second could involve certain tricks of the trade, or understanding the personal quirks of employees and customers.
- Before the sale, the emphasis is on the seller explaining the business operations to the buyer, and introducing him or her to the business's key managers and employees, customers, agents, suppliers, sub contractors, etc. The seller still owns the business and, if the sale falls through, this will remain the case. Because of this, certain highly confidential (or market-sensitive) matters might not be divulged.
- After the sale, the seller has no reason to hold back any information. Also, the buyer will be finding out for himself or herself what areas he or she has difficulties with and will be seeking specific guidance from the seller. Of course, the buyer is now in charge and will, probably, be changing the way things are done anyway, so the seller's help will become progressively less important.
- The length, style and type of handover should be covered in some detail in the sales contract. But, even with a formal agreement on how the handover is to take place, intentions are not always fulfilled in practice because both sides often become disenchanted with the process. Sellers find it difficult to be involved in businesses that are no longer their own, while buyers soon wish to be left alone to do things their way, without what they now consider to be the interference of the predecessor.

WHEN TO HANDOVER

A handover can take place, in practical terms, before a business sale is completed. This can occur when the potential buyer has made an offer, subject to knowing more about the inner workings and operations of the business. This requirement may not be satisfied by the buyer's formal due diligence process, as this often concentrates on accounting, legal and compliance issues, rather than on operational issues.

This pre-sale handover provides a challenge to business vendors as many find it difficult to know just how much they should be telling a potential, but as yet legally uncommitted, buyer about their business. There is, unfortunately, no easy answer to this dilemma, which relies on a judgement by the seller of the genuineness of the purchaser. You need to decide whether you are involved in a handover of information to a genuine purchaser, or satisfying the curiosity of a potential competitor. If in any doubt, you should hold back on sensitive information until you have a signed contract, which could be conditional.

ADVANTAGES OF PROPER HANDOVER

The reasons for a proper handover are more than just to provide information to the buyer. Other advantages of a properly organized handover are that it:

- reassures management and employees
- provides comfort to customers or clients that they will continue to receive personal service from the new owner whom they have now met
- demonstrates to the clients that the retiring owner cares about personal relationships, thus helping to preserve client goodwill for the buyer
- enables the seller to leave the business with his or her relationships intact, which is especially important in small communities
- provides the springboard for the buyer to develop new business opportunities with the new clients.

The disposal transaction

The disposal transaction will vary depending on the exit route you have chosen. Some aspects, such as due diligence will, however, be more or less the same. In the various appendices covering the different exit options we have explained how you go though the process of completing the disposal transaction and you should refer to the one relevant to your disposal route.

Payment

There can be several circumstances in a disposal where purchasers do not receive the full sale proceeds on completion of the sales transaction. You should refer to Appendix 8 on trade sales where we consider the most common ones – vendor finance, retention, earn outs and deferred payment – in some detail.

As we discuss in Appendix 8 the pertinent issue from a seller's point of view is whether the availability of vendor finance, or time payment terms, can enhance both the chances of disposal and the amount of the purchase price. Sellers should be aware that latitude with payment could be an effective sales tool, but that there is always a risk involved.

Summary

Implementation of your MESP is as important as its production, and the problems with implementation can arise from the way the plans were produced as much as from the shortcomings of those implementing them. Teamwork and commitment within the framework of commercial reality are important elements in both the production of your plans as well as in their implementation.

PART 4 *Appendices*

APPENDIX 1

WHAT ABOUT TAX?

This appendix discussess the importance of taxation planning in exit strategy planning. It provides:

- an overview of the taxes that apply generally to the disposal of a business and, in particular
- details of capital gains tax and inheritance tax
- information on the importance of time and timing in reducing tax liabilities and the consequent need to seek competent tax advice well in advance of your planned disposal
- a checklist to help you ask your adviser some of the important tax planning questions.

Mindful of the potential problems, we will use this chapter to give you a simplified overview of the main taxation implications of disposing of your business, if only to reinforce the need for you to plan well ahead and to get the relevant expert advice as early as possible. The advice is necessary both for the period before you exit your business and for the disposal itself.

DISCLAIMER

The taxation law that applies to the disposal of business assets is extremely complex and is changing all the time and a book of this kind can provide only a basic overview of the issues involved at the time of writing. You should note carefully the following points:

- The material in this appendix does not purport to provide taxation, accounting, financial or legal advice. Owners planning to dispose of their businesses should obtain independent legal and accounting advice early in the planning process.
- The circumstances of each business disposal are different. You cannot rely on the fact that the general principle will, necessarily, apply to you and your business. Consequently, independent taxation advice on your particular situation is always necessary.
- If you dispose of your business without taxation planning you might not be able to take full advantage of the various allowances and reliefs available to you, because many of them are complex and to comply requires a careful arrangement of your affairs well before the actual time of disposal.
- In all circumstances (and particularly if you are retiring) you should consider the effects of tax on your overall business and personal financial position, that is, you must take an integrated approach to your financial and business affairs.
- The Inland Revenue publish numerous leaflets and booklets on all aspects of taxation. Most of these are available without charge from your nearest Inland Revenue office. Most Inland Revenue publications are also available on the Internet at: www.inlandrevenue.gov.uk

WHAT TAXES ARE IMPORTANT?

Income tax, corporation tax, inheritance tax and capital gains tax will all have a bearing on your exit strategy planning. For all exit strategies, CGT is likely to be the most important, as it is the proceeds of disposal that need to be protected. However, for those owners considering a disposal through a family succession plan IHT could be equally important.

Income and corporation taxes will be relevant to the proceeds of the sale of trading assets in the accounting year in which you sell. Income tax, corporation tax and CGT will also be very important in the period leading up to disposal. For example, when you are considering how to allocate the potential trading surpluses in your business between income drawings and capital reinvestment (an issue we deal with in more detail in Chapter 10), the interplay of income and corporation taxes and CGT will be a key issue.

CAPITAL GAINS TAX

GENERAL PRINCIPLES OF CGT

As a general rule, CGT applies to the gain made on the sale of an asset owned and disposed of by the same person or entity. Gain is the difference between the cost of acquiring the asset and the amount received on disposal of it. The amount received is called the 'disposal proceeds'.

Where you dispose of an asset at less than cost, you incur a capital loss. Allowable capital losses can be offset against capital gains, but not usually against income profits.

Capital gains tax is payable on the 'taxable amount', which is an amount arrived at after calculating the 'total chargeable gain' and deducting from it various losses, allowances, costs, exempt amounts and 'reliefs'.

The 'annual exempt amount' is the fixed amount of taxable gain you are allowed in any year and is deducted from the total chargeable gain before CGT is payable. The annual exempt amount for 2002/3 is £7,700.

The order in which these allowances and reliefs are applied is important. We will examine these issues in more detail below.

Any form of property may be an asset for CGT purposes, including stocks and shares; machinery; land and buildings; and all business assets, including goodwill. Certain assets are exempt by the Inland Revenue (IR) from CGT, including private motor cars; proceeds from ISAs, PEPs, TESSAs and UK Government stocks; and betting and lottery winnings. The gain on sale of your private home is also usually exempt from CGT.

Disposal proceeds will, usually, be in the form of cash, which amount is clear. But where proceeds are not in cash, the concept of 'value' is used. Where the disposal is not at arm's length, 'market value' is estimated and used as the basis for calculating disposal proceeds.

ALLOWANCES AND DEDUCTIONS

Losses

Allowable capital losses can be for the current tax year or can be carried forward from previous tax years. Both sorts of losses can be deducted from capital gains, but where a gain is exempt from tax a loss on the same asset is not allowable. In calculating taxable gains, the first step is to deduct allowable losses for the same year, and if the resultant net amount exceeds the 'annual exempt amount' you can then deduct any carried forward losses you might have.

Indexation allowance

Indexation allowance (IA) is the allowance that adjusts gains for the effects of inflation. Its importance has been severely curtailed by the Finance Act 1998, which introduced taper relief and froze the IA at 5 April 1998, making the allowance available only for periods preceding 31 March 1998. To calculate IA up to April 1998, the taxpayer consults tables provided by the IR that give the indexation factor by which the gross gain is multiplied. For assets held on 5 April 1998 both IA and taper relief will apply on disposal.

DEDUCTIONS

The costs of acquisition, enhancement and disposal of an asset can be deducted from the gain. Also, the cost of defending your right to ownership of the asset can be deducted, while the normal cost of repairs and maintenance and interest payments cannot. Special rules apply to the costs of 'wasting assets' (which are defined as assets which had a predictable life of less than 50 years when acquired).

Acquisition costs are defined as being costs wholly and exclusively incurred in acquiring the asset. Where the asset is business goodwill, any capital costs expressly incurred wholly and exclusively in creating the asset can be deducted.

Enhancement costs are those costs wholly and exclusively incurred to enhance the asset as long as the costs are still reflected in the nature of the asset at the date of sale.

Incidental costs include costs of transfer or conveyance; and fees, commissions and remuneration for professional advice.

RELIEFS (OTHER THAN TAPER RELIEF)

Reliefs come in various forms. Some defer charges, others reduce the amount of tax before taper relief is applied. Some are allowed automatically, while others have to be claimed before the IR will allow them. Some of the more important reliefs as far as business owners are concerned are as follows.

Rollover relief

This allows gains on disposal of business assets to be deferred if replacement business assets are purchased with the proceeds.

Retirement relief

This provides relief for individuals aged 50 or over (or younger if they retire because of ill health) who dispose of a business or shares in a trading company and who retire. This relief will become less important as it is being phased out and will cease to apply to gains arising after 2003.

Special investments

If you dispose of shares in a business in which you were either receiving the Enterprise Investment Scheme income tax relief, or which was a nominated Venture Capital Trust, your gains are exempt if you meet certain qualifying conditions.

Business transfer relief

Where you transfer a business to a company in exchange for shares, your gains are deferred until you sell the shares.

Gifts hold over relief

This relief allows gains to be deferred when certain assets are given away or sold at less than arm's-length value (for example, a sale to a family member at less than fair market value).

TAPER RELIEF (ALSO KNOWN AS BUSINESS ASSET TAPER RELIFEF, OR BATR)

General principles

Taper relief, introduced in the Finance Act 1998, will become (if it is not already) the most important relief from CGT as far as private business owners are concerned. Taper relief reduces the proportion of gain chargeable to CGT according to the period of time the asset has been owned by individuals, trustees and personal representatives.

The rate of the taper depends on whether the asset is a business or non-business asset. The amount of relief is announced in the Budget and for business assets disposed of after 6 April 2002 new tables have been announced as shown in the table below.

As you can see, after two years the percentage of gain that is chargeable will be reduced to 25 per cent when CGT will effectively be charged at a top rate of 10 per cent (that is 25 per cent of 40 per cent).

Taper relief replaces indexation from April 1998, but not for assets held on or before 5 April 1998. This means that both the taper relief and indexation rules will still apply to some asset disposals. (You now know why we need tax advisers!) Taper relief is applied after all other reliefs and allowances have been given, but before the annual exempt amount is applied.

Taper relief is not available to company taxpayers for whom the indexation allowance will continue to apply.

Important terminology

The IR loves technical terms and the important ones to understand in taper relief are as follows:

- 'Qualifying holding period'. The percentage of gain chargeable depends on 'the number of whole years' in the qualifying holding period, which is simply the relevant period that the asset was owned by the seller. (Note that where an asset is acquired through an option, the qualifying holding period is deemed to be from the exercise of the option and not from the grant or acquisition of the option.)
- 'Business asset'. Any asset may be a business asset if it is used for the purposes of trade, profession or vocation or employment and if certain conditions are met. The holding of shares is a business asset where the company is a 'qualifying company'.
- 'Qualifying company'. A qualifying company is a trading company, or the subsidiary of a trading company, where the relevant individual can exercise at least 25 per cent of the voting rights in that company or if it is a trading company and the individual owns at least 5 per cent of the shares in the company and is working full-time in the company.

Whole years' asset held from 6 April 1998	*New rates (disposals from 6 April 2002)*		*Old rates*	
	Percentage of gain charged to tax	*Effective rate of tax for higher rate taxpayer (%)*	*Percentage of gain charged to tax*	*Effective rate of tax for higher rate taxpayer (%)*
Less than 1	100	40	100	40
1	50	20	87.5	35
2	25	10	75	30
3	25	10	50	20
4 or more	25	10	25	10

- 'Trade' and 'trading company'. Trade is deemed to be anything that is considered by the IR as trade for the purpose of income tax, and a trading company is a company substantially engaged in trade. (*Note* that there can be practical difficulties in this definition for some private business owners: see 'Common pitfalls' below.)

How to calculate CGT after taper relief

The IR states that the way CGT is calculated is aimed at reducing the amount of CGT payable on each asset by the taxpayer. Whatever the truth of the matter, calculating the CGT can have its own complications (for example, which losses to deduct from which gains), but in simple terms you go about calculating your CGT liability for business assets (that have been business assets for the whole period of ownership) in the following way:

Example 1 (where you have no allowable losses)

- Step 1: calculate your gain for the year. (You do this by deducting the cost of the asset, including incidental costs, from the disposal proceeds.)
- Step 2: if the asset was owned before 1998, calculate the indexation allowance and deduct this from the gain to get the chargeable gain.
- Step 3: calculate the number of whole years you have owned the asset to work out the taper relief and the resultant tapered chargeable gain.
- Step 4: deduct the annual exempt amount from the tapered chargeable gain to arrive at the 'amount liable to CGT'.

Figure A1.1 provides an example of this calculation.

Example 2 (where there are allowable losses)

- Step 1: calculate your gain for the year, as in Step 1 in Example 1, above.
- Step 2: deduct any allowable losses for the year and any losses brought forward from previous years from your gain. If the net amount is either negative, or is less than the annual exempt amount for the year, you do not have any CGT to pay and there is no taper relief to be calculated.
- Step 3: if the chargeable amount exceeds the annual exempt amount for the year you calculate the taper relief applicable to each asset. (This is where deducting the appropriate losses from the appropriate assets in the way most favourable for you is important.)
- Step 4: deduct the annual exempt amount from the tapered chargeable gain to arrive at the amount liable to CGT.

Common pitfalls with taper relief

Certain business owners will not receive full advantage from taper relief due to lack of planning and proper advice. Some of the more common pitfalls are as follows:

- Failing to qualify as a trading company: because the company owns too high a proportion of its total assets in investments or cash, or other assets that are not used in the trade.
- Selling shares to family members shortly before sale. This can arise when shareholdings are transferred to reflect previously agreed shareholdings that have not been formally documented, resulting in the taper relief 'clock' being restarted from the date of transfer and a loss of the benefit for the transferees.

This example is for when there are no allowable losses and is based on the relief available in April 2002.

You acquire a business asset on 10 July 2000 for £50,000 (including incidental costs) and you sell the asset on 8 September 2002 for £85,000.
Your untapered chargeable gain is therefore £35,000.
You have no other chargeable gains or allowable losses in the tax year.
There are two whole years in your qualifying holding period for taper relief purposes.
The taper relief percentage of gain chargeable for a business asset held for two years is 25%.

Assuming that your exempt amount is £7,700, the amount liable to CGT is computed as follows:

Chargeable gain	£35,000 @ 25% = £8,750	('total chargeable gain')
Less annual exemption	£7,700	('exempt amount')
Amount liable to CGT	£1,050	('taxable amount')

Figure A1.1 Calculating Capital Gains Tax

- Similarly, if an owner gives away shares or other assets (by putting them into a trust for his or her children, for example) the clock starts ticking again from the date of the gift.
- The corporate structure is such that the business being sold is owned by a holding company that sells the shares. There will be no taper relief granted in these circumstances, as it is not available to companies.
- Where an asset attracts both non-business and business taper relief it still takes 10 years (under current taxation rules) to achieve an effective tax rate of 10 per cent, and not two years from the date that business taper relief commences. However, with advice and the correct planning this can be minimised.

Some further points of note

1. One way of receiving the full benefit of taper relief even though the business has not been owned for two years could be to delay payment through instruments like bank guaranteed loan notes, cashable only when the full relief becomes applicable, because for CGT purposes the date of disposal is calculated from the date of payment and not when the agreement to sell is entered in to.
2. Other schemes for avoiding tax include giving up UK residence and being paid in a qualifying overseas country, but besides the question of whether the tax saving is worth this inconvenience you would need to establish from your advisors whether this loophole is still available.
3. Payment of a capital sum over time is still treated as capital (and not income) for CGT purposes, unless something in the sales agreement affects the amount of the selling price.
4. Goodwill is a business asset for CGT purposes and is subject to the same rules and allowances and reliefs as other business assets. However, it will be important to both vendor and purchaser to establish clearly what portion, if any, of the price being paid can be allocated to a goodwill component.

HOW MUCH CGT YOU PAY

Once you have calculated the 'amount liable to CGT' you still need to know how much to pay the IR. The rate at which CGT is payable depends on the individual taxpayer's income tax rate for the year in question. The amount liable to tax is treated as the 'top slice' of your income (that is, it is added to your income for the year) and charged to CGT at the rate applicable (sometimes known as the marginal rate). Depending on your total income for the year, the rate could be at the basic rate or the higher rate, or some at the basic rate and the balance at the higher rate.

It is useful if you can estimate in advance what the likely CGT consequences of your asset disposals will be. (You will be greatly assisted in this if you have kept your business records in an orderly fashion.)

As a minimum, you should establish the following facts with your advisers:

- what is being sold, the company's shares, or the assets of the business
- the dates you (or the selling entity if this is not you) acquired the assets
- if the shares in the company are being sold, the date on which the shares were acquired
- the costs of purchase, including acquisition and likely disposal costs (such as legal fees, commissions)
- the costs of any additions or enhancements to the assets
- the estimated date of disposal
- the estimated price of disposal
- the likely losses, allowances and reliefs available
- an estimate of the likely capital gains or losses for each asset.

INCOME AND CORPORATION TAXES

GENERAL PRINCIPLES

Income and corporation taxes are levied on income or profit. In the disposal of a business, proceeds from the sale of trading assets such as stock are included in the trading income of the business for the year in which they are sold and corporation tax might be payable on the resultant profit, if any.

Income tax could apply to a business vendor in many areas too numerous to mention in a book such as this. You should, as a part of your planning, review with your advisers the likely impact the sale of your business will have on your personal income tax, particularly with regard to the proposed timing of the sale. Early advice will give you the time to plan for the optimum outcomes. Also, it is difficult, and often illegal, to backtrack on transactions after they have been processed, so it is important to get it right the first time.

ESTABLISHING THE FACTS

Depending on the structure and nature of the sale, and your own circumstances, there are many questions you will need to raise with your advisers to establish the likely taxation consequences of your disposal. Some of these are listed in the checklist below.

The issues here will depend on your particular circumstances and the structure of your financial affairs, but there are some basic questions you should cover with your advisers, which include:

- What is being sold, the company's shares, or the business assets?
- The 'cut off' question: what income and expenditure items are likely to be included in the respective accounts of the vendor and purchaser, assuming the disposal goes ahead on the planned date?
- Is it possible and are there advantages in classifying some of the assets that are being sold as capital assets rather than trading assets, and vice versa?
- Is there the opportunity, or any advantage, in preserving income and/or capital tax losses within the company? (This will be relevant when you plan to sell the assets of the business and not the company that owns them.)
- What is the position regarding recoupment of depreciation expenses in a sale of the assets in question?
- Does the transaction involve transferring sale proceeds from your company (or trust) to your own hands as shareholder/vendor, and what are the taxation implications of this?

ALLOWANCES

Generally speaking, as corporation tax is paid on profits (that is, the difference between income and expenditure) the usual question of allowable deductions will arise. Once more, this issue is outside the scope of a book such as this and is something that will be addressed by your accountants when they prepare the tax returns for the year in which the business assets are disposed of.

INHERITANCE TAX

INTRODUCTION

Where a transferor transfers property to a transferee for less than market value (that is, as a gift) and the transferor dies within seven years of making the gift, IHT laws come in to play. These laws could have a dramatic impact on the way a business owner structures a family succession plan.

Inheritance tax law, like most tax laws, is complex and an understanding of its implications requires careful study. Business owners contemplating a family succession as an exit route should obtain early advice on IHT law from their tax advisers.

GENERAL RULES

The basic rule of IHT is that on death the transfer of an estate up to a certain value (in 2002/3: £250,000) is tax-free. Transfers to your spouse of any property either in life or after death, if both spouses are resident in the UK, are also free of tax.

The legislation also allows for gifts to be tax-free if certain conditions are met. These conditions include that the transferor lives for seven years after making the gift, or that the gift does not exceed a certain (relatively small) value, or that the total value of gifts does not exceed a specified amount in any single year.

Besides the exemptions for transfers after death and for gifts made in life, there is also significant relief under the IHT legislation for the transfer of business property, which could be very important to business owners wishing to dispose of their business assets to family members, either through a sale at less than arm's length, or through a gift, or a combination of both.

In a family succession you might decide to transfer your business to an heir for less than market value, as this could have several advantages to all concerned. To establish the likely IHT consequences of this you should clarify the following issues with your tax advisers:

- What is being transferred, the shares in the company, or the business assets?
- What is the value of the property being transferred?
- If shares are being transferred, is the company of the type to qualify for business property relief?
- Similarly, if assets are being transferred, will they qualify for business property relief?
- How long has the property being transferred been owned by the transferor?

- What are the likely consequences if the transferor dies within seven years of the transfer?

BUSINESS PROPERTY RELIEF

This explanation of the relief given on transfers of business property is a simplified one. Expert advice must be taken before you embark on any plans to dispose of your business asset through a gift to family members. Some of the more important aspects of the business relief are as follows:

- For the transfer of business assets both in life and on death, relief is available for certain property, known as 'relevant business property', subject to the property having been owned by the transferee for a certain time (usually two years) immediately prior to the transfer.
- The relief available is either 100 per cent or 50 per cent depending on the nature of the business and the property and whether the transferor has or had 'control' of the business. As a generalization, the more favourable rate applies to privately owned trading companies.
- Certain companies are not eligible for the relief, including those engaged wholly or mainly in dealing with securities, land and buildings and investments. (A bias similar to the definition of a 'qualifying company' in taper relief for CGT purposes.)
- If the property is an unincorporated business, or an interest in such a business, the value for the purpose of relief is the net value, that is the gross value of assets, including goodwill, less the value of liabilities.
- Where a transferor dies within seven years of a gift of business property, business property relief will be given if:
  - the property was relevant business property at the time of the transfer, and
  - it has been owned continuously by the transferee, and
  - it has remained relevant business property at the time of the transferor's death.

  Relief is reduced in proportion to value if part of the property fails any of these tests.
- Business property relief will remove the issue of whether to taper the relief according to the length of time the transferor has lived after the gift was given by him or her (assuming the time is less than seven years).

(*Note*: there are similar provisions for the transfer of agricultural assets.)

THE IMPORTANCE OF TIME AND TIMING

The need to plan is nowhere clearer than in the field of taxation. Planning is about giving yourself time and taking advantage of timing. It should be clear to you that timing your sale has a crucial impact on taxation liabilities, particularly now that taper relief is such a big part of the CGT regime.

You might need time to amend your corporate structure and you might need time to elapse before you can take full taxation advantage of this structure. Also, you will need to give yourself time if you are to be sure that your business qualifies as a trading company. Finally, you need time to plan, to ensure that you avoid the last minute panic that unplanned transactions invariably bring.

A FINAL WORD OF WARNING

This appendix provides a brief overview of extremely complex legislation that undergoes constant change. With relatively new law like the Finance Act 1998 there is little case law to support various professional interpretations of the legislation's application. Because of this, and as each business circumstance is different, extreme caution must be exercised when coming to any conclusions from generalized statements made here.

The observations in this appendix are not to be taken as advice and it is critical that you obtain independent, up to date legal, accounting and taxation advice prior to setting out on your exit strategy plan.

APPENDIX 2

VALUATION PRINCIPLES AND METHODS

In this appendix we examine in some detail the methods involved in valuing private businesses. We discuss:

- some introductory concepts of valuation, such as transferring value
- crucial issues in valuation, such as what are real profits and goodwill
- some of the more established methods of valuation employed in private businesses
- how you can value your own business, having considered particular problems such as establishing the appropriate price earnings ratio.

The information that follows will provide you with a working knowledge of valuation methods but will not, on its own, make you a business valuer. By reading this appendix you should gain a working knowledge of business valuations that will enable you to form an opinion as to the value of your business. For a formal valuation of your business you should consult an expert valuer.

SOME INTRODUCTORY CONCEPTS

BUSINESS AS AN INVESTMENT

Generally speaking, accepted business valuation methods place a value on a business by capitalizing its future cash flows or expected future profits. Whatever the approach, it is important for owners to recognize that business valuation should be based on the same objective criteria as the valuation of other investments and not on subject criteria.

TRANSFERRING VALUE

Business value will only exist if it can be transferred from vendor to purchaser. For example, if the price you ask for a sole trader business includes a goodwill value element, you will need to ensure that the goodwill value can effectively be transferred to the purchaser, rather than 'walking out of the door' when you leave.

BUYING A BUSINESS OR A COMPANY'S SHARES

When valuing a business for sale it is necessary to make the distinction between selling business assets (such as stock, plant, fixtures and fittings) and selling a company's shares (where all assets and most liabilities of the company are usually taken over). In the first case you could be valuing assets only (that is, with no goodwill component), while in the second case you would be valuing a business in total and the issue of goodwill value will need to be addressed.

TYPES OF VALUE

Valuers usually qualify their valuations by stating the circumstances under which the value pertains, for example valuations will be on a 'going concern', close down or 'fire sale' basis. These circumstances will determine the presence or otherwise of goodwill value, while the value of fixed assets can be greatly reduced when they have to be moved from the productive environment of an operating business.

In the case of exit strategy planning you will, hopefully, be considering the value of your business as a going concern, but if there is any question of a close down as a possible exit option then you will have to be aware of the affect this has on most asset values. (See Appendix 10 on ceasing to trade.)

'REAL' PROFIT, 'SUPER' PROFITS AND FUTURE MAINTAINABLE PROFIT

Profit is the cornerstone of private business valuation. Profit represents the return on a purchaser's investment and is, usually, the amount that is 'capitalized' to calculate business value. It is important, therefore to be clear what profit should be used in business valuation.

REAL PROFIT

The words 'real profit' are used to distinguish published profits (that is the profits that appear in the business's books of account) from the profit the business would be making if normal business expenses were included. Real profit can be either higher or lower than published profit and is also known as adjusted profit. Calculating real profit can be a problem in private businesses either because owners do not maintain a sharp distinction between business and private financial transactions, or because profit is shifted between business entities within the same group. You arrive at real profit by adjusting published profit by the following:

- non-business income and expenses
- non-recurring items
- income and expenses from other related entities.

The published profit of a private business often gives a distorted view of the real profit of the entity. This is because the business owners sometimes arrange matters so as to minimize taxation.

On the other hand, some businesses will publish accounts that overstate their profits (or understate their losses) by not including expense items such as rent (where they own the building), or by understating the realistic cost of running the business by not including full salaries for business owners and their families.

Some of the common adjustments which are necessary to arrive at real profits for private business are noted below.

Non-business items

A private business is a useful vehicle in which non-business expenses can be charged to provide benefit to its owners. Such matters as private motor vehicle, travel and telephone expenses are often included in business expenses.

Non-recurring items

Where a business has any income or expense that is not likely to recur in future this should be removed from the published accounts to arrive at real profit.

Owners' salaries

In calculating real profits it is sometimes necessary to deduct owners' stated salaries from published profits and to replace them with salaries (based on market rates) which would be payable to managers undertaking equivalent work to the owners. Simply, you could ask what it would cost for managers to undertake the owners' management tasks?

This is also a useful guideline for an investor/purchaser who does not intend working in the business, as real profit can be calculated for the circumstances where a manager is in charge of the business.

Premises

Where the business owns the premises in which it operates, ownership can reside in different legal entities controlled by the business owner. In these circumstances rental is sometimes completely excluded from published business accounts, or charged at excessive amounts to move profits from one business entity to another.

In calculating real profit it is important that a true market rental figure is included. The true market rent should be easy to establish. Advice can be sought from your local estate agent if you have any doubts.

Cost of goods sold and gross margins

It is easy to manipulate the profit of any entity that purchases goods by adjusting the value of the closing stock in the accounts at period end. A business can achieve continuously increasing published profits merely by increasing the value of its closing stock. Conversely, a business can often eliminate its profit by writing-down the value of its closing stock. In calculating real profits, an amount needs to be added to or subtracted from the accounting profit to allow for all unrealistic valuations of stock.

Super profit

'Super profit' is similar to real profit and is an expression used mainly in very small businesses. Some small business owners express their business's profit as being equivalent to their annual profit before deducting their own salaries (or any equivalent amount for market-related salaries that should be paid to compensate the owners for the work they undertake in the business). In these cases, super profit is the amount of profit after deduction has been made for these salaries. For example, if a business's real profits after adjusting for all non-business expenses, but before allowing for owners' market related wages of £80,000 is £250,000, then the super profits would be £170,000. Or, assume that in another business the profit is also £250,000 per annum, but market-related wages for the owners working in this business are £260,000: here the super profits are negative.

FUTURE MAINTAINABLE PROFIT OR FUTURE MAINTAINABLE EARNINGS

Business valuations are based on putting a capital value on future profits or cash flows and, because future profits are uncertain, business valuation is itself uncertain. The phrase 'future maintainable profits' (FMP) is used to describe the concept that future profits will recur at a particular level. (Some people also refer to these as 'sustainable profits'.) Strictly speaking, these are the profits that should be used to calculate business value. The phrase seems to imply that future profits can be predicted with some certainty which, of course, might not apply to the subject business. In private business valuations, FMPs are usually calculated by averaging a combination of past and projected profits; an interesting mixture of certainty and uncertainty! (See 'Establishing the FMP' below, where FMP is discussed in more detail.)

THE CONCEPT OF RISK

There are many risks involved in buying a business. Below we consider some of the more straightforward and common ones.

INCOME RISK

As stated above, most investment valuations rely on estimates of future profit. The risk that this future profit will not materialize will be greater with some investments than in others. For example, among the less risky investments is a cash deposit in a high street bank with a fixed interest return for a set period (with an undertaking to receive the capital back in full at the end of the period). At the other end of the spectrum, one could invest in the bonds of a highly geared start-up telecommunications business in a leading-edge new technology. The former investment will provide a lower rate of return because it offers you a relatively risk-free opportunity both in terms of income and capital. The latter has to offer you a much higher rate of return to compensate you for the much higher risk involved in both its income earning potential and certainty of a capital return.

Applying this theory to private businesses, some businesses are obviously more risky than others. For example, compare the purchase of a mobile phone shop on a high street (that has a month-to-month lease, where competitors can open at any time and where technology is changing rapidly), with purchasing an old-established newsagency (which is, the only one on the high street and that has a long lease). Assuming that both businesses have the same current annual profit and the same tangible net asset value, typically the capital value of the mobile phone shop would be less than the capital value of the news agency.

The reason for this difference is that in calculating their respective values you would use a lower multiple of profit for the mobile phone shop than for the newsagency. The different business values represent the difference in the risk involved in maintaining the cash flow (or profits) of the respective businesses. The buyer of the newsagency believes he or she is more likely to maintain profits and for a longer period than if he or she had brought the phone shop, and is, therefore, prepared to pay a larger capital sum for the newsagency. This brings us to a key building block in approaching private business valuations, namely, the higher the risk, the lower the multiple, and the lower the price.

(*Note*: in the public company sector, the multiple used to calculate value can also be viewed as indicating the probability (or risk) of future profit growth in the subject company. Should the probability of growth be strong, a higher multiple of current profits will be used. This is similar, but not identical to the approach used in the private business sector.)

ASSETS RISK

The risk of maintaining income is not the only risk in purchasing a business. Another is the risk in getting one's money back on termination (for example, in the case of a closure or on-sale).

Where a business has strong tangible assets, such as real property or modern plant and equipment, there is a greater chance of a recovery of capital on disposal than when a business has very few tangible assets. Consequently, the capitalization rate used to value an asset-rich business is usually higher than for an asset-poor business, although this theory was turned on its head during the recent 'dot com' boom.

OTHER RISKS

There are other risks involved in buying a business. These include the following:

- Losing key personnel and management; retaining key customers and suppliers; and non-complying use of premises and other environmental issues could all be seen as part of the risk involved in the business's ability to trade profitably, and its ability to expand its business and profitability in the future.
- Businesses face political risk (as the recent terrorist incidents have shown), and risks that legislation affecting the circumstances under which they trade can change. Naturally, this will affect future business values and they should be taken in to account when valuing businesses, especially large ones. However, it is difficult in the private business sector to build a methodology satisfactorily to take account of these factors.

WHAT IS GOODWILL?

The notion of goodwill is familiar to us all, although a precise description is more difficult. Valuing goodwill can prove to be even more difficult. So, what is goodwill?

LEGAL DEFINITION

Probably the best-known legal definition is by Lord McNaughten in the case of *I.R.C.* v. *Muller and Company* (1901) where he defined goodwill in the following way:

> It is a thing very easy to describe, very difficult to define. It is the benefit and advantage of a good name, reputation and connection of a business. It is the attractive force, which brings in custom. It is the one thing which distinguishes an old established business from the new one at its first start.

This definition recognizes that goodwill has a benefit (or value) to a business, but does not go much further than that. You could deduce from this definition that goodwill is the intangible component of a business that enables that business to earn a greater profit than could be generated by the net tangible assets alone. Which brings us to accountants.

ACCOUNTING DEFINITION

Accountants, being less philosophical than lawyers, look at goodwill more simply. A short accounting definition of goodwill is as follows: 'goodwill is the difference between total value and net tangible asset value'.

Although this definition does not necessarily make goodwill any easier for business people to understand, it does make it easier to value, especially after a business has been sold.

A PRACTICAL EXAMPLE OF GOODWILL

It will probably help our understanding of goodwill value to look at a practical example. Assume a retail business with three shops is being sold for £300,000 (excluding the real property). The value of the fixtures and fittings in the shops is £50,000 based on their written-down value and the value of the stock is £175,000 valued at cost. The value of goodwill would be £75,000.

VALUATION METHODS

There are many methods used to value private business and here we will examine the more common ones. The approach we suggest for private business owners to estimate the value of their businesses is to use two methods and compare the results. Your final opinion could be based on the average of these two results

THE 'SUPER PROFITS' METHOD

The super profits method is a simple method of business valuation which arrives at a total value of a business by calculating the goodwill value and the net asset value separately and then adding the two values together. It is used mainly in smaller private companies.

To calculate the value of a business using this method you take the following steps:

- Step 1: calculate the average super profits for the last three years – which we will call the maintainable super profit (MSP). Do not deduct taxation. (See previous 'Super profits' section, to calculate super profits.)
- Step 2: capitalize the MSP by a factor of between 1 and 2 to arrive at goodwill value. (The rationale for this is that the goodwill value of a small private business represents one or two years before tax MSP of the business.)
- Step 3: calculate the value of the net tangible assets of the business. (This is achieved by placing a gross current market value on a going

concern basis on all tangible assets, less any amounts owing on the assets and other liabilities.)
- Step 4: add the goodwill value to the net tangible asset value to arrive at total value of the business.

As an example:

- Step 1: assume MSP is £75,000.
- Step 2: assume the use of a multiple of 2, to arrive at goodwill value of £150,000.
- Step 3: assume total gross value of assets is £160,000 and total liabilities are £24 000: therefore net tangible asset (NTA) value is £136,000.
- Step 4: add goodwill value and NTA value to arrive at total value: £150,000 + £136,000 = total value of £286,000.

Where the company's shares are being sold it is assumed that the purchaser is buying all assets and taking over all liabilities, but where this is not the case the business's NTA should be adjusted accordingly.

THE PRICE EARNINGS RATIO METHOD

The p/e ratio method values a business as a whole by capitalizing its future maintainable after-tax real profits to arrive at total value, rather than by valuing goodwill and net assets separately as is done through the super profits approach. Thus, in a p/e ratio method the total value includes goodwill value.

The concept of the p/e ratio method is simple, but there are practical difficulties in establishing the FMP and in deciding what p/e ratio to use in each case. It is also important to note that assets that are not used to generate the business income (also known as 'surplus assets'), including such things as owned business premises or other real estate, are not usually included in the total business value calculated by using this method.

Establishing the FMP

This involves two distinct steps:

- adjusting the published profits to arrive at real profits
- deciding what combination of historic real profits and future profits should be used to arrive at the FMP figure.

The process of adjusting published profits in a private business to reach real profits was discussed previously, in the 'Real profit' section. Deciding on a final FMP figure is a matter of judgement. Although a purchaser is buying the future, he or she is more likely to believe that last year's profits are a closer proxy for FMP than next year's projected profits. It is usual to use a combination of historic and projected data to establish FMP and an average of the last three years' real profits and the next two years' projected profits (if available) is a good starting point. Note the figure used in this valuation method is the FMP after taxation.

Establishing the appropriate p/e ratio

You now need to establish the appropriate p/e ratio to use in your calculations. What you are looking for is a capitalization rate that truly reflects the profits risk and the growth potential of your business. Below we discuss some of the issues you need to consider and give you some pointers to establishing the appropriate p/e ratio.

The rate of inflation All investment returns, including official interest rates, are influenced in some way by the rate of inflation. So are p/e ratios. In times of high inflation, p/e ratios are also high, and in times of low inflation p/e ratios are supposed to be generally lower. However, this correlation does not always apply, particularly on the world's stock exchanges, which are often influenced by other considerations. Thankfully for our purposes, the p/e ratios (and hence the values) of private businesses are much more rational and are usually directly influenced by current inflation rates.

Alternative investments A first step in establishing the appropriate p/e ratio for your business is to find out the current returns of various alternative investments and to list them in order of type and risk. This will give you a point of reference to help you make your selection. Below we list some types of investment and their p/e ratios to which you could refer, and we ask you to consider some other issues that could establish an appropriate p/e.

- Relatively risk-free investments. Consider, for example, an interest-bearing cash deposit in a high street bank. Let us assume this pays 6 per cent before tax, or 4.5 per cent after tax. A 4.5 per cent after tax return is equivalent to a p/e ratio of 22. (*Note* this investment has neither capital gain nor loss potential.)

- Sale prices for comparable private businesses. Ask a company broker with knowledge of your industry sector what p/e ratios are usually applied to a business of your size in your industry (and for the sake of comparison in some other sectors of the market).
- London Stock Exchange. Find out what p/e ratios are applicable for public companies in your industry sector on the LSE. The *Financial Times* publishes average p/e ratios for the LSE for a range of sectors. In September 2002 examples of these were: Basic Industrial 14; General Industrial 19; Consumer Goods 23; Financials 20; Banks 15; IT 22; while the average for the FTSE 100 was 19.

Now consider your own company. How does it compare with the examples above?

- Put yourself in a potential buyer's shoes. What would be a reasonable return on investment in the business, given the risk of maintaining income and incurring capital loss? If you think 15 per cent is a reasonable figure this equates to a p/e ratio of 6.6; if you consider 10 per cent to be reasonable this equates to a p/e ratio of 10; and so on.
- Another way of looking at this (especially for smaller companies) is to ask: 'How quickly will the investor want to get his money back?' Or, 'How many years of after-tax profit is reasonable to repay the initial investment in this business?'

Comparisons with the LSE p/e ratios The average p/e ratio on the London Stock Exchange in the relevant industry sector could be a good reference point in deciding on the appropriate p/e ratio for your business. Public company p/e ratios are usually about twice those of larger private company p/e ratios, and three times those of smaller private businesses.

One also needs to be aware that there are times when stock exchange p/e ratios mirror the 'irrational exuberance' of the times, while private company transactions seldom follow this enthusiastic pricing model. In these circumstances (which have pertained recently), the discount for private companies in relation to public companies would be larger.

An American view of private company p/es Dewing, in his book *Financial Policy of Corporations* (1935), provides the following guidelines to choosing a p/e ratio for private businesses, also based on after tax profits. Although these multiples were used for companies in the USA some 70 years ago and are applicable to a time of low economic growth, they are still a very useful guide to p/e ratios for private companies in the UK, especially the smaller ones.

- For an old established business, with large assets and excellent goodwill: a p/e ratio of 10.
- Well-established business, but requiring considerable management skills: p/e ratio of 8.
- Well-established business, but subject to shifts in general economic conditions and products vulnerable to depressions: p/e ratio of 7.
- Business requiring small capital investment, but above average executive ability to manage: p/e ratio of 5.
- Small industrial business, highly competitive, relatively small capital (which virtually anyone could run): p/e ratio of 4.
- Business which depends on special, often unusual skills of one, or a group of managers, small capital, highly competitive, high mortality: p/e ratio of 2.
- Personal service businesses, requiring virtually no capital. Management has special skills and intensive knowledge of the business. Earnings reflect his or her skill and it is questionable whether the business can continue without him or her: p/e ratio of 1.

Private company p/e ratios Most business markets around the world have a two-tiered structure with quite different p/e ratios applying to the private and public company sectors. Private company valuations are, however, influenced by public company sentiment and there is a trickle down effect to the private business sector. Generally speaking, private company valuations do not fluctuate as much as public company valuations, except where private companies are being listed on the Stock Exchange when very high multiples can be applied to a fashionable business going public.

Recent flotations of Internet-related, or high-tech, companies were based on values that obeyed few valuation rules. It was not only that p/e ratios were high, but also that in many cases they did not even apply because the businesses had never made a profit. In these cases the only rule of valuation that applied was to capitalize hopes and expectations. Here we must rely on the forecasting powers of City bankers, which is beyond the comprehension of mere business people.

As a generality in the UK current (2002) multiples for larger private companies are in the range from 4 to 9, while the p/es for smaller companies range from 2 to 4. The average p/e on the LSE, outside of the purely speculative stocks, is 21, although there are large variations between industry sectors. Also, there is increasing volatility between sectors and across the market generally, while p/e ratios are historically high.

Valuing a business using the p/e ratio method

The steps in using this method are as follows:

- Step 1: establish the FMP of the business after taxation.
- Step 2: select the appropriate p/e ratio (or capitalization rate).
- Step 3: multiply FMP by the p/e ratio multiple selected, to arrive at total business value.
- Step 4: add the value of surplus assets (that is, those assets not necessary for the production of the business income or profits) to arrive at total value.
- (Step 5: to value the goodwill, subtract the net tangible asset value from the total business value. If the total value of the business does not exceed its net tangible asset value there will be no goodwill value. If total value is less than net tangible asset value there is 'negative goodwill value' and it can be assumed that the value of the assets in some other use exceeds the value of the assets in the business itself as a going concern.)

A note on asset values

It is important to be clear about the difference between asset values and business values. Our approach in this appendix has been to value a business as a going concern; that is, to value a whole collection of assets, tangible and intangible, together as an entity in their current business use. Asset value alone is not the same as business value because asset value alone can be more or less than the value of the business in which they are currently being utilised.

If the assets alone are worth more than the total business value, it is worth considering whether the business should sell its assets and close down, or whether some of the assets could be sold and the business continued without them.

A note on the value of shares in private companies

The approach to valuation has been to value the whole business. If you wish to value the individual shares of your company, it is obvious that you could divide the total value of the company by the number of shares on issue. However, in private companies this will not necessarily mean that a minority shareholding (or any parcel of shares) will have the same value pro rata as the value of the total shareholding.

One of the reasons that private companies are worth less than public companies is because there is a lack of liquidity in private company shares. This is particularly true of a minority shareholding in a private company, which can be unsaleable. If you are valuing a private company for the purpose of disposal of a minority interest in the company that will remain private, you need to be aware that a substantial discount will usually apply to a less than a 100 per cent holding. A value pro rata to total value will usually only apply if you already have a buyer who is prepared to accept a value on this basis (such as in a shareholders' agreement).

THE DISCOUNTED CASH FLOW (DCF) METHOD

The DCF method of valuation differs from the other methods we have discussed in this appendix, in that it actively takes into consideration the present value of money. (Note that, while some valuers argue that a p/e ratio multiple recognizes present values, it is difficult to know precisely how this applies to choosing an appropriate p/e ratio.) Another way of saying this is that the DCF method recognizes that a pound in your pocket today is worth more than the same pound in your pocket next year.

The other difference is that the DCF method capitalizes (or discounts) cash flows rather than utilizing accounting profits.

The DCF method is used in most public company valuations (and by public companies when assessing the worth of their potential acquisitions). Its weakness for private business purposes is that it relies exclusively on discounting the values of projected (or estimated) future cash flows. All business forecasting is notoriously unreliable, and forecasting for private business is even less certain than for public companies. For this reason we do not recommend that you attempt to place a value on your business using this method.

Should you be considering a public listing, the valuation experts or your sponsoring broker will probably value your business on this basis (and probably in conjunction with at least one other method). Similarly, should the potential buyers of your business include a venture capitalist in their ranks, the VC could use the DCF method to value your business.

If you are interested in learning more about the DCF method, most standard financial or valuation textbooks cover the topic.

INDUSTRY YARDSTICKS

In very small businesses, short-cut methods of valuation are common. These are often referred to as 'industry yardsticks' or 'standard formulae' valuation methods. These methods place a value on a business based on gross turnover (or sales) rather than on profit or return on investment. These short-cut methods could be viewed as merely a different way of expressing value in relationship to a multiple of profits, as they are usually used in those businesses where a fairly standard relationship does exist between gross turnover and net profit. Such businesses include small professional practices or small retail outlets, where total value can be expressed in terms of a multiple of weekly or annual gross sales. For example, some insurance brokers are valued at between one and two times the total annual commissions earned.

CONCLUSION: VALUING YOUR BUSINESS

This appendix should have enabled you to form an opinion of the value of your business in order to place your plans in the correct context. Having the right information about the current and future values of your business will also clarify your decisions as to when to start planning and how long you need to plan.

Where you are going to estimate the value of your business yourself we recommend that you take the following steps:

1. Gather together all the relevant financial information, including historical accounts, profit forecasts and asset values.
2. Value your business using two different methods. You should compare the valuations and average them.
3. If your business is very small, you should compare the valuations with the relevant industry yardstick or standard formula, if one exists.
4. Compare your valuations with recent market sales of comparable businesses, if available.

Note: you should be aware that your valuation estimation (and comparable market sales) might not strictly apply to your business because of potential risks associated with your business or, put more precisely, because of the risk that profits will not be maintained. Also, your business's value could, in practice, be worth less than its theoretical value (arrived at using conventional methods) because of its impediments to sale. We would hope that through planning you will remove these impediments, but in your initial valuation estimates these problems could still be present and you will have to bear them in mind.

Where you are using valuers to provide a formal valuation for your business, they will require certain minimum information. Figures A2.1 and A2.2 are checklists that will assist you in providing this information.

You will need to assemble the following information when you are preparing an opinion as to the value of your business. Professional valuers will, as a minimum, also require this information to provide you with a formal valuation.

1. Background
- ☐ A short narrative background of the business. (Type of business, date commenced, location, number of employees, number of owners, plus anything else you think is relevant.)
- ☐ Legal structure of business; company or trust or partnership. Provide diagrammatic structure if necessary.

2. Financials
- ☐ At least three years' full financials (profit and loss and balance sheets) of all entities involved in the business.
- ☐ Profit and loss and cash flow projections for at least two years.
- ☐ Full debtors' listing.
- ☐ Stock details.
- ☐ List of assets – depreciation schedule.

3. Premises details:
- a) Location of business, clarify whether city, suburban or country where this is not obvious.
- b) Number of branches and locations.
- c) Properties owned or leased?
- d) Lease details, plus a copy of all leases.
- e) Owned property details, including:
- ☐ Description and estimated value.
- ☐ Is property to be valued? (If so, the valuer will advise what information is required.)

4. Taxation returns

Where business is sole trader or partnership, taxation returns for the last three years should be provided. Taxation returns are not usually required to value companies.

5. Franchises, licences, and so on

If the business operates under a franchise or licence agreement, or is reliant on agency agreements for its trade, full details of these and copies of the relevant agreements should be provided.

6. Staff details

These should include:
- ☐ Management: number and qualifications.
- ☐ Technical: number and qualifications.
- ☐ Support staff: number and qualifications.

7. Business plan

A recent business plan will greatly assist any valuer to understand the business, especially its markets and its marketing plans and, hence, its growth potential.

8. Other information

All businesses are different and unless a comprehensive business plan is provided, the valuer will usually request further information before completing a formal valuation.

Figure A2.1 Valuation of Businesses: Checklist of Information Required

The following information is required for the preparation of a valuation for accountant or solicitor practices.

1. Background
- ☐ A short narrative background of the firm. (Date commenced, location, number of partners, type of practice, number of employees, plus anything else you think is relevant.)
- ☐ Background of partners training, experience, special skills, etc.
- ☐ Is practice part of a franchise group?

2. Financials
- ☐ At least three years' full financials, including profit and loss and balance sheets of all entities involved (practice, service entity, family trust, where relevant)
- ☐ Profit and loss and cash flow projections for at least the next two years.
- ☐ Full debtors' listing.
- ☐ Work in progress (WIP) totals.
- ☐ List of assets and depreciation schedule.

3. Practice details
- ☐ Partnership agreement.
- ☐ Full details of partners and managers and support staff.
- ☐ Lease details (copy of the lease if possible).
- ☐ Details of real property owned. (Is it to be valued?)
- ☐ Type of work undertaken, including the mix of work and the percentage each comprises of the total billings. (*Note*: accountants' tax returns are often expressed as a percentage of the number of returns between private and corporate. A more meaningful figure is the percentage of total billings.)
- ☐ Location of practice: clarify whether city, suburban or country where this is not obvious.
- ☐ Structure, that is:
  Partnership or company?
  Service entity company?
  Family trust?

4. Taxation returns

Ideally, returns for the last three years should be provided.

5. A note on WIP

In solicitor practices WIP is of two kinds:

a) Work completed, but not billed.
b) Work to be completed on current files.

The estimated totals of both should be provided where possible. Most solicitors have an idea what the amount under (a) is, while the total under (b) is more of a rough estimate. The amount under (a) is the important figure, however, and do not worry unduly if (b) is not known too precisely.

6. Business plan

It will greatly assist the valuer if a current business plan is available. This will not only improve the understanding of the business's operations but will also provide an insight into the practices' prospects and future expected profitability.

Figure A2.2 Valuation of Professional Practices: Checklist of Information Required

APPENDIX 3

AGENTS AND FRANCHISEES

In this appendix we will look at the special position that agents, licensees and franchisees find themselves in when they wish to exit their businesses.

We explain:

- that your agency or franchise agreement is vital to establishing whether you own a business or not
- what your rights are when you wish to exit
- that these rights could determine your choice of exit options
- the usual routes to exit available to agents and franchisees
- the buyer of last resort facility that might be available to some agents and franchisees
- what your principal could be doing to facilitate your exit for value from your business.

THE VALUE OF AN AGENCY OR FRANCHISE

If you are a self-employed agent, or trade under a franchise (or license), you own a business that has a value in the sense that you earn an income from it, but does it also have a capital value? It could have a value if it generates some form of recurring income or profit and you are able to transfer this ownership to a third party. But to do this, of course, you need to own the business.

Leaving aside the question of ownership for the moment, an example of recurring income in agencies is where income comes in year on year without you having to do much extra work, such as repeat (or 'trailer') commissions in the insurance or financial services industry; while a retail franchise store will probably have recurring trading profits as long as it retains its premises and maintains its ability to trade under its franchise agreement.

(You can read more about how businesses are valued and how value is transferred in Appendix 2.)

DO YOU OWN A BUSINESS?

Assuming your business has the qualities that enable it to be sold for value, the next question that arises is whether you own the business and whether you are able to sell it for a capital sum, as opposed to losing all rights once your licence agreement has expired. The answer to these questions will depend on the nature of your business and the exit strategy policy that your principal has adopted. (Please note we will use the word 'principal' here to cover the principals of self-employed agents, or licensees or franchisees.)

'Ownership' of a business can become intertwined with the notion of owning your clients. It is particularly relevant in industries where agents provide a professional or financial service, or product to clients on behalf of their principals. The insurance industry is a good example of this. The legal relationship here is between the client and the principal (with the principal having continuing legal responsibilities to the client), and the principal 'owns' the client and the rights to the income generated by the client. The principal bestows certain rights to income generated from the client to the agent under the agency agreement, but the agent does not own the client and will usually lose all rights to the client income when the agency agreement comes to an end. Furthermore, the agent has no right to sell the benefit of the client income to another person.

Although there is no legal right to income, or capital benefit to an agent under these circumstances once an agency agreement has terminated, the principal can at its discretion agree that income benefits to the agent will continue after the agency agreement has terminated, or that benefits will continue to be paid to his or her beneficiaries after his or her death. Similarly, principals can, if they so choose, allow agents to sell their benefits of the income to a third party (usually another agent) for a capital sum, subject to approval by the principal.

In the case of many other franchise agreements, ownership *per se* is not an issue. It is usually clear that franchisees own their franchise businesses; the questions that arise are how, and to whom, are franchisees able to dispose of their businesses when they wish to do so.

Your position regarding these important issues should be clear from your agency or franchise agreement, as all principal firms should have policies governing the important question of sale or succession.

AGENCY AND FRANCHISE AGREEMENT ('YOUR AGREEMENT')

Your agreement should cover the question of ownership of your agency business, the ways you are able to dispose of your business, how the business is to be valued on sale and what conditions need to be fulfilled by you and the prospective purchaser before you can sell.

The market value of your business might also be influenced by your agreement, because it could dictate that you are selling in a market controlled by your principal, rather than in one that is free. This could depress your business's sale value. On the other hand, there could be positive factors in your agreement, such as if your principal offers funding to purchasers, or itself offers to buy your business through what is often known as a buyer of last resort (BOLR) facility.

CHECK YOUR AGREEMENT

From what we have said above, it is obvious that the first thing to do if you are an agent or franchisee thinking of selling your business is to check your agreement to see what it says about this matter. If it is not clear from the agreement what your principals' policy is on exits, you will need to clarify this with them.

A well thought out exit policy will not only include restrictions on disposal (such as the potential purchaser having to meet certain requirements and be approved by the principal), but should also include guidance and help for agents and franchisees on the question of sale or succession and even provide for the granting of loans on favourable terms to purchasers by the principal.

Unfortunately, in many cases, there is no clear policy laid down or assistance given on exit strategy in agency or franchise agreements, particularly with new franchise groups, and you could be left somewhat in the dark as to exactly what you can and cannot do. But, obviously, the existence or otherwise of policy on exit strategy is the first thing you must clarify.

GROWING YOUR BUSINESS

Growing a business first to sell it later is a basic part of an exit strategy. One of the strongest motivations for a business owner is the hope of realizing a substantial capital sum on disposal of his or her business. This capital can be used as a retirement fund; or as the means to acquire a bigger, better business; or as a legacy to pass on to an heir. A progressive, business-like principal will recognize the advantages both to its agents and to its own business of motivated agents or fanchisees who wish to build a valuable business. From the principals point of view, the more success its agents have, the more success it will have.

Business growth can be organic, or it can be through acquisition. In agencies or franchises, acquisition is usually undertaken by acquiring another agency under the same principal, or another franchise under the same franchise system. You should check to see what your principal's policy is on acquisitions and what support it provides you to acquire another business within the group. Similarly, you should understand what assistance (for example, managerial or financial) is available from your principal to assist you in organic growth.

There could also be other advantages to your principal if you build your business through acquisitions. In the insurance industry for example, in some companies, if an agent dies or retires, his or her clients (contained in what is known as a 'client register') revert to the management of the company and become what is known as 'orphans'. Research has shown that less repeat business is written and there are more lapses with orphans than when client registers are acquired by a new agent under a managed exit strategy policy.

CHOOSING THE OPTIMUM EXIT OPTION

Assuming your agreement allows you some freedom to plan your exit, we will now examine the exit options available to agents or franchisees. Most agencies and franchises are small businesses. This fact, and the fact that they are operated under licence, restricts the choice of disposal options open to them, but there still might be more exit options available than you may realize.

Exit options that might be available to agents and franchisees include the following:

- a succession to a family member
- a management or employee buyout
- a trade sale
- a sole trader merger
- a sale to your principal under BOLR.

Most of these options are dealt with in depth elsewhere in this book, but we will examine each one briefly, pointing out the differences in approach for agents and franchisees compared with other businesses.

FAMILY SUCCESSION

How to exit your business through a family succession has been covered in full in this book and especially in Appendix 4. The only difference for agents and franchisees could be the restrictions in planning a family succession placed on them by their agreement.

It should be possible in all franchise systems under your agreement to pass on your business to an heir in your lifetime. Many principals encourage this option, as the advantages for all are plain to see. If this is allowed by your agreement, you should follow the steps outlined in this book to plan and implement your succession plan.

Some principals will not allow family inheritance of agency businesses during the agent's lifetime, but they will allow the benefit of recurring commissions to be inherited by nominated next of kin, usually a spouse, when the agent dies. This is, of course, not the same as passing on a whole business, as the next of kin is not permitted to write new business either for existing clients or for third parties. Usually, the principal will take over the new business side of the client base once the agent has died and, thus, what is inherited is a diminishing income stream with a limited lifespan. The details of how this works in your particular agency could be of extreme importance to you and you should check your agreement, or discuss it with your principal.

A MANAGEMENT OR EMPLOYEE BUYOUT

The principles of management buyouts are covered fully in this book in Appendix 5. Many people think that MBOs are reserved for larger businesses and involve venture capitalists and sophisticated financial engineering, but this is not true. An MBO is like a trade sale where the buyers happen to be your management or employees. Of course, this option is not available to very small franchises and agencies where there is no management structure, but for all other businesses it is an option you should consider.

The reasons why an MBO might be a suitable option for you are covered elsewhere in this book, but it is worthwhile repeating these advantages especially as they apply to agencies and franchisees. They include:

- Your management knows your business better than any outside buyer. For example, it will be familiar with the franchise system under which you operate; or, where you are providing personal or financial services as an agent, it will know the clients intimately.
- You know your own management personally, you understand its strengths and weaknesses (which helps enormously in the grooming and the handover periods) and you should be able to negotiate the buyout in a spirit of positive goodwill.
- You should be able to structure the sale arrangements to suit your retirement planning needs, including arrangements for continuing to work in the business after its sale if you so wish.
- As the seller, there is a great deal of personal satisfaction in seeing people you have worked with and like taking over a business that has probably been built up through your joint efforts.

A TRADE SALE

Whereas franchisees (especially if they employ senior management) will have various exit options open to them, sole trader agents (especially those without suitable heirs to take over the business) are more limited in their choice. The obvious exit choices for sole traders without heirs are a sole trader merger and a trade sale. The problem with a trade sale could be the transference of knowledge of the business because sole traders have no senior management, so even this option is not necessarily open to them.

Trade sales are covered more fully in Appendix 8, and impediments to sale are discussed in Chapter 6. You should carefully read both if you are considering a trade sale.

To assist you to understand the special problems faced by agents and licensees in a trade sale, we list below the main points that you need to clarify before you begin to plan a trade sale. The first part concerns issues that should be resolved in your agreement, while the second concerns issues of a more general nature.

Agency agreement issues

- Does your agreement allow you to sell your business in a trade sale?
- If it does, what restrictions does it place on you? (For example, does your buyer have to be another agent or current franchisee and does the principal have to approve the buyer?)
- Are you allowed to advertise the sale?
- Are you allowed to set the asking price, or is this the preserve of your principal?
- Does your principal provide finance to approved buyers?
- Will your principal provide training to the purchaser? (This will be particularly important if you are unable to stay on after the sale to hand over to the purchaser.)

Other issues

- Are you able to assist the purchaser with vendor finance?
- Are you able to stay on and execute a proper hand over to the purchaser?
- Is your business so specialized that the purchaser pool is severely restricted?
- Is your business of the sort that the purchaser is likely to find a lender willing to assist with the purchase price?

Having addressed these issues and come up with a positive result, you are now in a position to plan your trade sale accordingly.

SOLE TRADER MERGER

If you are a self-employed agent with no suitable heirs or management staff, a sole trader merger might be your only viable way of exiting your business for a reasonable price (see Appendix 9). The family succession and MBO routes are closed to you and you might have difficulties with a trade sale. The problem with a trade sale is how to ensure that the business has a going concern value, because all the operating knowledge is in the owner's head and disappears when he or she leaves.

The first step in going about a sole trader merger is to confirm from your agreement whether you are able to go down this exit route and what sort of restrictions are put on you by your principal. The questions you should be asking are similar to the ones covered in 'agency agreement issues' in 'A Trade Sale' above.

Appendix 9 covers sole trader mergers in some detail and you should refer to it for detailed information on how you go about this exit option and for questions of personal liability and taxation. There are some particular points of note for agents or franchisees who are considering sole trader mergers, which are as follows:

- Finding potential merger partners should be relatively easy within your network.
- Your business cultures should be very similar, as you have both been working under the same regulated system.
- The concept of 'mentoring' (where older agents train and support younger agents) is well established in some networks and it is not a large leap to go from mentoring to working together in a merged entity.
- Some principals strongly favour mergers between agents or franchisees, as questions of approving the purchaser and training new franchisees do not arise with mergers between people already within the group. (Note that other principals have rules against ownership of more than one franchised business.)
- Principals will usually have more confidence in providing financial help to an acquiring owner who is already in the group than to an outsider.

BUYER OF LAST RESORT FACILITY

Where principals wish to encourage agents to build up a capital value in their businesses and to encourage, or facilitate their exit strategy planning, they will often provide a BOLR facility. A BORL facility is an undertaking by the principal to purchase from agents their businesses at a certain price, subject to certain conditions. We will now examine briefly how this might apply.

The conditions

Usually the BOLR facility will only come into play if the agent has gone through certain steps to sell his or her business and has failed. These steps might be laid down in the agency agreement, or they could be more ad hoc. The idea is generally that agents must have planned their exit along the lines of the exit strategy policy laid out in their agreements or, if there is no such policy laid down, in a way considered reasonable by the principal.

The price

Usually, the BOLR facility is not meant to be a full substitute for a successfully planned exit. The idea is that it is a last resort disposal and the price paid reflects this fact. For example, in businesses with few hard assets, the principal could use a valuation formula to arrive at a purchase price at a discount of say 30 per cent to true market value or, where there is a large asset content in the business, the principal could set the BOLR price at a figure that reflects the market value of net tangible assets only.

CONCLUSION

In this field there are nearly as many different agency agreements as there are principals, so it is impossible to generalize on what agents can do with regard to exit strategy planning. Your agency agreement is the key as far as your rights are concerned and you must start by understanding what you can and cannot do under this agreement.

Proper exit strategy planning is a fast-developing area of principal and agency arrangements. You might find that where your principal has not yet developed a policy that fully covers these issues, that it might be prepared, in consultation with its agents, to address the highly important matter of ensuring that you have a capital value in your business and that you can realize it on exit.

APPENDIX 4

FAMILY SUCCESSION PLANNING

In this appendix we will:

- describe some of the difficulties encountered in family succession planning and show you how through planning, you can overcome some of them
- take you through the succession planning process, from training and grooming your heir to producing your master succession plan
- show you how a well-planned family succession could be the ideal way (in terms of personal satisfaction, financial reward and retirement planning) for you to exit your business.

THE DIFFICULTY WITH FAMILY SUCCESSION

Two-thirds of small to medium-sized enterprises (SMEs) in the UK are family businesses and yet only 15 per cent of them reach the third generation according to research from the Manchester Business School. Other research shows that family succession is the preferred exit strategy for most family business owners. So what is going wrong? What is it about families and family businesses that make family succession so difficult? Is it because reconciling business and family cultures is so hard, or because children do not wish to follow their parents' way of life? Or is it because family succession planning (like most other succession strategies) is left too late, or not planned for correctly?

There is no simple answer, but most family businesses owners face most of these problems when attempting to pass their businesses on to an heir. This means that a careful, systematic approach to family succession planning, which recognizes the special problems facing the average family business is needed if a succession is to be a success.

But what is 'success' in family succession? Whereas in other exit options, success can usually be measured in terms of the optimum after-tax financial return to the owner from the disposal of the business, in family succession planning success could mean merely the act of transferring the business to a favourite child and the fact that the business continues to survive under that child's management. So, before one attempts to measure success, the aims and ambitions of the owner within the context of the business must be understood. Other differences in family succession planning are considered below.

THE NATURE OF FAMILY SUCCESSION PLANNING

Family succession has some important differences from the other exit strategy options that could be of advantage to you when planning your exit. These include the following:

- Because the sales transaction is usually not fully at arm's-length, you can have a larger degree of control over its structure, including its price, funding and method of payment, than you can in other exit options (which assists you in your retirement planning).
- If you wish, you should be able to arrange for your continued involvement in the business after the sale more easily than in other exit options.
- You might not be seeking to maximize the sale price, but you could be able to arrange for payment over time on terms that can have taxation advantages for you.
- The needs of the business and family can be balanced.

Because of these factors, the disposal price and its terms of payment will often be determined by how much you need to live on in retirement and how much the heir can afford to pay, rather than on the real value of the business. The respective taxation implications for the owner and the heir could also be a major consideration in structuring the transaction.

On the negative side, you could have an ethical dilemma in balancing your own interests with feelings of responsibility for the interests of your successor. This could result in your not receiving full value for the business.

CHOOSING YOUR HEIR

The first step in any family succession plan is to choose the appropriate heir to the business. Where there is only one heir, it is necessary to decide whether he or she wishes to, and is capable of, taking over the business. If there is more than one candidate who has both attributes, it is necessary to decide which one is suitable. The factors to consider include business aptitude and management potential. Potential is more important than experience, because you should plan to groom your heir for the role as owner-manager over an extended period.

In theory, the steps involved and the logic employed in choosing the appropriate heir should be similar to those involved in choosing the best CEO for the business, or the lead manager in a management buyout; that is, the heir you choose should be the one most capable of running the business when you leave. In practice, however, the choice may be made for various personal and family-related reasons, rather than on solid business-based grounds.

Where there is only one heir (or only one heir who is interested in taking over the business), it might still be a mistake, on purely business grounds, to hand over the business to that heir. But, if this is to be the case, your task is to make the best of a dubious decision and to prepare this person as best you can for the role of running the business. This appendix will assist you in grooming your heir for the owner-manager's role.

COMMON MISTAKES IN CHOOSING AN HEIR

Where there is a choice of more than one heir to take over the business, mistakes (viewed from a purely business point of view) are still made. The usual reasons why these mistakes are made are as follows:

- The chosen heir is considered to be the one with the most need, rather than the one with the most ability.
- Because the first-choice candidate is not willing to take over the business, a second and less suitable candidate is chosen.
- The heir is the family favourite (for personal rather than business reasons).
- Because the business owner has two children, both are chosen, although one might be totally unsuitable.
- The best choice is female and is, therefore, considered unsuitable. An unsuitable male heir is chosen instead.
- The chosen heir is the dominant personality among the children, but is not the best candidate from a purely business point of view.

In short, the choice is often a subjective one based on family sentiment and/or family values rather than on business criteria. But even a bad choice is better than no choice at all; and far better than deciding it is all too hard and 'the children can sort it out themselves when I am dead!'

THIRD PARTY OBJECTIVITY

If you are looking for an outcome that will be best for you, your business and your heir, you could seek advice from a third party that can bring some objectivity to the task. If you have a non-executive director in the business, or if you use the services of an outside consultant whom you trust on a personal basis, you could seek this person's opinion on your choice of a suitable heir. Using the services of someone whom is too close to the family, like your long-standing accountant or family solicitor might not be such a good idea.

If the outsider's opinion is the same as your own, this should give you confidence to proceed with your succession plan. If this opinion is different from yours, you should discuss it in depth with the outsider to test your original ideas before making a final decision.

Your objective should be to make a rational decision and, if you believe that having considered all the relevant views no one in the family is suitable to take over the business, you should consider another exit strategy. You should bear in mind that the wrong decision could have unfortunate long-term implications, including your return from retirement to save the business.

MORE THAN ONE HEIR

A particular problem in succession planning is where there are two heirs who both wish to take over the business. In order to solve this problem in an apparently fair way you might be tempted to give equal shares to the two heirs, but to give ultimate executive power to only one (instead of, for example, making them joint managing directors). This gives the business one executive leader (which is in line with accepted management principles) but, because both heirs have equal voting power, a potential stalemate at shareholder level is created.

If you try to address this problem by giving equal executive and voting power to both heirs, you could leave the company with a similar stalemate, but this time both at board and shareholder level.

THE FUNDAMENTALS OF VALUE AND LIKELY PURCHASE PRICE

A key issue in your planning will be the value of your business. The value will determine the level of borrowing possible against the business and could establish the sale price your heir can pay. You will wish to know what the true value of your business is likely to be on the open market compared with the likely purchase price from your heir. This will be important for your retirement planning and in deciding whether succession is financially feasible for you.

You will also need to consider whether the succession will be through an arm's-length sale (that is, at fair market value) or whether there will be a gift element involved, and you need to be aware of the various tax implications of these transactions. You also have to consider what amount is necessary for your retirement.

These various considerations might not be reconcilable. A purchase price based on the true market value of the business might be adequate for your retirement, but may be more than your heir can pay (either through his or her own resources, or through borrowings). Alternatively, although you might be prepared to partly finance your heir into the business (or even gift part of it), you might be unable to fund the purchase and retain enough money for your retirement.

TAXATION

The impact of taxation on business transfers and disposals is considered in Appendix 1. Inheritance tax could also be a vital issue in family succession planning and you should get expert advice on the potential impact of this tax and capital gains tax at an early stage in your planning.

THE FOUNDATIONS OF YOUR MASTER SUCCESSION PLAN (MSP)

Once you have decided that the transaction is feasible from both your and the heir's perspective, you should now prepare the foundations of your MSP. To do this you should take the following steps:

1. Consider your business continuity arrangements.
2. Have your business valued.
3. Prepare an operational business plan, or if you have already have a plan in place, review and update the plan.
4. Write down your initial thoughts on the key components of your plan, including the following:
   (a) The preferred time frame for the hand over (but subject to taxation advice).
   (b) Your financial requirements up to retirement.
   (c) Your financial requirements for retirement.
   (d) The nature of the succession transaction, including purchase price, how funded, terms of payment, amount (if any) of vendor finance.
   (e) The preferred heir you have chosen.
   (f) The steps necessary for completing the heir's grooming and training and the likely timetable.
   (g) The likely taxation implications of the disposal (and their effect on the preferred timing of the handover).
5. Prepare a draft MSP.

Once you have established the basis for your plan you should draw it up in draft form and present it to key family members for discussion and, if necessary, modify it following these discussions. You will also need to discuss the plan in detail with your heir before getting all parties to sign the plan as confirmation of their acceptance. We will address these issues in more detail below.

THE MSP IN DETAIL

Before we examine in detail how you put your MSP together, you should note that family succession planning takes longer to complete than most other exit options. Opinions vary on whether it should begin at least five years, or at least 10 years prior to handover, while some say it should begin as soon as you have decided who your heir is to be.

Your MSP is made up of the following component parts.

BUSINESS CONTINUITY PLANNING

Issues you need to consider here are as follows:

- If you have shareholders or partners, do you have an agreement with them that makes your plans possible?
- Is your business structure tax efficient?
- Do you have a will and does it ensure that your succession plans will be fulfilled should you die before you intend to hand over the business?
- Should you consider putting the business in to trust for your heir now?

A important addition to a family continuity plan could be to introduce a 'family constitution' or family agreement which sets out how the business is to run and how responsibilities are to be shared out between family members. The agreement could be similar to a normal shareholders' or partners' agreement and set out spending limits, dividend and salary policies, and so on.

(You should refer to Chapter 2 where business continuity planning is covered in more detail.)

OPERATIONAL BUSINESS PLANNING

The preparation, updating or reviewing of the operating business plan has the same objectives as in all exit strategy planning options: namely, to set the foundation on which the MSP is built. (This subject is dealt with in Chapter 7.)

PREPARING THE MSP

Generally speaking, a family succession plan should be prepared in consultation with all family shareholders or partners. (It is a moot point whether family members who are outside the business should be involved in the planning, but most family business experts advise against it.) As a retiring owner you should consider using a non-executive director (or an outside consultant) for expert, objective advice to assist you in finalizing your MSP.

It is advisable to prepare your draft plan prior to discussions with family shareholders, rather than attempting to prepare a plan from the beginning with them. The reasons for this are as follows:

1. You, as the retiring owner with a long intimate experience of the business, rather than the successor and family members, are most likely to have a more balanced and mature judgement of what overall structure and business strategies are likely to be successful.
2. First and foremost, you need to look after your own interests. Once in retirement, and having lost control of the business, your financial options will be greatly diminished, or eliminated, if anything goes wrong with the succession. Once the business is transferred, the heirs can probably look after themselves, while it is probably too late for you to rebuild your business and your life.

DISCUSSING THE DRAFT MSP WITH FAMILY SHAREHOLDERS

If your family is concerned with not being consulted in drawing up the draft plan, you could explain that it was a joint effort between you and the non-executive director (or consultant) because of its technical nature and because it required an objective viewpoint. The plan as presented to family shareholders should not, however, be a *fait accompli*, and it should be altered if family shareholders raise reasonable objections.

(*Note*: The question of whether non-executive family shareholders should be involved in succession meetings needs to be considered. In the end, this will depend largely on the personalities of the family members involved. If there are problems with difficult family shareholders who are not executives of the company, efforts should be made to exclude them from the meetings.)

REVISING THE DRAFT MSP

If there are major objections to the draft plan in the family shareholders' meetings, it is probably advisable to ask for time to review the plan with your outside adviser, rather than to agree to changes during the meeting. This provides you with a useful negotiating strategy and time to reflect.

You should privately reconsider your position with the outside adviser and present the changed plan to the family again (or re-present those areas of disagreement only). You should aim to gain complete acceptance of the plan by all parties and have the revised document signed by the heir as recognition of this acceptance.

DISCUSSING THE DRAFT MSP WITH THE HEIR

It is vitally important that discussions with heirs start as early as possible. They need to understand the plan's implications and their obligations under it from an early stage. Depending on your relationship with the heir, you might decide that it is wise for your outside adviser to meet the heir privately to discuss the draft plan. In such private discussions, it is more likely that there will be complete openness and lack of inhibition from the heir.

It is necessary, when these meetings have come to a conclusion, to confirm with the heir that all terms of the plan are fully understood and agreed.

FINALIZING THE MSP

Following agreement from the family and heir, your draft plans can now be incorporated in to a final MSP. The following are the major points that will need to be incorporated:

- the identity of the heir
- the timing of your retirement and your financial requirements up to and after retirement
- the final structure of the sale transaction as to price, terms and method of payment, vendor finance, etc.
- the corporate structure of the acquiring entity
- the taxation implications for both parties
- a business continuity agreement. If there is more than one heir, they should enter into a new agreement (outline the provisions of the agreement that the new owners should finalize before they acquire the business – see Chapter 2)
- the heir's involvement and role in the business up to the handover period
- the training (or grooming) of the heir for the role of owner-manager (see below)
- mechanisms for the owner to regain control of the business should circumstances arise that make this desirable.

(You should refer to Chapter 9 and Figure A4.1 for how a master exit strategy plan should be prepared and presented.)

GROOMING YOUR HEIR FOR SUCCESSION

Probably the most important aspect of a family succession is to groom your heir for the task of owner-manager of the business. It is important that the succession timetable is framed not only to suit the retiring owner, but also to enable the heir to go through all stages of grooming or training at a pace that is suitable for him or her. A period of hands-on management and simulated 'ownership' could be necessary before the handover is completed.

It is usual to divide the heir's grooming into the following stages:

- learning
- doing
- managing
- leading
- outside experience.

We will consider each of these steps in turn.

LEARNING

This will have stared when the heir first joined the business. An involvement with all aspects of the business (even if only superficial) will be important to the heir's future development, so you should involve the heir in as many functions of the business as possible.

DOING

The heir should be given freedom to partake in all business functions. If the heir has any obvious weaknesses, these should be worked on, or you should ensure that these can be covered, or compensated for in the heir's eventual management team. Undergoing this objective assessment of the heir's weaknesses is a valuable contribution to his or her future management success.

MANAGING

The heir's operational management skills can be gradually developed, so that by handover he or she should have had sufficient experience to manage all aspects of the business.

LEADING

Besides learning how to manage, the heir needs experience in leading other managers and running the business. Although leadership is largely an inherent skill, team leadership and decision-making can be taught to most competent managers. By the time of the handover, the heir should be capable of making the strategic decisions necessary to be an owner-manager.

OUTSIDE EXPERIENCE

It is essential that heirs have some business experience outside the family business. Preferably,

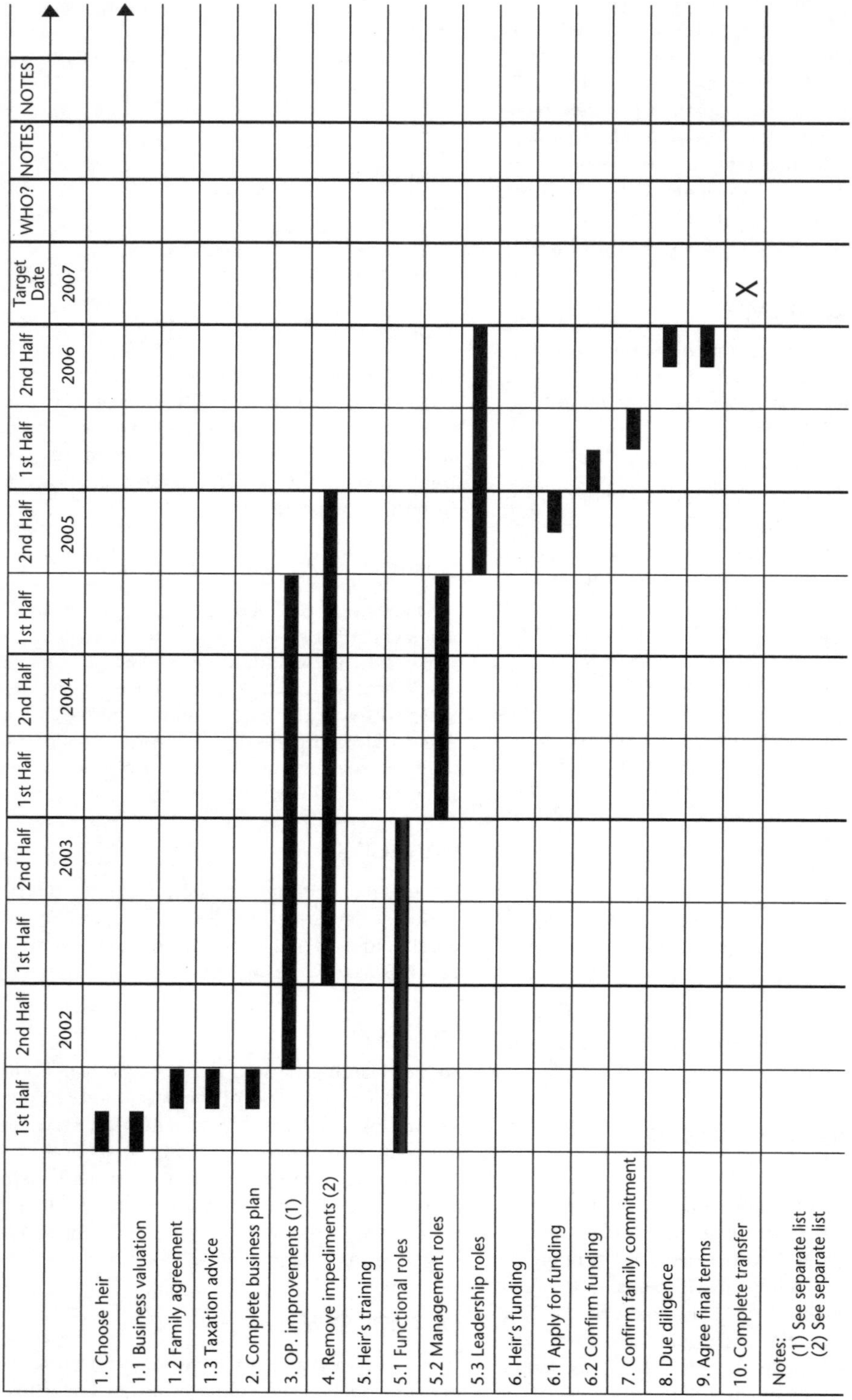

	1st Half	2nd Half	1st Half	2nd Half	1st Half	2nd Half	1st Half	2nd Half	1st Half	2nd Half	Target Date	WHO?	NOTES	NOTES
		2002		2003		2004		2005		2006	2007			
1. Choose heir														
1.1 Business valuation														
1.2 Family agreement														
1.3 Taxation advice														
2. Complete business plan														
3. OP. improvements (1)														
4. Remove impediments (2)														
5. Heir's training														
5.1 Functional roles														
5.2 Management roles														
5.3 Leadership roles														
6. Heir's funding														
6.1 Apply for funding														
6.2 Confirm funding														
7. Confirm family commitment														
8. Due diligence														
9. Agree final terms														
10. Complete transfer											X			
Notes: (1) See separate list (2) See separate list														

Figure A4.1 Master Exit Strategy Plan: Family Succession

this should be early in their careers and before the grooming for ownership process has begun. If this has not happened, time must be set aside (a minimum of two years) for heirs to gain this experience. This will be of great benefit to the heirs themselves, and ensure greater credibility and respect in the eyes of the management and employees of the family business when they return.

TIME REQUIRED FOR A FAMILY SUCCESSION

As was said earlier, you must allow considerable time if you are to plan for a successful family succession. It is generally accepted that it takes at least 10 years for an heir to be trained to take over a business. This time is required for the heir to acquire the skills and experience necessary to run the business and for there to be full acceptance of him or her by business contacts and customers, and to secure the support of employees.

The time required to train a particular heir to be fully competent in the owner-manager role of a particular business will, of course, depend on many things, including the following:

- the ability and personality of the heir
- the effectiveness of the training
- the nature of the outside business experience
- the time spent working outside the family business.

Taking all these matters into account, the total period for training and grooming will probably need to be a minimum of 10 years. You should begin to address the other aspects of your MSP about four to five years before your target exit date.

SETTING STANDARDS AND MONITORING

Family businesses should be managed like any other business: that is business values rather than family values should be paramount. In reality, this is not always the case and reward and status are provided to family members based on non-business criteria. There is no harm in this while a strong, experienced businessperson is running the business, but a succession based solely on these sorts of subjective family judgements is unlikely to succeed.

The prospective heir should be set a series of performance benchmarks throughout his or her learning, doing, managing and leading stages. There should be continuous monitoring and reviews of performance, preferably involving all family executives. Serious deficiencies in performance along the way might cause you to reconsider your choice of successor.

Handing over your business to an inadequate heir could do a great disservice to all concerned, particularly to the heir.

THE ROLE OF FAMILY MEMBERS AND NON-FAMILY EMPLOYEES

The needs of family members who have been passed over for succession must not be ignored. It is generally accepted that it is not wise to give minority shareholdings in the business as compensation to those members who have been passed over as heir, but rather that they should be compensated with other assets. You could also consider compensating those overlooked with an agreed annual payment, or dividend, from the business (without an attached shareholding).

Family members and executive shareholders who are not in line for succession could still feel they have played a useful role in the plan by being involved in, and perhaps being signatories of, the final MSP. This could also ensure their continuing support of the heir.

Non-family management and key employees within the business need to have their concerns addressed. Animosities could exist towards the next generation and, if they do, they need to be discovered as soon as possible. Remedial action, or sensitive politicking, could be necessary to ensure the loyalty of important staff members is retained.

RETAINING CONTROL

A family succession plan provides the owner with the ideal opportunity to implement an integrated financial plan. In no other option are you more able to exercise the same degree of control over the disposal transaction (in its price, timing, method of payment, and so on) and, therefore, to structure the disposal to suit your exact personal financial needs. In other options, you as seller take from the buyer only as much as the market (and the desirability of your business) will allow. Control over the business (and its cash flows) ceases with arm's-length disposals, whereas in a family succession the transaction could be structured so that ultimate business control (and control of the cash) remains with you until you are sure that your heir has got to grips with the business.

Some ways of retaining control that you could consider are as follows:

- Do not transfer voting control until you are sure that the heirs are capable of handling the business successfully.
- The ownership of the business remains in the old company ('Oldco') and a new company owned by the heir ('Newco') is set up. Newco leases the business assets from Oldco. Only when you are fully satisfied with the heir's handling of the business and that it is trading successfully, does Oldco sell Newco the business. (If you are interested in this approach, you should first take taxation advice.)
- Buy/sell agreements (or put and call options) can be included in the contract, which would give the owner the right to re-enter the business on the happening of certain events. Such events could include the death or disability of the heir, or unsatisfactory trading results. This would be part of the business continuity plan if there were more than one heir.
- Similarly, if a third party financier funds the acquisition with security over the business assets and with your guarantee, a default by the borrower heir could give you the right to re-enter the business.

The downside of this sort of continued involvement with the business should also be recognized. Some family business experts believe that it is essential for retiring owners to give up all their equity in the business so they do not continue to interfere with the new owners. Others point out that the 'shadow' left by the retiring owner (in terms of employee loyalty and devotion to his or her ways of doing things) is hard enough for the heir without having the former owner still exerting direct influence. New owners need to be free to introduce change in the way the business is run. An acceptable compromise for all concerned could be for the owner to sell all his or her shares and retire, but remain as a consultant to the board. In this way he or she can act as a sounding board and provide help when requested, without stepping on the heir's toes.

CONCLUSION

With such a large number of family-owned businesses, family succession is an important part of the exit strategy planning process in the UK. It is often a difficult task, more because of personal and family-related issues than because of any inherent difficulties in the planning and implementing processes themselves. For owners of family businesses, choosing a successor could be the hardest thing you will ever have to do in your business life. But the potential rewards of family succession are great, not least the thought that by implementing a successful succession you have bequeathed a stable, profitable business, instead of a mess, to the next generation.

SUMMARY OF STEPS NECESSARY TO IMPLEMENT YOUR FAMILY SUCCESSION

1. Choose your heir.

   1.1 Make your own choice.

   1.2 Seek independent advice on your choice.
2. Establish the value of your business.
3. Decide the basis of transfer of the business (for example will it be at fair market value or at some other value?).
4. Obtain taxation advice.
5. Consider your business continuity (risk management) planning, including:
   (a) Shareholders' agreement or 'family constitution'
   (b) Insurance and wills
   (c) Need to place business into trust.
6. Establish the timeframe for succession and your personal financial requirements.
7. Draw up a draft MSP and discuss it with family members. (Consider whether you need outside advice.)
8. Revise, or produce, your business plan. Identify your business's shortcomings – this is analogous to identifying its impediments to sale.
9. Discuss the MSP with your heir and finalize it.
10. Embark on, or continue with, grooming your heir for succession.
11. Implement the MSP. Regularly monitor your progress.
12. Consider steps for retaining control, or re-entering the business.
13. Complete handover.

APPENDIX 5

MANAGEMENT BUYOUTS AND BUY-INS

In this appendix we provide a brief overview of the process where managers or directors purchase all or part of private businesses in which they work, so that private business owners can better understand the considerations that govern a successful MBO transaction.

We do not cover the activities of public companies divesting businesses or subsidiaries to their directors and the many complicated legal and ethical issues that can arise, such as providing security for the purchase of their own shares, or the conflicts of interest that directors might face where they have a part in both deciding a divestment and participating in the buyout.

We hope that by better understanding the mechanics of a private business MBO (even in the simplified form as described in this appendix) business owners will be assisted in deciding whether this form of exit could be suitable for them and their businesses and, where it is, to plan for an exit in which they maintain a measure of control. We believe that by taking this approach, business owners are more likely to maximize their return from this, sometimes rather stressful, exit route.

THE OWNER'S PERSPECTIVE

Most literature on management buyouts is written from the point of view of the acquiring party, its aim being to assist directors or managers in the difficult task of undertaking an MBO. This review of the MBO process, in common with this book as a whole, is written from the point of view of the business owner. Its aim is to assist you in understanding the MBO process and the requirements of the various parties involved, so that you can decide whether an MBO is a viable disposal option for your business and, if it is, to plan for a rewarding exit through this route.

The key objective of this book is to enable business owners to achieve full value for their businesses from the exit option that they choose. This can be achieved through an MBO that is planned by the owner, but is unlikely to be the case when the owner has no understanding of the forces at work in the MBO transaction, or how to negotiate a favourable deal with his or her managers and their highly skilled and experienced financial advisers.

WHAT IS AN MBO?

An MBO is simply a sale in which managers acquire part (or all) of the business (or the assets of the business) in which they work. Usually, the management is supported by banks and venture capitalists that provide them with the funding required to purchase the business. This funding will usually be a mix of debt and equity.

Managers, VCs and other financial institutions (rather than business owners) often initiate MBOs themselves, especially in the larger transactions. Managers do this for a myriad of reasons (including a desire to be their own bosses) and financiers do it because of the potentially large financial returns available to them if the MBO, and the subsequent business building, is successful. Financiers will usually view an MBO as a two-staged process: the initial investment in the MBO, followed by an exit within a relatively short period (say five years) through a trade sale, secondary buyout, or flotation.

MANAGEMENT BUY-INS

The MBO team usually consists of the key managers of the business, one of whom is the potential CEO. Where the CEO and/or the management come from outside the business, the transaction is usually known as a management buy-in. An MBI can arise in several ways including:

1. A business owner could approach managers outside the business with the idea that they might wish to buy the business with the support of financiers.
2. Potential buyers outside the business could approach a VC requesting financial support for a proposed buyout for a business that they think is a good MBI prospect.

3. Financiers already involved with a potential MBO could bring in outside management when they feel that the current management team is weak in certain areas. Or they could become aware of an opportunity of a buy out and approach an 'industry expert', or someone that is known to them through previous transactions, to lead an MBI team. These sorts of transaction are also known as a management buy-in/buyouts, or BIMBOs.

In a pure MBO, the management has inside knowledge of the business, an advantage it has over outsiders who might launch an MBI. Hence, MBOs are usually considered by VCs to be less risky than MBIs. Also, the owner of the business is usually more favourably disposed towards internal managers rather than external managers, which can facilitate negotiations in an MBO.

(*Note*: the balance of this appendix will refer mainly to MBOs, but most of the principles involved apply equally to MBIs or BIMBOs.)

HOW DO MBOs ARISE?

As we have said, MBOs can arise through a number of circumstances some initiated by managers, some by VCs and some by the owners themselves.

1. Typically managers initiate MBOs when they become aware that owners wish to sell and where they believe there is a reasonable commercial opportunity to increase business value and their own wealth.
2. In public companies, MBO opportunities arise through business restructuring or selling of subsidiaries. These decisions to divest can sometimes be made by directors who themselves may decide they wish to acquire the business, thus giving rise to potential conflicts of interest.
3. Venture capitalists will initiate what are known as institutional buyouts where they formulate the deal and negotiate direct with the owners and offer the management an opportunity to participate. Institutional buyouts are increasing in number, but are usually limited to the very large transactions
4. Finally, in private companies owners can initiate an MBO by planting the idea in the minds of management and assisting them with the MBO process.

INSTITUTIONAL PREREQUISITES FOR AN MBO

Subject to the owners consent, any business can be purchased by its managers as long as they have the desire and the money to do so, but what are the guidelines if they need financial support?

There are no hard and fast rules to determine which businesses VCs and banks will support in an MBO. Investment fashions are subject to change, while each financial institution will have its own particular investment policy. The following guidelines will be a good starting point to assist you in understanding whether your business could be suitable for an MBO.

1. Businesses in most industries qualify for MBOs.
2. There is no upper limit, in theory, to the size of the deal, but most VCs are unlikely to be interested in deals smaller than £2 million, although VC Trusts will invest in deals as small as £500,000.
3. The business itself should have the following characteristics:
   (a) It should be able to generate consistent positive cash flows sufficient to service the borrowings necessary in a leveraged transaction. Proof of this ability should be evident from recent performance and not merely based on projections.
   (b) Ideally, the business should be in a position to borrow heavily against its own assets. The equity injection from VCs and management is usually relatively small and the business will need to borrow heavily to complete the purchase. (It should be noted that there are certain legal constraints on a company using its own assets as security to purchase its shares and owners and managers would need to get expert legal advice in this area.)
   (c) Where a business has limited capacity to borrow, the strength of the cash flows and the banks' willingness to lend against them will become paramount.
   (d) The business should be well established and, ideally, have a strong position in its market.
   (e) Current investment fashion can affect investment decisions. Traditionally investors have preferred high- or medium-technology businesses because they are perceived to have higher growth potential, but currently (2002) it is

extremely difficult to attract VCs to certain high-tech sectors.

(f) The business should have strong growth prospects. This is especially important to VC investors.

(g) The business should have a multiskilled management team, lead by a competent CEO, which has a strong desire to acquire the business. The CEO must have the respect and support of the management team. Where there is no one suitable for the role of CEO (or other key function), outside expertise must be brought in to cover this deficiency.

4. Business plan: It is essential that the management team has a current, professionally prepared, well-reasoned and realistic five-year business plan for the business it hopes to purchase, if it is to attract the interest of banks and VCs in an MBO proposition. Most management teams will seek assistance with the production of the plan from their accountants, or from a corporate finance specialist.
5. Advisers: In the case of an IBO, the institution itself will undertake the assessment of the transaction and lead the negotiations with the vendor. In all other cases, the management team will usually need the support of advisers as well as banks and VCs to complete a successful MBO. Venture capitalists can undertake the functions of financial advisers and negotiators as well as arranging the financing, but in most cases management will prefer to use the services of specialist corporate financial advisers (who are often from large accounting firms) to assist them in completing the deal.

   The role of financial advisers is to assist in the production of the business plan and to undertake a financial feasibility analysis that confirms the suitability of the business and its industry for financier support and, if required, to be involved in the negotiations with the various parties (vendor, banks, VCs, and so on) on behalf of the acquiring management. Advisers should also be aware of suitable VCs that they could introduce to the proposition, or be able to find alternative financiers if the original VC withdraws from the deal. The presence of competent financial advisers will also assist in making the investors comfortable with the proposition.

   The management team will also need the assistance of other advisers such as lawyers.

THE CEO AND THE MANAGEMENT TEAM

The calibre of the management team is the major concern of any financier considering investing in an MBO. The strength of the team will also be the determining factor of the success of the buyout, regardless of how it is funded. The following questions will assist you in determining whether your current management could be suitable for an MBO:

1. Is there someone in the business who could be an effective, strong CEO who can also lead his or her team through the purchase negotiations?
2. Does the management team include people who are experienced in the essential functions of the business, for example, production, sales, research and development, marketing?
3. Does the team include a strong financial manager?
4. Does the management have the ability to be involved in a hands-on way in the business's activities, and to adapt to the role of owners?
5. Can the management team assist in the production of a well thought out, achievable, strategic, operational and financial business plan?

MANAGEMENT GROOMING

Besides failure to attract the requisite financial support, a major reason that MBOs fail to be consummated is because of the inability of the management team to hold together through the stresses and frustrations of the purchase negotiations. An important part of the planning process for an owner-initiated MBO is to have a stable management team in place well before negotiations begin.

THE THREE TESTS

Generally speaking, three questions should be asked before you proceed with investigating the MBO option, these are:

1. Does the business have suitable management?
2. Do historical financial reports and cash flow projections show that the business has adequate maintainable cash flows to service the requisite borrowings?
3. Does the business have strong growth prospects?

As has been stressed previously in this book, an effective, realistic operational business plan is an essential prerequisite for any exit strategy, and the examination of the viability of an MBO as an exit option should also begin with a business plan, which must demonstrate the suitability of the business as an MBO target, especially from a financial viewpoint.

FINANCING THE TRANSACTION

If the management team is able to acquire the business though its own financial resources and borrowings secured against the company assets (where this is legally permissible), then no VC involvement is necessary. This would be ideal from the management's point of view, as it would hold all the equity and reap all the rewards. This could be the best option for the owner also, because dealing with your own management should be easier than dealing with institutional investors. However, most MBOs are leveraged transactions that require financing. Besides the management equity, this financing is usually a mixture of VC equity (such as preference shares), loan capital and conventional bank debt.

EQUITY

Managers and VCs will subscribe to equity in the business. Other institutions or individuals could also take up equity. This could be in the form of ordinary shares, or preferred shares convertible into ordinary shares at a later date, or preference shares with a fixed or variable dividend, or a combination of the above. The precise requirements of the equity investors will vary from transaction to transaction.

Equity investors will be looking for a high rate of return on their equity investment in what they believe is a high-risk, highly geared private business. They will aim to make the bulk of their profit through an exit and, therefore, a viable exit strategy (often through a trade sale, a secondary buyout, or a public listing) is usually a prerequisite for attracting institutional investors.

DEBT

Bank debt underpins most MBO transactions. Debt to equity ratios of between 5 to 1 and 10 to 1 are not unusual. Secured borrowing from commercial banks is usually the cheapest form of finance. These borrowings are typically secured by the business's assets and are known as 'senior debt'. This debt will usually take the form of a term loan, with scheduled repayments. The obstacles to raising senior debt are the ability of the business to borrow based on the security of its assets and its ability to meet the interest and capital repayments from its cash flows.

Further bank finance would come in the form of an overdraft to meet the working capital requirements of the business.

MEZZANINE FINANCE

Where the business is unable to achieve a buyout based on equity and bank debt alone it will need to raise what is known as subordinated debt, or 'mezzanine finance'. Mezzanine finance, because of its subordinated nature, is considered to be of a higher risk and, therefore, attracts a high rate of interest.

The mezzanine loan often has attached rights to acquire shares for an agreed amount on sale or flotation of the business, thus giving the lender a potential equity premium. The security for mezzanine debt is usually similar to that of the senior debt, although it is subordinated to this debt.

UNDERSTANDING THE VARIOUS FORMS OF FINANCING

As a business owner you should be aware, in general terms, of the various types of finance available. It is the managers themselves who will need to have an understanding in specific terms of their options, or procure expert advice. It is more important for you that, by following the steps outlined in this book, you are able to put the business into such a shape of profitability and good management that both the management team and the investors are attracted to it. Once you have identified and groomed a suitable management team, the management team will have the prime responsibility of raising the funding.

NEGOTIATING THE PRICE

As we said earlier, most literature about MBOs is written to assist the purchasers in negotiating with the vendor to acquire the business at a favourable price. It is important, therefore, that you understand the tactics that will be adopted by the MBO team and its advisers in negotiating with you to acquire your business.

Generally speaking, the management's financial advisers will carry out all negotiations with the various parties involved in the buyout (banks, VCs, institutions and owners) on behalf of the MBO team. However, it is likely that you will also have direct dealings with the VCs. This means that you as owner will be up against formidable negotiators whose strengths include the following:

- They have considerable skill and experience in MBOs.
- As outsiders, they are able to drive a hard bargain without endangering the relationships that have been established between management and owners.
- They are able to be tough in their negotiations because they have the money and the reputation and, at the end of the day, if the negotiations fall through there is always another deal tomorrow.
- They have the experience to identify and highlight any weakness in the vendor business, which helps to drive down the price.

REMOVING THE IMPEDIMENTS TO SALE

This part of planning is crucial in all exit strategies and you should remind yourself of the contents of Chapter 6. Your operational business plan should have identified the impediments to sale, and by implementing the 'things to do' in your MESP you should ensure that the major impediments are removed. This will ensure that when the time of final negotiations for sale come round your business is in good shape, what some call 'investor ready'.

OWNER'S DUE DILIGENCE

During the implementation of your MESP, we advise you to commission your own due diligence report on the business. You can present this report to your management (and other interested parties if you are conducting an auction – see 'The auction process' below), but even where you are not approaching the MBO in this way, the due diligence process will add to your confidence in your business's current and future prospects, and help you eventually to secure the optimum price on disposal.

It can be part of the acquirer's tactics that during negotiations and due diligence you are put under pressure to reduce your price. Negotiations can become strung out while you are incurring professional fees and not spending as much time on your business's operations as you might like. With proper planning (including preparation of your own due diligence report) you can relieve some of this pressure, especially during the important final negotiations.

EXCLUSIVITY (OR 'LOCK-OUT') AGREEMENTS

When negotiating an MBO, VCs will attempt to enter into an agreement with the owner, which seeks to exclude any competitive offers. You should be aware of the fact that this gives the VCs certain advantages without any legal obligations to purchase. The commitments are all from the vendor, while the purchasers enjoy what is virtually a commitment-free option period to consider whether they wish to make you a formal offer.

The MBO team and their investors undertake their due diligence investigation during this option period. You should be prepared (particularly if you have not undertaken your own due diligence) for all sorts of problems (real and supposed) to be uncovered during the VC's due diligence, which could be reasons the purchasers give for reducing their offer price. Without the ability to court competitive offers, the owner is at a considerable disadvantage should this occur.

However, exclusivity agreements are a usual part of the MBO process and it is usually difficult to get a VC to commit to the time and expense of their due diligence without an exclusivity agreement.

THE NATURE OF DUE DILIGENCE

The exact scope of the due diligence will depend on a number of factors, including the knowledge that investors have of the industry and the complexity and diversity of the business being acquired.

Although due diligence is conventionally concentrated on accounting and legal matters, it should not be the same as an audit. The purpose of a due diligence is for the purchasers to understand the business and its potential and to identify any hidden problems that could deflect it from achieving this potential. Effective due diligence will analyse historic accounting records, investigate legal agreements, the extent to which the proprietary rights and technology are secure in the business, address the warranties and indemnities offered by the vendor, scrutinize all aspects of the business plan, including its financial projections and the background and experience of the CEO and his or her MBO team, all with the purpose of deciding whether there is a realistic prospect of increasing the business value and realizing an attractive return to the investors and financiers.

Due diligence will, in some cases, be a deal breaker and in this respect some have likened it to a house survey. But if you have already undertaken the survey and fixed the problems uncovered, hopefully this will not be the case for you.

INVESTIGATING ACCOUNTANT'S REPORT

This is the crucial due diligence operation and can be extremely wide-ranging. The purpose of the accountant's report (also known as the 'acquisition review') is to provide the investors and the management team with a thorough understanding of the business's trading, balance sheet and taxation position. The investors instruct the accountants on the scope of their investigation and the owner should ensure that the cost of these investigations is to be borne by the investors.

The investigating accountant's report can be terribly disruptive to the vendor business and the more that has been done in advance to ensure that the business complies and is well organized and managed, the less disruptive this will be.

The accountants, of course, will take particular care with the financial projections, examining closely the assumptions on which they are based. The investigation accountant's report can take four to eight weeks to complete. You should prepare for this eventuality and, where possible, have a member of your staff available to assist with the investigation so that the least possible disruption is caused to the business.

LEGAL AUDIT

Depending on the nature of the business, the investors may conduct a legal audit. This will be particularly important where the business relies on agreements with key suppliers of products or technology for its future profitability. Lawyers will also be involved in drawing up the legal contracts for the sale, which can be quite complex.

INDEPENDENT INVESTIGATIONS

As well as the accountants' and lawyers' reports, the investors may require independent investigations into such things as the business's production processes and their efficiency, products and product development, and the markets in which it operates. This will be particularly important if the investors are unfamiliar with the industry, or if serious doubts exist regarding the accuracy and assumptions of the management team's forecasts.

MANAGEMENT AUDIT

Because the investors place so much reliance on the management team, they will investigate thoroughly the background of its key members. It is very important here that the vendor has chosen, trained and groomed the potential CEO and the management team that will be responsible for the MBO. This is one of the very good reasons why you should plan for an MBO well in advance.

THE MBO TEAM: THE HUMAN ELEMENT

Exit strategy planning aims to create a market for your business. Our experience has shown that unless a great deal of care has gone into choosing the right CEO and management team, negotiations can fail at the last minute, causing great damage to your business.

You must never overlook the human element in an MBO. Even if your managers have the right mix of technical and financial expertise, it is still very important that they are personally compatible and able to work as a team. Equally important is that the CEO has the loyalty, support and respect of his team. If these are not present, problems could emerge during the strenuous and stressful period of negotiating the MBO, leading to its possible collapse.

OTHER ISSUES

An MBO involves negotiations between many parties. The most obvious parties are the owners, the financiers and the management team. However, customers and suppliers are equally important to the longer-term viability of the business that is being transferred from one owner to another. Care must be taken to preserve the customer base, while the continued support of creditors should be secured.

THE LEGAL CONTRACTS

In a MBO, the legal contracts are usually more complex than in a normal business sale, as there are at least three parties involved rather than two. It is usual that the business acquired is sold into a new company that is funded by the investors, who are made up of the MBO management team, the VCs (and other investors) and the lenders (or debt providers).

An example of how the agreements could be structured is shown in Figure A5.1.

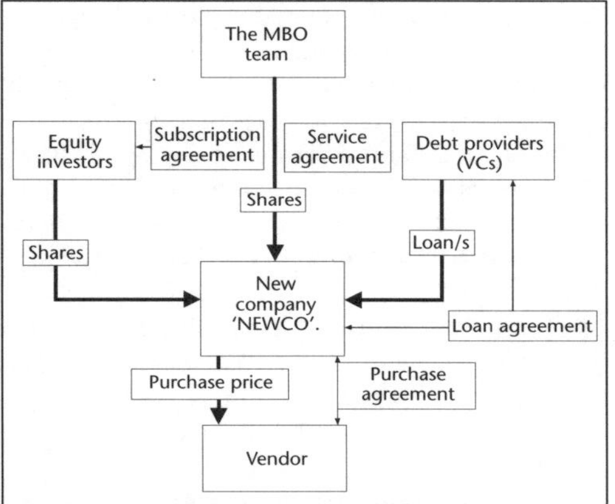

Figure A5.1 Management Buyouts: The Legal Contracts

Besides the sale agreement, there are two other legal documents that you should be aware of, namely, the subscription agreement and the Articles of Association.

THE SUBSCRIPTION AGREEMENT

This is a legal contract between the equity investors, the management and the new company, which contains provisions whereby the institutional investors have the right to approve certain significant actions of the business, such as capital expenditure, acquisition and disposal of major assets.

The agreement also covers such things as warranties and indemnities from the management, rights to appoint non-executive directors, provision of information to directors and rights of investors to approve certain actions by the management team.

THE ARTICLES OF ASSOCIATION

These determine the capital structure of the new company and the rights and obligations attaching to each class of shares. The articles of association will cover the normal matters contained in the company article of association, such as appointment of directors, transfer of shares, powers to issue new shares, redemption of shares, dividends, voting rights.

OWNER'S UNDERSTANDING

It is not necessary for you as the owner to have a detailed understanding of all the potential agreements at the planning stage. Rather, it is important that you understand the principles of what is involved so that you are able to plan accordingly.

Figure A5.2 summarizes the contents of a heads of agreement for a MBO.

Heads of agreement are drawn up 'subject to contract' and would usually contain the following provisions:

1. A description of the business and assets to be acquired (or shares to be acquired).
2. A purchase price.
3. Arrangements for calculating the price if based on future earnings, and so on.
4. The nature, methods and timing of settlement of the purchase price.
5. Matters needing to be completed before settlement; for example, due diligence review.
6. Matters to be undertaken before completion, for example, transfer of assets, settlement of debts, precompletion dividends, and so on.
7. Conditions of the sale, such as receipt of taxation clearances, approval of major customers, trade unions, lessor of premises, and so on.
8. Terms of any restrictive covenants and of any future trading arrangements.
9. Timetable and procedure for preparation, signing and completion of agreement and the arrangements for bearing or sharing costs and fees.
10. A statement on warranties and indemnities.
11. Arrangements for key executives other than MBO members.
12. Arrangements for public announcements and notification to employees of the sale.

Figure A5.2 Contents of MBO Heads of Agreement

THE AUCTION PROCESS

An MBO is an increasingly used exit strategy. Its growth is driven by management and financial institutions because of the profits they perceive to be available through this type of acquisition. But an MBO is usually a drawn out and highly stressful experience for management and owners alike. In all this stress there is a danger for the owner-vendor that your business could be sold for less than its market value. One of the aims of this book is to alert business owners to the opportunities of maximizing their business equity through planning and control of the disposal process, and nowhere is it more important than in MBOs.

In this appendix we have concentrated on the owner assisting the management in acquiring the business. Another way for owners to exert control on an MBO is through an auction process. The philosophy behind this approach is that you believe that your business is suitable for an MBO, but rather than management driving the deal themselves, you approach a selected number of VCs with the proposition. An important part of the process is that the owner commissions his own due diligence report and sends it to a limited number of carefully selected VCs (selected on the basis of reputation, experience and industry expertise) and leaves it to the VCs to put together an MBO or MBI team. This widens your field of potential purchasers and injects an element of purchaser competition, although you will still probably have to sign an exclusivity agreement with whoever comes up first with an agreement in principle to proceed, or a conditional offer, so that they can complete their independent review.

STEPS TO IMPLEMENT THE MBO

In conclusion, we summarize the steps that you should take in an owner-initiated MBO as follows:

1. Decide whether the business is suitable for an MBO or MBI and whether this is likely to be the optimum exit strategy for you. You should take whatever advice is necessary to reach a reasoned decision.
2. Consider whether the business has the surplus cash flow to service its likely borrowings and whether it has the growth prospects likely to excite potential VC backers. You should be able to establish this through your business plan, or the due diligence report that you comission.
3. Value your business now and estimate its value at the time of disposal once you have groomed it for sale. (If you are retiring, confirm whether the sale proceeds are likely to be sufficient for your retirement.)
4. Consider whether the current management is interested in making an offer for the business at the value you believe is reasonable.
5. Assess the quality of the management and abilities of the potential CEO. If these are wanting, you need to decide whether, first, the current management can be groomed for the tasks, or whether it will be necessary to bring in and train management and a CEO from the outside. You might need outside advice for this.
6. Commission your own due diligence report.
7. Assist the management to find, and have initial discussions with potential suitable financial backers or VCs; assess the reaction of these potential backers to the proposition. Alternatively, proceed along the auction path and elicit VC interest. You should obtain expert advice before you embark on the auction course.
8. If this is all positive, prepare an MESP (see, for example, Figure A5.3) that includes all the relevant 'things to do', impediments to sale removal and a timetable for disposal. (Note that if you decide not to proceed along the MBO route having commissioned a due diligence report, the report will not be wasted as it is necessary for any exit route you adopt.)
9. Implement all aspects of your MESP.
10. Finally, the MESP should be completed through the MBO or MBI disposal route.

SUMMARY

An MBO is an exit strategy that takes longer to accomplish than almost anybody in the business believes is likely when they embark on the process. This is partly because of the many different parties involved (who will also all have their own advisers), and partly because of the complicated nature of the deal itself. However, it can be a rewarding process for owners, managers, investors and lenders alike. From an owner's point of view, it is important not to be overwhelmed by the process and the parties involved. Being prepared is probably your best way of ensuring that you retain some control of events (and achieve the most favourable outcome) and we hope that this appendix will give you some ideas in this regard.

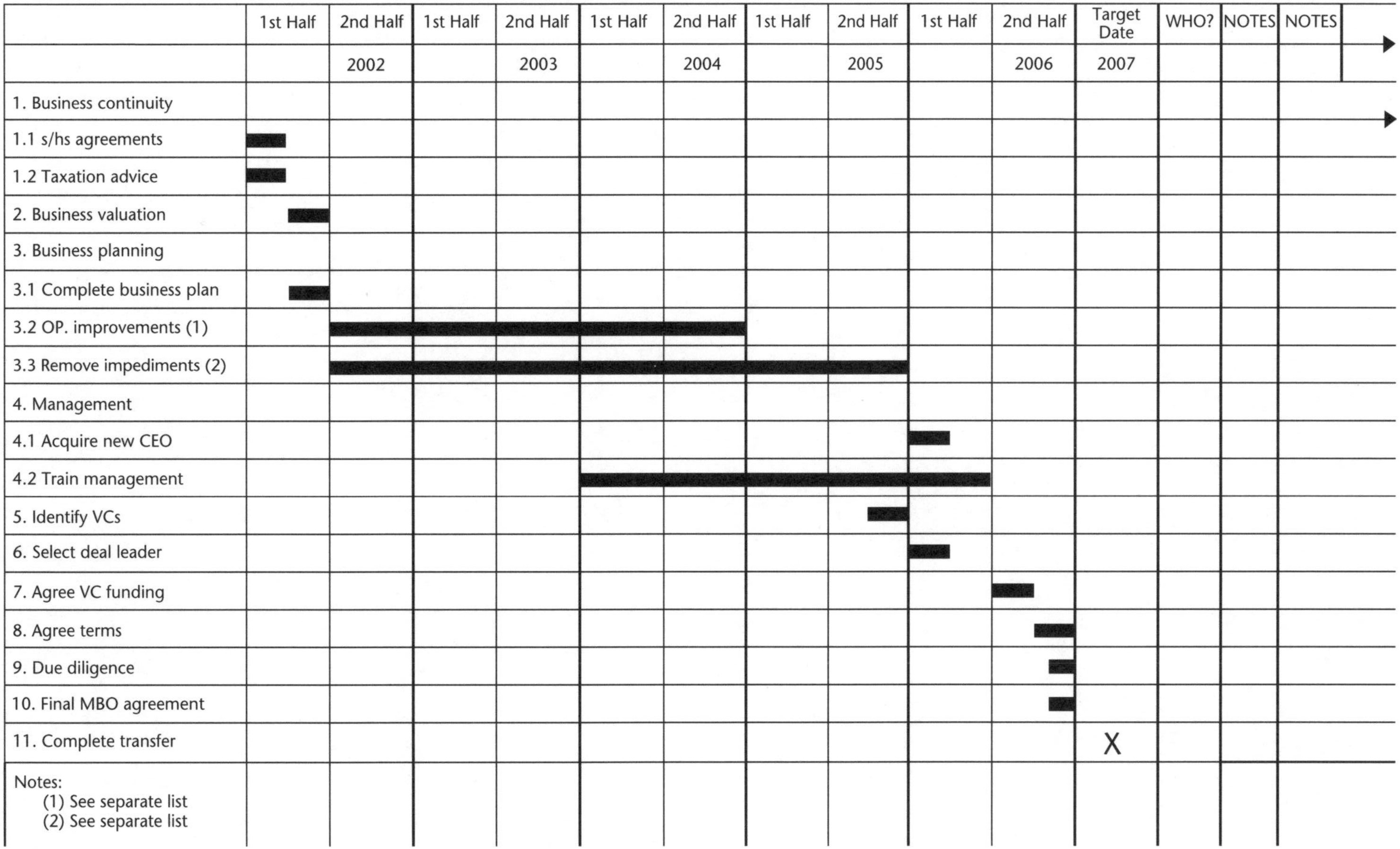

	1st Half	2nd Half	1st Half	2nd Half	1st Half	2nd Half	1st Half	2nd Half	1st Half	2nd Half	Target Date	WHO?	NOTES	NOTES
		2002		2003		2004		2005		2006	2007			
1. Business continuity														
1.1 s/hs agreements														
1.2 Taxation advice														
2. Business valuation														
3. Business planning														
3.1 Complete business plan														
3.2 OP. improvements (1)														
3.3 Remove impediments (2)														
4. Management														
4.1 Acquire new CEO														
4.2 Train management														
5. Identify VCs														
6. Select deal leader														
7. Agree VC funding														
8. Agree terms														
9. Due diligence														
10. Final MBO agreement														
11. Complete transfer											X			
Notes: (1) See separate list (2) See separate list														

Figure A5.3 Master Exit Strategy Plan: Management Buyout

APPENDIX 6
FLOTATION OR PUBLIC LISTING

In this appendix we will look at floating your company on the London Stock Exchange as a possible exit strategy. We will:

- set the historical scene for the public company marketplace
- examine the general issues concerned with flotation, including the pros and cons of flotation both for you and your company and the advantages of flotation as an exit strategy for private businesses
- consider the two markets (or boards) on the LSE; and the OFEX market; and compare the criteria for joining them, and what investors will look for when investing in your company float (this will enable you to check whether your business might be suitable for listing)
- look at how a business owner goes about the listing process itself and some aspects of life as a public limited company (plc).

FLOTATION AS AN EXIT OPTION

'Floating', 'listing' and 'going public' are all terms used to describe the process whereby owners of private companies sell their shares to the public (including institutions) and arrange to have these shares traded on a recognized stock exchange.

Flotation is a very attractive exit option for the right business. It is a way for a private business owner to dispose of his or her equity in stages at, hopefully, increasing values at each stage. Historically, listing has been available only to the very largest of private companies but, with the advent of 'secondary' or 'alternative' exchanges, the opportunity now exists for a wider range of businesses to float.

Flotation is, however, still reserved for a small minority of private businesses. Attaining a maintainable pre-tax profit of £5 million (which will provide a value on flotation of between £50 and £75 million) is considered to be a practical minimum for a conventional (or 'traditional') business before it can seriously consider listing on the Main Board. The barriers are lower for the secondary markets, but in normal times they are still too high for most private businesses.

The material in this appendix will help you to decide whether flotation could be a viable exit option for your business.

A RECENT HISTORICAL PERSPECTIVE

During most of the 1980s, going public made many business entrepreneurs into multimillionaires but, after world share markets crashed in 1987 and the Western economies went into recession, the opportunities for flotation were greatly diminished.

During the next decade the world economy improved and by the end of the 1990s boom times had returned. Share prices improved and the appeal of investing in shares returned. The number of all kinds of public listings on the world's exchanges increased greatly. Initial public offerings (IPOs) of 'new economy' businesses (that is, those in the high-technology, computers and telecommunications sectors) proliferated, while there was an insatiable demand for the stock of any company with 'dot com' at the end of its name. The value put on these companies at flotation bore little resemblance to their current or even future potential profitability, but investors ignored these fundamentals, once again enabling most owners and promoters of businesses that floated to make a great deal of money.

But, as the economy has slowed in the new millennium and the allure of 'high-tech' and 'dot com' stocks has faded, the market has turned down once again and some investors have suffered huge losses. This has resulted in the market's appetite for new issues being greatly diminished. Even where flotation is possible, the value placed on private businesses by investors is likely to be significantly reduced.

The fluctuations in value of more traditional businesses with a consistent history of profits and competent management (or 'old economy' businesses as they are sometimes called) has been less dramatic during both recent business cycles: never so hugely in demand, they have not been so widely shunned. Nevertheless, steep price fluctuations in the market carries general sentiment with it, making it harder for all when economic times are tough, so that even solid companies find it difficult to raise funds after a downturn, even if the downturn has been concentrated in sectors outside of their own.

It is hoped that a more balanced approach to the advantages and disadvantages of going public for both business owners and investors will now return to the market for an extended period but, in the public company arena, history shows that wild fluctuations of value and sentiment always occur.

TIMING AND SENTIMENT

Flotation is a high-risk strategy, not least because factors external to the business can have such a significant impact on its value. One of these factors is timing.

Listing a company on a stock exchange requires the enthusiastic support of a wide range of people and institutions that are, by the nature of their work, strongly influenced by market sentiment. Consequently, the economic climate has a big influence on whether or not a float will be successful at any particular time. For example, there is currently (2002) a much more sceptical attitude in the financial markets towards all public offerings and particularly those of smaller companies. This has resulted in a more difficult climate for smaller companies in which to attract underwriter and institutional investment support for listing than was the case in the late 1990s.

But these things are cyclical: as financial markets become more buoyant the opportunities for smaller companies to list should increase. For those business owners who have planned their exit, the important thing is to be flexible in their approach to timing. It is important to get the internal factors that you might be able to control in order (such as current and future profitability and the ability of your owners and managers to run a public company) and then choose the right time to list.

WHICH MARKET?

There are two strongly traded markets on the London Stock Exchange, either of which could be suitable for your business. These are the Main Market and the Alternative Investment Market. Each of these has its own advantages and disadvantages as far as any particular business is concerned. From this appendix you will gain an understanding of how they operate, which will help you to form an opinion of your business's suitability for listing on either.

Listing requires conforming to sets of rules and regulations, including those of the UK Listing Authority (UKLA) and the LSE. Your decision whether to list, and on which board, could be influenced by the ability of your company to comply with these requirements. Of course, you should not be making any plans or spending too much money on the listing route until you have had expert advice, including that from your prospective sponsoring broker.

Besides the two main markets, you could consider joining OFEX, which is an 'off exchange' share matching and trading facility launched in 1995. OFEX is discussed in more detail in the 'OFEX' section below.

THE OWNER'S UNDERSTANDING OF THE LISTING PROCESS

There is quite a lot to digest before you can fully understand the various issues involved with flotation, but you need not try and become an overnight expert in the listing process. It is sufficient to have a general understanding of the subject and the ability to recognize whether your company could have a future as a public company. This appendix will attempt to convey this general knowledge to you. Once you have decided that a listing is worth considering further, it would be usual for you to turn to the experts for specialist assistance.

FLOTATION AS AN EXIT STRATEGY

When considering whether to float, owners must not only consider the suitability of their company for flotation in relation to the market in which they are trying to float, but also compare flotation with the other exit options available to them. Some of the questions to consider are as the following:

1. Is my business suitable for life as a public company in terms of its ethics, management approach and ownership aspirations?
2. Is the management capable of meeting the onerous compliance and corporate governance issues involved in running a public company?
3. What is the likely value of the business through a float compared with its value through other exit options, such as an MBO or a trade sale?

4. What is likely to be my personal satisfaction and potential stress in being the CEO of a public company?
5. What are the restrictions in any particular exit route (for example, complying with an extensive set of rules in public listing, or dealing with difficult 'people in suits' in a venture-capitalist backed MBI); and what are the costs compared with the likely benefits?
6. What are the risks involved in trying to list compared with other exit routes?

(Some of the advantages and disadvantages of flotation compared with other exit options are summarized in Figure 5.1 in Chapter 5.)

REASONS FOR FLOTATION

Owners of private companies will wish to float their businesses for different reasons. For example, raising capital for growth will be the dominant reason for some, while for others it will be a key part of a possible multi-staged exit strategy. The main reasons for owners of private companies to float from an exit strategy point of view are usually the following:

1. To dispose of an initial part of their investment and to create a liquid market in which they can sell (or gift) the balance of their equity, at prices higher than would have been the case if they had not floated.
2. To create a legacy for their heirs that is easier to sell than minority shares in a private company. This is particularly useful where there are several heirs.
3. To create easier access to funding for future growth of the company, which will lead to an increase in the value of their residual shareholdings.
4. The personal satisfaction of being involved in a successful float and the status derived in being a director of a plc.

ADVANTAGES TO THE COMPANY IN BEING A PLC

Some of the advantages of being a public company from an exit strategy point of view are listed above. There are others, which include the following:

ACQUISITIONS

The company's ability to acquire other businesses is enhanced by the cash it will raise on listing and by its ability to issue its own shares to business vendors rather than having to pay them cash.

ACCESS TO CAPITAL

A plc will usually have raised capital at the time of its listing and will have the ability to raise new equity capital through issuing new shares in the capital markets. It is also usually easier for plcs to borrow the capital necessary for growth or acquisitions.

STATUS

There is a general perception that a plc has financial strength and this, together with the higher public profile associated with being listed, will elevate its status in the eyes of financiers, customers, employees and suppliers.

EMPLOYEE BENEFITS

Besides the increased prestige, a plc has more flexibility in the areas of stock options and employee share schemes, enabling it to attract and retain key management and staff.

RIGOROUS DUE DILIGENCE

The listing process involves a rigorous investigation of the company's operations and structure by accountants, lawyers and advisers, which usually enhances the company's long-term operational efficiency.

DISADVANTAGES FOR A COMPANY IN BEING A PLC

There are disadvantages in a public listing both for owners and the company. These include the following:

COSTS

The flotation process itself is expensive and the ongoing costs of being a plc, such as annual registration fees, investor relations, annual report to shareholders, are significantly higher than normal private company compliance costs.

PUBLICITY

Being a plc involves much more exposure through the press (which can often be hostile) and onerous Stock Exchange disclosure requirements.

VULNERABILITY

A plc is more vulnerable to fluctuations in the market and to being taken over. Controlling shareholders and directors (sometimes the previous private business owners) are, therefore, more likely to lose control of the business. This is especially true if the business is either particularly successful, or is underperforming its sector or competitors and its share price is depressed.

MANAGEMENT TIME

The amount of time management spends in plcs, on what private business owners might consider as non-core activities, is considerable. This will include such things as investor relations, press briefings and Stock Exchange reporting requirements.

SUITABILITY OF THE BUSINESS FOR FLOTATION

Having considered the pros and cons for you and your company of going public, you will need to decide whether listing is worth exploring further. If you believe it is, the next step is to understand what is required of the company by the authorities and the marketplace before it can be listed.

We will look initially at the two main markets on the LSE, namely the Main market and the AIM. For both markets there are two broad tests that a company needs to pass before it can be considered suitable for listing, which are:

- complying with the regulatory requirements for listing
- convincing the investing community that it is worthwhile investing in its business.

These tests overlap to the extent that the investment community is unlikely to find a business that has failed to meet the regulatory requirements attractive, but it is necessary to pass the regulatory test before you can even consider the second one, so we will consider them separately.

REQUIREMENTS FOR LISTING ON THE MAIN BOARD

These requirements are in two parts: first, compliance with the UKLA listing rules and, second, being accepted by the LSE to be traded on the Main market as a public company.

We will summarize these requirements below, but if you require more detailed information it is available from the LSE either on their website or in their excellent CD, *A Practical Guide to Listing on the London Stock Exchange*. We acknowledge both as the source of much of what is written below.

MAIN BOARD: UKLA'S RULES

The first thing to note is that although the rules have general application, they are not rigid. For example, high-tech companies in their pre-profit phase have been allowed to list on the Main market despite, strictly speaking, not meeting the rules on trading history.

The UKLA, as part of the Financial Services Authority, ensures that its listing rules are met. A summary of the UKLA's Listing Rules is as follows:

- Incorporation: the business must be incorporated, and usually as a plc.
- Accounts: the company must have published audited accounts for a period covering three years prior to listing and ending no more than six months before the planned listing date.
- Trading history: the company must have traded and earned revenues for three years prior to listing, and any significant businesses it has acquired in the previous three years must have the same trading record.
- Directors: directors and senior management must show that they have the collective experience and expertise to run all areas of the business. There must be evidence that there will be no conflict of interest between directors and the business.
- Working capital: the company must have sufficient working capital for its current needs and for the forthcoming 12 to 18 months.
- Independent operations: the company must demonstrate that it can carry on its business independently of its controlling shareholders (who are defined as holding more than 30 per cent of its shares).
- Shares sold to the public: on listing, at least 25 per cent of the shares in the company must be sold to the public.
- Market capitalization: the minimum value of the business on flotation must be £700,000.

MAIN BOARD: LSE RULES

Parallel to the requirements of the UKLA, the LSE is responsible for admitting companies and their securities to trading on the Main market. This entails complying with its admission and disclosure rules, which are designed to sit alongside the UKLA's rules. Thus the LSE and the UKLA are jointly responsible for the regulations that govern the admission of companies to the Main Board. The LSE's rules are available from the LSE, and your advisers should be thoroughly familiar with them.

THE APPOINTMENT OF ADVISERS FOR A MAIN BOARD LISTING

Having decided that your business is suitable for flotation, you would now address the question of appointing advisers for the float. These include:

- A sponsor, who will co-ordinate your entry into the market and assist you in a wide range of issues (including the general suitability of your company for listing) and who will help you in choosing other advisors. Your sponsor needs to be approved by the UKLA, who can provide you with a list of approved sponsors.
- A corporate broker, who will provide the vital link between the market and investors. He or she will advise on the UKLA's Listing Rules, the timing of the float and the important issue of pricing your stock. The broker will assist you in marketing your float up to listing and in the 'after market' trading and promoting of your shares.
- Reporting accountants, who will review all accounting information and produce the accounting reports, which form a key part of the information contained in the prospectus.
- Lawyers, who will produce the necessary underwriting agreements and verify the information in the prospectus.
- Taxation specialists, who will advise on such things as capital gains and inheritance taxes.
- Public relations advisers, who will deal with promoting the issue and with relations with potential investors, including Institutions.

REQUIREMENTS FOR LISTING ON THE AIM

The AIM is specially designed to suit smaller, growing businesses. Its entry rules are less onerous than those for the Main market. Besides being the potential long-term home of a plc, it could be used as a stepping-stone to the Main market. There are no sector limitations with the AIM, and the LSE itself sees the AIM as appealing to a wide range of businesses, from large family businesses to venture-capital backed private companies looking for an exit strategy.

THE AIM AND UKLA'S RULES

The advantage of the AIM for private businesses considering a listing is its greater regulatory flexibility compared with the Main Board. Some examples of this are as follows:

- Trading history: no trading record is required (compared with the main market's requirement of a three-year trading period).
- Percentage of shares sold to the public: there is no minimum percentage of shares that must be in public hands (compared with 25 per cent for the Main market).
- Admission documents: these are not pre-vetted by the Stock Exchange (they are for the Main market).
- Minimum capitalization: there is no minimum requirement for capitalization for an AIM listing (currently £700,000 for the Main market).

THE AIM AND THE LSE'S RULES

The business's suitability for listing on the AIM is decided by the company's 'nominated adviser', who will be a firm of professional advisers drawn from a panel nominated by the Stock Exchange. This adviser is responsible for explaining the AIM rules to you.

A broker will play the same role for AIM companies as in the Main market, as will legal advisers, reporting accountants and public relations professionals.

As in a Main Board flotation, a prospectus (also known as an 'admission document') is the key document for an AIM listing, and this together with an application form, a declaration by the nominated adviser and a letter from the company broker confirming his or her appointment must be lodged with the LSE at least three days prior to your company's admission to trading.

Additional information required by the exchange includes:

- advice on the director's skills and business history

- names of shareholders entitled to control more than three percent of the votes at a shareholders' meeting
- an undertaking that there is sufficient working capital to meet the company's present requirements
- names of any party that has received fees of more than £10,000 from the company in the last 12 months.

APPEALING TO INVESTORS

The second aspect of successfully floating your business on the LSE, whether it is on the Main market or the AIM, is to convince investors that your business is an attractive proposition whose shares are worth buying. Your sponsor and broker will need convincing first and the price they set for the shares will be pitched at a level that they believe will attract investment support.

From an exit strategy point of view, if your business currently lacks some of the qualities required for listing, your task is to remedy these shortcomings during your planning period. You will be aiming to improve the business both by improving its operations (for example, by improving profitability or repositioning its activities to a more highly rated sector) and by removing those impediments to sale that are making listing impossible, or are likely to reduce its offer price. (See Chapter 6 on impediments to sale.)

Your advisers and investors will be looking for various attributes from the business and its management before they are likely to support its flotation.

These are that the business must:

- have a consistent record and good prospects with regard to its trading operations (this might not be relevant to high-tech businesses in their development, or 'pre-profit' stage)
- have management systems and operational procedures robust enough to withstand the strains of a public company
- not be overreliant on one, or a few customers, products or ideas, or on products that could go out of fashion quickly
- have a viable and realistic business plan (*note*: such a plan will form the basis of your master exit strategy plan and the prospectus required by the UKLA; and is vital to the operational development of your business, including the chances of a successful float)
- have a quality management team, with the expertise and experience to carry the business forward
- have a stable board (preferably with non-executive directors) whose members have been present for some time and who are united and committed to the business and the float.

The directors and management of the business must display:

- an understanding of the *Combined Code* of corporate governance (which is published by the UKLA and compliance with which is voluntary) and an enthusiasm for implementing its recommendations, including such things as separating the roles of chairman and CEO
- an understanding of the difference between the way private and public companies are run, including a strict segregation by owner-managers of personal and business assets and income and expenditure
- an awareness of the importance of undertaking those steps that will make the business as attractive to investors as possible, including seeking out strategic acquisitions and taking all available steps to reshape the business to move it into a more highly rated sector if possible
- an awareness of the impact and importance of timing on the share value, and planning that allows the company to float at the appropriate time
- an understanding of what investors expect from a company, including the importance of investor relations.

THE METHODS OF LISTING

Your advisers will clarify the ways in which you can list your company's shares and the pros and cons of each method. In brief, there are three main ways in which a listing can be achieved, which are:

1. An initial public offering where the company's shares are offered for sale to the general public and institutions to raise capital for the company and its shareholders. This is the most expensive process, but has the advantage of ensuring a high degree of liquidity for your stock.
2. A placement of shares to specific investors. This is cheaper than an IPO, but has the disadvantage of less liquidity for the stock.

3. An introduction to the market where no shares are sold and no capital is raised. Twenty-five per cent of the shares of the company must already be in public hands. This is the cheapest and easiest route, but is not suitable for those wishing to exit their equity holdings, or for companies wishing to raise capital for expansion through organic growth or acquisition.

THE PROSPECTUS

Whatever method of listing you adopt, you will have to have a prospectus (which is also known as 'listing particulars'). The form and content of the prospectus is laid down by the UKLA (who need to approve it) and your advisers will guide you through its production.

A prospectus has two functions, namely:

1. It sets out all the information about the company that has to be made public under the UKLA's Listing Rules.
2. It provides a comprehensive description of the company's past and current areas of activity, including trading performance, and a well-reasoned forecast of its future trading prospects.

Lawyers need to verify that all the facts in the prospectus are correct.

THE COST OF LISTING

THE MAIN MARKET

Because of the wide differences in the size and type of businesses that come to market, it is impossible to be precise about the cost of going public. Gaining admission to Main Board of the LSE will cost not less than £300,000 in advisers' fees alone, excluding fees to the UKLA and the LSE itself. It is usual to estimate fees as a percentage of the value of shares sold (or total capital raised) and in these terms it will usually be between four and eight per cent of the total value.

Besides the cost of listing, there are the ongoing costs of being a public company that are levied by both the UKLA and the LSE. Details of these costs, which are of both a fixed recurring nature and based on capitalization, can be obtained from the relevant authorities.

THE COSTS OF LISTING ON THE AIM

Although it is theoretically possible to list on the AIM for as little as £100,000, recent research by the accounting firm, HLB Kidsons, shows that the average cost of a company seeking to raise £2 million on AIM is between £400,000 and £500,000. A large proportion of this will be for advisor, legal and accounting costs, which will vary with the nature of each business that floats. The problem for companies raising smaller amounts of equity is that any flotation requires a certain amount of fixed costs and, therefore, the costs as a percentage of funds raised can seem prohibitive. AIM has an admission fee and annual fees which vary on the market capitalization of the company. Annual fees start at £5,000 based on a market value of upto £350 million plus £7.50 per £1 million of market capitalisation over £350m.

You can obtain full details of admission fees and annual charges from the AIM itself.

PREPARATION FOR LISTING

It could take about two years from the decision to list to actually being admitted to the main market of the LSE. For those who are planning to list their businesses as an exit strategy, the actual time taken will depend on the overall timetable for exit and whether a decision is taken to delay the float even further because of market conditions.

Once flotation has been chosen as a possible option, you should take the following steps:

- Commission an expert to investigate the company and prepare a report on its suitability for public listing, including advice on which market is the more suitable.
- Request that this report includes an estimated valuation, highlights the impediments to listing and provides a timetable for removing these impediments.
- If the report is favourable on the prospects of listing, approach a sponsor to advise you on your business's suitability for listing and to assist you with the steps described in this appendix.

AFTER ADMISSION

Following admission, a plc is subject to onerous continuing obligations from which private companies are free. These obligations include maintaining an informed market about the company's affairs, publishing financial accounts on a timely basis and complying with restrictions in dealing in the company's shares. Directors must have a clear understanding of these rules and regulations as transgressions can cause them to fall foul of the criminal law, particularly as laid down in the Criminal Justice Act 1993.

Your sponsoring broker, or adviser, will advise directors on all these issues before the float and keep them up to date on their responsibilities after the company has listed.

In summary, a plc has to exhibit tighter management control and greater transparency and will incur higher compliance costs than a private company.

OTHER MARKETS

The information covered so far in this appendix has concerned the Main and Alternative markets of the LSE, but there are other markets to consider.

SUBMARKETS

Within the LSE itself there are submarkets, which are groupings of companies of similar type, such as LANDmark or TECHmark.

As an example, TECHmark is a submarket for innovative technology plcs regardless of their size, industrial classification or location. Admission to TECHmark is conditional on:

- gaining a listing from the UKLA, and
- admission to TECHmark, via the LSE.

OFEX

The information provided below is a brief overview of OFEX listing requirements. Further information can be obtained from OFEX itself, whilst a very useful booklet, *A Guide to OFEX*, is produced by the accounting firm Baker Tilly, from which some of the information in this section is taken.

As mentioned above, OFEX is an 'off exchange' share matching and trading facility, rather than a share market. OFEX is neither a Recognised Investment Exchange nor a Designated Investment Exchange under the Financial Services Act 1986.

Transactions in OFEX securities of unlisted and unquoted companies are only undertaken by member firms of the LSE and the shares are not quoted or dealt in on the LSE itself, neither are they subject to LSE rules.

JP Jenkins, an LSE member firm, started OFEX in 1995. Its object was to attract entrepreneurial businesses in the 'new economy', so it could be considered as a natural home for smaller, riskier businesses in the e-commerce, new media and telecommunications sectors.

OFEX has its own code of practice, and deviation from it can lead to suspension of the guilty party's securities from trading. However, the regulations for trading on OFEX are not as strict as for companies whose shares are traded on regulated exchanges and costs for gaining admission to OFEX are considerably lower than for the AIM. Documentation required for applicants is, however, extensive.

Businesses can join OFEX either through a fundraising or an introduction. There are no formal restrictions on the type of business or industry sector in which the business operates. The decision on whether a company is suitable to apply to OFEX is made by the company's authorized corporate adviser.

OFEX rules state that to qualify for trading, companies must meet the following criteria:

- The securities must be freely transferable.
- The company must be legally incorporated.
- The company must be supported by an authorized corporate adviser.
- Satisfactory settlement arrangements must be in place.

OFEX issues guidelines for a company's suitability to be traded. These include that the company must have the following characteristics:

- a strong management team
- good prospects for growth
- strong financial records
- established systems of management reporting.

LISTING AND EXIT STRATEGIES: A SUMMARY

The objectives of a company float are not only to maximize the funds raised by the company and the amount receivable by the vendors, but also to ensure the company is actively traded in the market after its flotation at a price appropriate to its existing value.

From the point of view of exit strategy planning, a very important third objective is that the owners are able to sell the balance of their vendors' shares at a reasonable price at some time in the future, if they so wish.

For these objectives to be accomplished, naturally, the pricing of the initial issue becomes crucial and there needs to be a demand for the company shares in the market once it has been listed.

It is not necessary for the private business owner to be involved in the detailed matters of pricing a float, or marketing the flotation or, indeed, making the final decision to float. This is the province of experts whom owners should consult once the initial appraisal of the business has taken place and the decision is made that a public listing is possible.

Going public can be a highly traumatic event for a business owner. The listing process itself is strenuous, complex and costly. The aim of exit strategy planning is to prepare the company for listing and to remove the impediments that stand in its way before it embarks on the final listing process.

If you believe that your business is in a position to float or could be in a position to float at some time in the future if certain targets are met, you should begin the process of planning for the flotation, which can be summarized as follows:

1. Establish the suitability of you and your manaagement and your business, for listing. This will include obtaining expert advice; considering the advantages and disadvantages of being a plc; considering whether your reasons for seeking a listing are likely to be fulfilled by the process and whether listing is the optimum exit option for your company, assuming you are able to reach certain financial targets at some time in the foreseeable future.
2. Commission an expert's report and valuation of the business.
3. Consider on which exchange you are aiming to list in the light of your company's profile and the exchange's requirements.
4. Prepare your business for flotation (see Figure A6.1 below). This will include:
   (a) Business continuity planning.
   (b) Operational business planning.
   (c) Identifying and removing impediments to sale.
   (d) Growing and 'positioning' your business to achieve your targets of necessary size and market acceptance. (This could include acquisitions as well as organic growth.)
5. At the appropriate time, consider whether your business is now likely to be ready for listing (that is, has it reached its targets?) and, if so, appoint a sponsor. On the sponsor's confirmation of your business's suitability for listing, proceed with the flotation with the assistance of the sponsor, including doing the following:
   (a) Decide on which market and method of listing (for example an IPO, or a placement or an introduction).
   (b) Appoint a corporate broker.
   (c) Appoint reporting accountants, lawyers, taxation specialists and public relations (PR) advisers.
   (d) Prepare prospectus (listing particulars).
   (e) Prepare new business plan and profit forecasts.
   (f) Undertake presentations to institutions and analysts.
   (g) Fix issue price.
   (h) Complete underwriting.

	1st Half	2nd Half	1st Half	2nd Half	1st Half	2nd Half	1st Half	2nd Half	1st Half	2nd Half	Target Date	WHO?	NOTES	NOTES
1. Business continuity		2002		2003		2004		2005		2006	2007			
1.1 Corporate structure														
1.2 Taxation advice														
1.3 s/hs agreement														
1.4 Expert's report														
2. Business planning														
2.1 Strategy meeting														
2.2 Complete business plan														
2.3 OP. improvements (1)														
2.4 Remove impediments (2)														
3. Make acquisition/s														
4. Listings														
4.1 Appoint sponsor														
4.2 Prepare long form														
4.3 Prepare prospectus														
4.4 Profit forecasts														
4.5 Presentations														
4.5 Fix issue price														
4.6 Complete underwriting											X			
Notes: (1) See separate list (2) See separate list														

Figure A6.1 Master Exit Strategy Plan: Flotation

APPENDIX 7

FRANCHISING OR LICENSING

In this appendix we will consider a little used exit route for private businesses, namely the franchising of their operations. We look at:

- the way you are able to check the suitability of your business for franchising
- the advantages and disadvantages of franchising and how you can get help in making the decision as to whether your business is suitable for exit through the franchising route
- who are likely to be your franchisees and how you can find them
- pilot schemes, operating manuals, training and franchise agreements
- the steps you should take to set up a franchising business in the UK.

FRANCHISING: A LITTLE USED EXIT STRATEGY

The decision to franchise a business, rather than to sell it, is not widely used as an exit strategy in the UK. Although franchising is usually associated with retailing (particularly food retailing), it should not be considered as being limited to this sector of the market. Its usefulness as an exit strategy has wider application than most business owners think.

The act of franchising is not, by itself, a complete exit, but could be the first step in a strategy that maximizes the value of your business equity. It is often necessary and, indeed, highly beneficial for a business owner to exit their businesses in stages. Public listing and franchising are both good examples of effective, multistaged exit strategies for business owners with the appropriate businesses. In franchising the first step is to franchise your operating business and become a franchisor. The second step is to sell the franchisor business.

Through franchising as an exit option you are able to either dispose of the total operations of the business to franchisees and remain as the owner of the franchisor business, or franchise only part of the operations, becoming a franchisor and retaining ownership of some operations, thus being involved in both sides of the business. A good example of this is where a franchisor retains some outlets as 'company stores'.

In both cases, you have opened up your opportunities to dispose of the business in total over the longer term. If the franchising is a long-term success, you have the opportunity to dispose of the whole business at a higher price than was originally possible. Even if the franchise business is not a long-term success, you have unlocked a part of your equity through the initial sale of franchises.

So, franchising can be viewed as an integral and important part of exit strategy planning, not least because of the flexibility it provides to private business owners.

WHAT SORT OF BUSINESS CAN BE FRANCHISED?

When considering whether your business is suitable for franchising, the following guidelines will be of assistance:

- The business should have a distinctive brand or operating system.
- The operating system must be of a kind that can be taught to reasonably intelligent business owner-managers.
- The business products or services must be new, or presented in a new or unusual way.
- There must be sufficient gross margin in the business for the franchisee to pay a royalty to the franchisor and for both parties to make a reasonable profit, taking into account the franchisee's initial capital outlay.
- The work must be attractive enough to attract franchisees, and suitable franchisees must be available for this type of business.
- Ideally, the business must be well established and profitable (although some start-ups with exciting potential can be franchised).
- The franchise businesses should be able to be operated profitably in various geographic areas.

OTHER IMPORTANT CONSIDERATIONS

When you are considering whether to utilize franchising as an exit strategy, the suitability of your business is only the first hurdle. The next, and more important, one is whether the franchising route is the optimum exit strategy for your business. This is a difficult decision because of the many unknowns, but by reading this book and taking the appropriate expert advice, you should be able to make a reasoned judgement on this matter.

An important issue that you should consider from the outset is franchisee retention. There are two important periods in any franchise operation. At the beginning, franchisees will need to be sure that they are getting fair value through buying into your franchise scheme. New franchisees are often inexperienced in business and are easily caught up in the excitement of their new venture. They can be less than discerning and it might be relatively easy to persuade them that they cannot hope to be successful without your product or system and ongoing support.

Once the initial period of euphoria is over, however, and the hard grind of business reality takes its toll, franchisees will start to question what continuing value they are getting from the franchisor. This is when you as the franchisor must be able to provide them with sufficient added value to ensure that they are retained as franchisees.

BUSINESSES FOR WHICH FRANCHISING MIGHT NOT BE SUITABLE

Certain businesses might not be suitable for franchising. These would include businesses:

- whose products or services are likely to have market appeal for only a short while
- whose gross margins are too low to provide an adequate return to both franchisee and franchisor
- in which a high degree of operating skill levels need to be imparted to the franchisee
- in which the goodwill value (residing, for example, in customer loyalty) attaches to the business owner's special skills and is difficult to transfer to the franchisees
- which are operating in a geographically defined market that cannot be replicated outside this area
- with complicated and detailed audit requirements that could not be easily handled by franchisees
- that are failing and are using franchising as a way to save their operations.

(I am indebted to the British Franchise Association [BFA] for the above guidelines.)

THE ADVANTAGES OF FRANCHISING

The following reasons are usually given as to why a private company might franchise its operations:

- Franchising provides a means of expanding the business without the normal strains that expansion places on capital and human resources.
- Franchising is a way of selling parts of the business to various owners. This could be both more profitable and more easily accomplished than selling the business as a whole.
- It is generally easier for potential franchisees to raise money for a franchise opportunity than for an acquisition through a normal trade sale, as lenders (usually banks) consider the risk to be lower in franchising.
- Franchising can raise the profile of the business as a whole and, subsequently, its long-term value.
- Having more outlets leads to greater volumes of purchasing, with resultant bulk purchase discounts and potential for higher profits.
- From an exit strategy viewpoint, franchising provides another option to private business owners (one that they might not normally have considered).

THE DISADVANTAGES OF FRANCHISING

Franchising places a large burden on the franchisor, being more costly and time-consuming than many realize. The disadvantages of franchising a business include:

- The setting up costs for a franchise system are considerable. These could include running a pilot project; producing manuals and franchise agreements; advertising and recruiting franchisees (including, perhaps, the production of a prospectus); and legal expenses in copyrighting and protecting trademarks and brands. There could also be increases in national advertising and promotional costs, which might not be matched by franchise revenue in the early stages. Cash flow could be negative for some time, although up-front franchise fees can alleviate this.
- Although one of the advantages of franchising is said to be the fact that self-employed

franchisees work harder than employees, one of the disadvantages of franchising is that the franchisor relies heavily on the business abilities and honesty of his or her franchisees, who are largely independent of the franchisor's control.

- Over time, franchisees can either become disillusioned with the franchise, or feel they can run a business independent from the franchisor. The franchisor must, therefore, be prepared to provide continuing benefit to his or her franchisees and to motivate them over a long period. (Note that franchisees might not only leave the franchise business, they might also compete against it – using the knowledge they have gained while being a franchisee. This is a double disadvantage to the franchisor.)
- From an exit planning viewpoint, franchising is a high-risk venture compared with a trade sale, but is probably no more risky than an MBO, which is prey to the uncertainties of the management team and the financiers' requirements.

As a business owner considering franchising as an exit option, you need to undertake two preliminary tests, one objective and one subjective. First, you need to seek advice to see whether your business has the degree of brand awareness and/or uniqueness conducive to franchising. Second, you need to ask yourself whether you have the personality to be a successful franchisor and whether the potential outcome justifies the time and stress involved in putting together the franchising business. If these issues are positive, the question boils down to an economic one: is franchising likely to be your optimum exit strategy?

THE STEPS NECESSARY TO SET UP A FRANCHISE IN THE UK

Once the decision has been made in principle to go down the franchising route (having considered all the potential advantages and disadvantages), we suggest you now take the following steps:

1. Ask an expert to provide a report on the potential of your business as a franchised network. (The British Franchise Association (BFA) can provide you with a list of suitable franchise consultants.) You should ask the expert to include, as a minimum, the following matters in the report:
   - The suitability of the business for franchising particularly with regard to the business brand strength (awareness) and its operating systems.
   - The type of franchise system or model contemplated.
   - What the franchise system is to be called and what management and marketing support systems will be provided to franchisees?
   - The steps necessary to put the business into a position to be franchised and the estimated time required to complete this task.
   - Projections of the expected income of the franchisor; and projections for profitability for different franchisee models over, say, the next five years.
   - The financial details of the proposed franchise offer, including advertising costs and the initial franchise fee and continuing royalties.
   - An estimate of the costs involved in the launch. (A full cash flow projection will also need to be produced. You might require assistance with this from your accountant.)
2. Should this report confirm the suitability of your business for franchising, the next step is to consider whether a pilot scheme is necessary to prove the franchise's potential. If the business has been operating with autonomous branches, utilizing branch accounting and management systems, a pilot scheme might not be necessary.

   (*Note*: the pilot scheme usually has the dual purpose of demonstrating the feasibility of the franchise system to the potential franchisees, and being a way in which you can test and refine your operating system and financial model for your franchise. Most franchise experts are strongly in favour of franchisors running a pilot scheme before they officially launch their franchise business.)
3. The company's business plan should be reviewed and a master exit strategy plan drawn up to include the steps contemplated in setting up the franchise. These steps will include the recommendations in the expert's report.
4. Once the pilot scheme has proved successful (or if one was not considered necessary), it is now important to protect the business by registering trade names, brand names and patents and to prepare to launch the franchise network.
5. Lawyers should now be instructed to draw up proforma agreements covering all aspects of the relationship between the franchisor and the franchisees. (A checklist of the minimum information that should be included in a franchise heads of agreement can be seen in Figure A7.1.)

Like all legal agreements, any particular franchise agreement should be tailored to meet its own special circumstances and legal assistance should be sought in producing agreements. As a general guideline, the matters below would be included, as a minimum requirement, in most franchise agreements:

1. The name of the franchisor and franchisee.
2. The standard clauses covering:
   - The term of the agreement.
   - The franchise fees, both initial and continuing (also sometimes known as royalties).
   - Renewal of the agreement.
   - Exclusivity (geographic or other).
3. Date of commencement of business.
4. Training to be provided by franchisor and franchisee.
5. Operations manuals, and operational assistance from the franchisor.
6. The franchisee's operational undertakings.
7. Insurance.
8. Trade or operational secrets.
9. Reporting, inspections and audits.
10. Advertising budgets and undertakings by franchisor.
11 Trademarks, logos and name.
12. Franchisor's business transfer (or exit strategy planning) policy.
13. Termination and consequences of termination.
14. Post-termination covenants. (*Note*: an area that is often neglected in franchise agreements is exit strategy planning for franchisees themselves! Franchise agreements should include the franchisor's guidelines and rules for franchise disposal, including agreed types of disposal, valuation methods, 'buyer of last resort' contingencies, etc. Besides being important for franchisees, the inclusion of these policies in the franchise agreement should assist franchisors to attract and maintain quality franchisees. This subject is covered in more detail in Appendix 3.)

Figure A7.1 Contents of a Franchise Agreement

6. You could now produce the prospectus, or offer document, for franchisees. This should be in a form that presents the opportunity in a clear, optimistic way, without exaggeration or hyperbole. (*Note*: although bodies such as the BFA recommend the production of a prospectus, it is not a legal requirement to produce one.)
7. Concurrent with advertising and recruiting potential franchisees, a comprehensive franchise manual should be produced. This will cover all aspects of the business's operations and training. (The operating manuals are dealt with below.) The detail and size of this document will depend on the complexity of the business, but is likely to be at least 30 pages.
8. Now you need to review your management resources and gear up for the planned expansion and increased training and monitoring activities.
9. Complete the first round of franchise recruitment. (*Note*: the success of the business will rely, among other things, on recruiting a sufficient number of competent franchisees.)

THE OPERATING MANUALS

The franchisor's operating system is contained in the operation manuals. The manuals must be a comprehensive and explain clearly all matters involved in the franchise business, including what the franchisee does and how he or she does it. The manuals set quality and performance standards and cover the setting-up stages and the continuing operations details.

If you do not already have manuals for internal use, it will be necessary for you to produce franchise material from scratch. This is a large task, which could take up to six months to complete. There are companies that specialize in the production of franchise manuals and you should get quotations from them to see if you wish to use their services. (Refer to the BFA's website for more information.)

TRAINING AND CONTINUING SUPPORT

The franchisor will need to provide training for the start-up period and on a continuous basis to ensure that a complete understanding of the operating system is transferred to the franchisees. The extent of this training will depend on the nature of the business and the capabilities of the franchisees. Where franchisees were former branch managers or company employees, the training might be limited to financial and ownership issues only, as they should have competence in operational matters.

You as the franchisor must be able provide continuing support to your franchisees for the complete term of their agreements. Franchise agreements can be for a period of up to 20 years and the franchisor must have the personnel, expertise and capital to meet support obligations.

As mentioned previously, a franchisor must also have a personality which is capable of dealing with a group of strong-willed, self-motivated, small business people who, on the one hand, want autonomy but who, on the other hand, expect the franchisor to contribute to their growing profitability.

WHO ARE YOUR LIKELY FRANCHISEES?

Recruiting suitable franchisees is probably the hardest, most costly and time-consuming process in setting up a franchise and, if the business is to grow, the recruiting process will be a continuing one.

As mentioned above, if a business already runs various branch offices or shops, the obvious franchisees are its own managers. If it is a well-established business with a strong profit record, it should also be able to attract franchisees from outside. Once the business has a record of success it becomes increasingly easier to attract franchisees.

When you have finalized the production of the memorandum of offer document (or prospectus) you are in a position to proceed with the recruitment of franchisees. The franchise industry is strongly entrenched in the UK and there are many well-tried ways of recruiting franchisees.

(*Note*: most experts advise against using a recruitment consultant to find franchisees, as the consultant's aim could be to fill the posts regardless of the quality of the candidates.)

Successful ways to recruit suitable franchisees include the following:

- Advertising: several newspapers have franchise sections, which are widely read. There are also several franchising trade magazines in which you can advertise.
- Franchise exhibitions: these events are held regularly and are usually well attended. Some are more prestigious than others.
- Referrals: this is the best way to get new franchisees and will transpire when you have current franchisees who are happy and operating successfully under a fair and reasonable franchise agreement. Referrals are less likely to occur with a new franchise operation.
- The British Franchise Association: Many potential franchisees look to the BFA for guidance. The BFA's information pack is sold to thousands of potential franchisees each year and franchisors can advertise their opportunity in this publication.

EXPERT ASSISTANCE

You will need to use various experts, including consultants and lawyers to assist you in setting up your franchise business. If you do not have contact with the appropriate experts, lists of consultants and lawyers who specialize in franchising can be obtained from the British Franchise Association. Other information on availability of experts can be obtained on the Internet. Most importantly, as the franchise agreement is a central part of any franchising system, a specialist franchise lawyer should draw up contracts, etc.

SUMMARY OF STEPS TO SET UP YOUR FRANCHISE

In summary, the steps you should take if you wish to use franchising as an exit route are as follows:

1. Make a preliminary assessment of your business's suitability for franchising. If you believe this is positive, go to the next step.
2. Commission an expert's report on your business's suitability for franchising and ensure the report provides a comprehensive list of things to do to make up any deficiencies in this regard.
3. Consider setting up a pilot scheme. If you set one up, assess the success of this. If it has been successful, go to the next step.
4. Write a brief policy outline, including how many outlets you will franchise, number of retained company outlets, advertising policy, etc. Decide on the financial structure of the franchisee arrangements, including upfront fees, franchise fees (or royalties), etc.
5. Review and update your operational business plan. Begin to produce your master exit strategy plan (see Figure A7.2) for exit through franchising, and include the actions recommended in the expert's report to bring the business up to standard for franchising. Include your policy outline in your MESP.
6. Register brand names and patents.
7. Instruct your lawyers to draw up proforma franchise agreements.

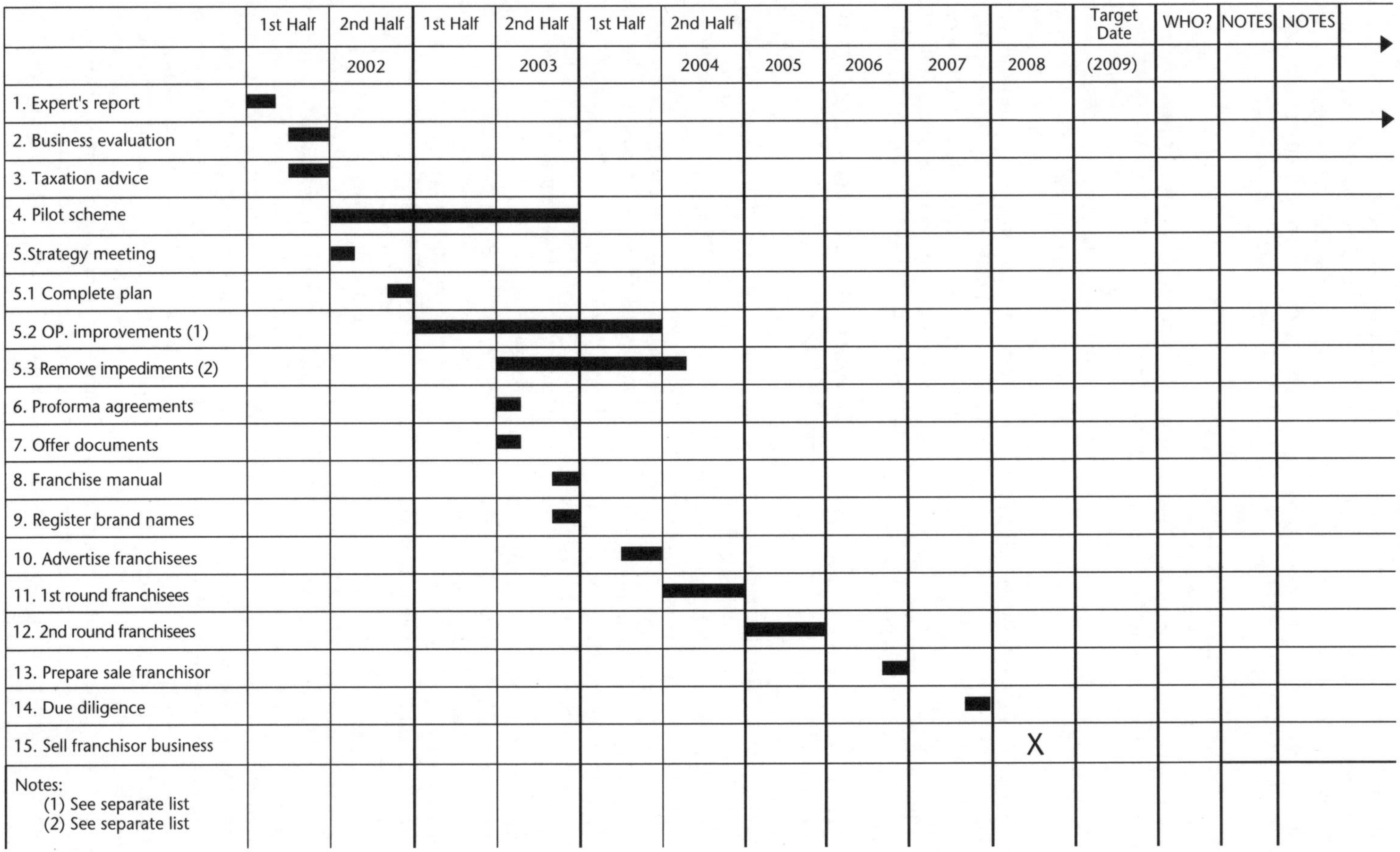

	1st Half	2nd Half	1st Half	2nd Half	1st Half	2nd Half					Target Date	WHO?	NOTES	NOTES
		2002		2003		2004	2005	2006	2007	2008	(2009)			
1. Expert's report														
2. Business evaluation														
3. Taxation advice														
4. Pilot scheme														
5.Strategy meeting														
5.1 Complete plan														
5.2 OP. improvements (1)														
5.3 Remove impediments (2)														
6. Proforma agreements														
7. Offer documents														
8. Franchise manual														
9. Register brand names														
10. Advertise franchisees														
11. 1st round franchisees														
12. 2nd round franchisees														
13. Prepare sale franchisor														
14. Due diligence														
15. Sell franchisor business										X				
Notes: (1) See separate list (2) See separate list														

Figure A7.2 Master Exit Strategy Plan: Franchising

8. Produce a memorandum of offer document (or a prospectus) and franchise operating manual.
9. Begin the franchisee recruiting process.
10. Review your operating resources, which incorporate franchisee support systems (including training resources), accounting systems, distribution (where this is appropriate), management (including monitoring resources).
11. Sign your first franchisee and get your exit strategy under way!

CONCLUSION

Franchising as an exit route is often not considered by private businesses in the UK. This is probably because of the following:

- Business owners do not consider franchising as an exit route as such, because most think of exit planning as a short-term, single-stage event rather than a longer-term planned process.
- Franchising is still inextricably linked in some business owner's minds to the food industry.
- Some business owners mistakenly believe that franchising is for larger businesses only (a common misconception with MBOs also).

We hope that this appendix will cause you to consider franchising as a viable exit option, which, in your case, could turn out to be the optimum one.

APPENDIX 8

TRADE SALES

We have shown you so far in this book how to plan and groom your business for sale. In this appendix you will learn about the trade sale process in more detail. What you learn here will not turn you into a qualified business broker, but it will enable you to be prepared for the stressful process of selling your business and equip you to gauge the level of competence and experience of the agents you might engage to assist you in the sale.

INTRODUCTION

In April 1998, new capital gains taxation legislation was introduced in the UK that provides what is known as 'taper relief' on business disposals. It is expected that over the next two to three years a record number of business owners will wish to dispose of their businesses to take advantage of these taxation measures. The majority of these businesses will be disposed of through sale to third parties, in what is known as a 'trade sale'.

A trade sale appears to be the most straightforward method of business disposal from the business owner's point of view, because all you have to do is to hand over your business to a business broker who (you hope) will do the rest. But in reality this very 'easiness' could also be your problem, because an unplanned trade sale in the hands of the average business broker will seldom realize the optimum exit price for the business owner.

To get the optimum price you must, first, be certain that a trade sale *is* the optimum exit strategy for your business, then you must have put your business into shape for disposal and then you must ensure your business is sold properly either by yourself or by a competent, experienced agent. Finally, you must ensure that you will receive the optimum after-tax price for your business, which means getting sound taxation advice from a competent taxation adviser at an early stage.

WHAT IS A TRADE SALE?

A traditional trade sale involves selling 100 per cent of the business to a commercial buyer (who often owns a similar, or compatible business) and the owner exiting the business (usually after a reasonable handover period). However, especially for larger private businesses, there are variations on this theme. The most common variation is for a part of the business (either a minority or majority stake) to be sold. A minority sale can be to another business or individual, but is often to an investor or venture capitalist, or to an industrial partner.

MINORITY SALE TO A VC

Here the sale of equity could be by a minority shareholder who wishes to exit the business; or it could be the sale of part of the total equity held by the owner, who has other aims and ambitions.

The advantages to an owner in selling a significant minority of his or her holding (say 40 per cent) to a VC include the following:

- The introduction to the business of a bigger entity which not only has cash itself to invest in the business, but can also attract finance from a bank for growth or acquisition.
- This sale can be part of a multistaged exit strategy, the next stage being either the sale of the balance of the holdings in a trade sale, or (with the VC) a secondary buyout, or a public listing.
- The introduction of the VC will bring added prestige to the business and enable it to attract quality management and employees, while the VC's resources will strengthen the balance sheet if necessary.

MINORITY SALE TO INDUSTRIAL PARTNER

Where a company has attractive technology, but is perhaps new or small and consequently lacks the firepower to assure its growth, a positive step could be to sell a minority interest to a larger, or more established business in the same sector (which might notionally be a competitor) and participate in what is commonly called 'corporate venturing'. The advantages of such a sale could include the following:

- The new partner could have the infrastructure (such as storage and distribution) that the smaller business lacks.
- The new partner should have the financial resources to capitalize on the technology or innovation of the smaller business, while the smaller business might have the innovative culture that the larger partner lacks.
- The larger partner should have the management and systems to help the smaller business achieve its objectives, including administrative, financial and marketing expertise.
- The association with the new partner could make access to institutional finance easier for the smaller business.

THE STEPS OF A TRADE SALE

The first step is to decide on the right sale price, as asking the wrong price will probably jeopardize your sale plans. The valuation techniques described in Appendix 2 will help you to establish the approximate market price for your business. (To ensure you have established a true market value you will probably require a formal valuation from an experienced business valuer.)

The second step is to obtain taxation advice on the implications of your planned disposal. The third step is to decide what portion of the equity you wish to sell. The fourth is to put your business in to the optimum shape for sale. The final step is to arrange the sale itself.

IMPEDIMENTS TO SALE

To ensure your business is sold for its optimum price you need, among other things, to go through the same steps necessary to ensure that you will not be impeded in your sale and to improve your business's attractiveness to buyers as you would for any other exit strategy option. In brief, this involves the following steps:

- Addressing ownership and shareholder issues, such as business continuity planning and retirement planning.
- Obtaining good taxation advice so you can plan the timing of the sale and your financial planning generally to your maximum advantage.
- Identifying those aspects of your business which will make it hard to sell or will depress its price. We call these 'impediments to sale'.
- Grooming your business for sale by removing these impediments to sale.
- Preparing yourself for the important aspects of the sale process, such as due diligence, preparation of memorandum of offer document.

Figure 6.1 lists the usual impediments to sale (or current defects) in a typical business. But, of course, all businesses are different and you must undertake a rigorous analysis of your business to see which impediments apply in its case. Having identified these, you must include the ways you plan to remove them in your operational business plan. This plan will, in turn, be incorporated in to your master exit strategy plan.

An impediment to sale that needs highlighting (and probably the most common one, especially in smaller businesses) is lack of management to replace you, the owner. In Appendix 4 on family succession planning we point out the necessity of identifying and grooming an appropriate heir to be the future owner-manager. In a trade sale, the need for management continuity after sale is equally important for two reasons. First, if the business is offered for sale with no trained management in place, potential buyers will be limited to other owner-managers with the same skills as yours; which eliminates as potential buyers those investors who do not wish to manage (or are incapable of managing) the business after they have bought it. Second, even if an owner-manager buys the business, most of the knowledge essential to the running of the business (including customer relationships) could be lost. The goodwill value in many private businesses lies in the expertise of their owners and to preserve this goodwill value it must either be transferred to the new owner (through a handover and training period); or reside in the management which stays on after the sale; or, if practicable, be committed to writing in operating manuals.

One result of failing to transfer management skills and knowledge is that the vendor-owner might need to spend a very long period of time in the handover of the business, which might be costly, frustrating and highly inconvenient.

IMPROVING PROFITABILITY

Your accountants will tell you that the way to improve profitability is to increase sales revenue and decrease costs. If only business life was so simple. The desired outcome might be obvious, but it is the steps necessary to achieve the outcome that are not so obvious. The costs you are trying to reduce are those whose reduction will not have a corresponding long-term negative impact on sales and profits; while increasing sales revenue is about increasing gross profits. (Unprofitable sales for sales' sake can, indeed, increase your losses.)

In most private businesses there is an amount of discretionary spending, usually related to owners' benefits. You can identify this when accounts are adjusted to show 'real' profits. But this is not what is meant by reducing business expenses to increase profit. What we mean is a real reduction in the costs of doing business, while maintaining, or improving, gross profit. This is a much more difficult exercise and is one of the reasons you need three years at least to groom your business for a successful sale. (Another main reason is usually the time needed to train the management team.)

WHAT IS BEING SOLD?

When you are selling a business you need to decide what exactly is being sold. There are a number of alternatives available to a buyer. These include the right to acquire:

- the business name, licences, patents, brands, etc.
- specific assets and liabilities owned by the business; but not the business operations or staff
- the business as a going concern, including its name, tangible (or fixed) assets (such as plant and equipment), intangible assets and the taking over of staff. Specific liabilities are often excluded from these transactions
- and, when the business is a company, all the company's shares, the purchase of which will result in the buyer acquiring all assets and liabilities (unless specific assets and liabilities have been previously sold by arrangement) and taking over all operations and staff.

You need to be aware that there are now specific taxation reasons why company owners will wish to sell the shares of a company they own, rather than having a company sell its assets. These matters are covered in some detail in Appendix 1.

SALE OF THE ASSETS AND BUSINESS AS A GOING CONCERN

If you plan to sell your business as a going concern you will need to provide a wide range of documentary information to the prospective buyer, including the following:

- narrative description of business, including date established, date acquired by you, length of time in current premises, etc.
- profit and loss statements for the last three years
- copy of current business plan
- registration of business name (if applicable)
- bank statements for the past 12 months
- aged debtors' listing
- client files (where applicable)
- schedule of plant, equipment, fixtures and fittings
- schedule of employees including:
  - position
  - experience
  - salary package
  - leave entitlements
- details of any key employees and whether there are current service contracts in place
- details of in-house pension schemes
- your accountant and solicitor's details
- copy of lease of premises. In particular, the buyer needs to know:
  - the balance of term left to run
  - the current rent
  - the rent review provisions
  - who pays the rates and taxes
  - if there are any renewal options
  - if the lease can be assigned and, if so, what the conditions of assignment are
  - if there are any unusual conditions, such as options to purchase
  - the name and address of the landlord
- real property sale contract, if freehold is to be sold.

You might also need to provide information on the following matters:

- Reason for sale – the buyer will want to know this to determine whether you are selling because the business is going bad.
- The degree of ongoing assistance/tuition that you are prepared to provide following settlement, and for how long. Do you expect to be paid for all or some of it? (See also the

comments above concerning transfer of goodwill and management information.)
- Are you in a position, and are you willing, to provide vendor finance?

SALE OF COMPANY SHARES

If you intend to sell the company structure through the sale of its shares you will need to provide the information listed above and have the following additional documents available for the purchaser:

- full financial accounts of the company including balance sheets, for a minimum of the past three years
- tax returns for a minimum of the past three years
- company's Memorandum and Articles of Association
- depreciation schedule
- aged debtors' listing
- full details of all liabilities including loan contracts, lease agreements, creditor arrangements, and taxation liabilities
- annual returns for a minimum of the past three years
- corporate records including share register, share transfers, names of directors, shareholders
- location of registered office.

(*Note*: Because taper relief under capital gains tax is only available to individuals, the sale of the company structure by individuals selling the shares in the company they own is now the favoured method of disposal for sellers [where the shares are owned by individuals and not by holding companies]. But buyers prefer to buy assets and not companies with their unknown risks and liabilities. This will lead to some interesting negotiations over the ensuing years.)

THE VALUE OF YOUR BUSINESS

When you have taken the decision in principle to sell, you will want to know the current market value of your business before you make a final decision to dispose of it. Some of the technicalities of valuations are dealt with in Appendix 2. Before you fix the price of the business you must bear in mind the following important points:

- The price at which the business is listed for sale (that is, the asking price) often determines whether or not it will be sold.
- All prices are negotiable and business people expect to haggle, but if you start with a price that is too high you are at a disadvantage for several reasons. For example:
  - Buyers can be frightened away even before they make serious inquiries.
  - You will have started off with unreasonable expectations and will find it hard to accept what might be a reasonable market price.
  - You will have lost confidence in your advisers for letting you put the business on the market for that price and will be uncertain what to do next if the business fails to attract your asking price.

It is better to face up to what your business is really worth at the beginning, rather than going through the costly and stressful business of trying to sell a business that is overpriced. Think carefully about market value based on sound valuation principles and not subjective issues like 'this business has taken me all my life to build'. Seek professional help from a reputable valuer. Make your decision when you have all the relevant facts and outside advice.

TAXATION

Your aim under your exit strategy plan is to receive the maximum net price for your business when you sell it. This means you need to be aware of the impact taxation will have on your sale. In Appendix 1 we discuss some of the taxation issues surrounding exit strategies. Capital gains tax and Inheritance tax are obviously important, but so are corporation tax and income tax. Appendix 1 is only an introduction to the complex area of taxation and you should get advice from a taxation expert as early as possible in your exit strategy planning. The advice should cover both your personal and your business taxation situations, and you should aim for an integrated approach to your overall financial position, particularly if your business sale is to coincide with your retirement.

It is important to get advice as early as you can, because certain taxation reliefs are based on the period of ownership of assets, while others are based on the time that has elapsed since transfer or your retirement. You do not wish to find that you are being penalized on timing issues because of lack of foresight and planning.

PREPARING A MEMORANDUM OF OFFER DOCUMENT

When selling a business you need to produce preliminary information to show initial enquirers, followed by more detailed information to show those with genuine interest (and who have signed a confidentiality undertaking). This means you would usually produce the following to give to prospective purchasers:

- the preliminary advertising and/or mailer
- a memorandum of offer document.

PRELIMINARY INFORMATION

This should consist of the basic facts, presented simply. Avoid making rash claims or extravagant statements and keep the document brief: one page should do. You should not disclose the identity of your business at this stage. The information is designed merely to wet the appetite of potential buyers and to sort out the genuinely interested from the time wasters. You would invite those who are interested in taking matters further to contact you for a full memorandum of offer and to sign and return a letter of confidentiality. When this happens you can go to the next stage.

MEMORANDUM OF OFFER DOCUMENT

You can now send out the memorandum of offer document. To assist you, the usual contents of this document are outlined in Figure A8.1.

You could also at this stage commission a due diligence report on your business (which could be viewed as a more comprehensive and more independent assessment of the business) to provide to prospective buyers, especially if you anticipate strong interest and the possibility of having several parties interested. You could now be in the position of conducting what some call a covert auction.

Even at this stage it is usual to hold back the business's name and any other market-sensitive information. Only after you are satisfied that the enquirer is not a competitor seeking market-sensitive information about your business but is genuinely interested in progressing the enquiry should you provide the highly confidential information like the company's name, your reason for selling, names of key employees, client lists, etc.

The information required for a memorandum of offer document advertising a trade sale would be different for each business being sold. However, the following information is usually necessary as a minimum:

1. Background of the company: ownership and history.
2. Management organization and control.
3. Products, services, nature of services.
4. Company's markets, customers and competition.
5. Administration and personnel.
6. Raw materials and suppliers.
7. Arrangements with principals and agents.
8. Facilities, plant and real property.
9. Financial information in summary:
   - Profit and loss: last three years
   - Profit and loss forecast: next two years
   - Current asset and liability (balance sheet) information
   - Interim financial accounts, not more than six months old (see also schedules, below.)
10. Asset information/depreciation schedule.
11. Analysis of trading operations.
12. Future plans and developments.
13. Asking price and reason for sale.
14. Schedules:

Schedule 1: Financial accounts (last three years)
Schedule 2: Profit and loss and cash flow forecasts (next two years minimum)
Schedule 3: Principal and agency agreements
Schedule 4: Investigating accountant's reports
Schedule 5: Asset valuation reports
Schedule 6: Background of key managers and employees
Schedule 7: Asset depreciation schedule
Schedule 8: Up-to-date business plan*

* *Note*: a great deal of the information required in a memorandum of offer document should already be contained in a professionally produced business plan.

Figure A8.1 Memorandum of Offer Document for a Trade Sale

This is a sensitive area and must be handled on a case-by-case basis. In some situations, certain information will only be divulged when a conditional written offer to purchase has been received and an exclusivity agreement has been entered into which gives the prospective purchasers the confidence to spend money on their own due diligence. The conditions of purchase would usually include the completion of a satisfactory due diligence investigation and all sensitive information being divulged.

Your aim must be to keep as many interested parties as possible vying for the business until you receive a conditional offer. You could find that using an experienced business broker here will assist not only in the production of the memorandum, but also with the question of confidentiality.

There are rules governing the offering of interests for sale under the Financial Services Act and you might wish to take advice on this if you are handling the sale yourself.

MARKETING YOUR BUSINESS FOR SALE

To attract interest you might feel that the only way is to advertise your business to potential buyers. However, to advertise the fact that your business is for sale is to alert competitors and employees and, potentially, to inflict damage to your trading prospects and company morale. This is the basic dilemma that faces the owner who wishes to sell his or her business. But 'advertising' does not necessarily mean putting advertisements in the newspaper. You (or your agent) have several choices in spreading the word, including:

- contacting potential buyers personally
- using your networking contacts
- using your local Business Link
- advising other intermediaries like accountants who could have interested clients
- mailing to targeted mailing lists
- advertising in specialist trade journals.

PERSONAL CONTACTS

It is possible you will know of potential buyers in your industry. Some of them may have mentioned to you in the past that they could be interested in buying your business should it come up for sale. Hopefully, you will know whether this interest is genuine or just a ruse to find out useful information. You could make personal contact with these industry people or send them the preliminary information. Similarly, if you use a broker, he or she could know the names of potential buyers.

NETWORKING CONTACTS

Most industries have networking opportunities; either through trade association or more general bodies like Chambers of Commerce. You should discretely spread the word through your contacts in these organizations.

BUSINESS LINK

It is usual for Business Links to have sector groups for such things as the food industry, or manufacturing, or retailing and you could advise the chairman of the relevant group that your business is for sale.

OTHER INTERMEDIARIES

Intermediaries, such as accountants or solicitors could have clients interested in your business and the word can be spread in a controlled and confidential way. Some brokers use this method of selling businesses almost exclusively.

MAILING

The advantage of mailing is that only the recipient should see the information, unlike media advertising that could be seen by anyone. You (or your agent) could mail to specific industry sectors or to any potential buyers who you think might be suitable for whatever reason. Industry-specific (and other) lists can be obtained from professional mailing houses. Professional business brokers have mailing lists that can be targeted geographically, by size of business and industry sector, etc. Another advantage of using an intermediary for mailings is that confidentiality can be maintained.

TRADE MAGAZINES

Whether you advertise in your trade magazine will depend on two issues. First, is your industry sector large enough for your advertisement not to give the game away that you are the advertiser? Second, is the magazine a successful medium for businesses for sale? (You can usually tell by checking how many other people are using it for this purpose.)

GENERAL MEDIA ADVERTISING

The advantage of media advertising is that it often attracts potential buyers whom you were not aware of, or did not expect to be interested. You have to weigh this up against the confidentiality issues we mentioned earlier. If you do decide to advertise, the choice of a suitable advertising media is important. Here you need to consider the number of potentially interested parties you will reach compared with the cost of the advertisements.

1. For a business of a reasonably large size with national appeal, you could consider the national press, for example the *Sunday Times* or the *Weekend Telegraph*. Regional newspapers, like the *Yorkshire Post*, also have a large circulation and could be suitable.
2. Local dailies or weeklies may be suitable. Use the classifieds if the business is small.
3. You might consider whether a trade or specialist publication is suitable for your business. A good way of gauging whether you are likely to find the publication successful is to see whether businesses for sale advertisements appear regularly in it. Be cautious in choosing these publications.

The important thing to realize with advertising is that only a small percentage of potential buyers will see any one advertisement. Persistence is very important. Should you fail to find a buyer through one approach, try another. Try different styles of advertisements, or different publications. Remember, you only need one buyer and you never know how he or she is going to find you. You must, of course, work within your budget.

If you are going to use an agent to handle your sale (there are many different types ranging from company brokers to mergers and acquisition specialists), your choice of one could be determined by the way they promote the businesses they are selling. Some company brokers only use media advertising and if you are not comfortable with this approach you might choose an agent who uses more focused mailings, or has good industry contacts.

SALES FILES

When you are handling your own sale, the way in which you store and organize your information will have a large bearing on how successful you are in selling your business. Develop an orderly system in which:

- all inquiries are recorded (with telephone numbers)
- records are kept of all types of information sent to inquirers (preliminary information, memorandum of offer, etc.)
- records of visits to the business by potential buyers are kept, with dates and any other pertinent information.

The more parties you have interested (even if their interest is not particularly developed) the more confidence you will have in negotiating the sale and, of course, the more chance you will have of selling the business. Always try to advance negotiations with more than one party to each stage. Do not put all your eggs in one basket and neglect some parties because you think you have 'an absolutely certain' buyer all tied up. The only certainty that a sale is complete is when you have the contracts signed and the buyer's money is in your bank. So keep all interested parties on the go until then.

COMMON MISTAKES WHEN SELLING A BUSINESS

Most business owners will only sell a business once in their lifetime. Some may sell two businesses, but only very few have much experience in this activity. If you decide to handle the sale yourself you should be sure that you are aware of, and avoid, the misconceptions that many buyers have about the process. Below are listed some of the more common mistakes that are made by vendors:

1. They overprice the business. (We have already discussed this in chapter 6 on impediments to sale, but it is worth repeating that you must price your business realistically if you want to sell it.)
2. Their sales documentation is inadequate. (You must have a professionally prepared memorandum of sale document available, which not only gives a true picture of the business, but shows also that yours is professionally run. An independent due diligence report commissioned by you will have an even stronger impact on potential purchasers.)
3. They try to sell the past and not the future. (We have mentioned previously this failing by vendors: they ignore the fact that buyers are interested in future profits and growth and not what the business has done in the past. Vendors must have a current business plan available that sets out the business's

probable future direction, with realistic profit and loss projections, if they are to attract quality buyers to their businesses.)
4. Most vendors have limited vision when it comes to their target market and usually think that the best buyer will come from their local competitors. (In the small business sector most competitors' real desire is to see the seller go out of business. Alternatively, they will find out all about a business during the sales negotiations and then walk away. In today's open marketplace you seldom know where your best buyer will come from; and remember that you only need one.)
5. They fail to understand that a buyer buys what he or she wants, which is not necessarily what you have for sale. (An eventual lack of interest by a buyer once he or she has analysed your business is not necessarily a negative reflection on your life's work. Another way of putting this is to say that a buyer seldom buys what a seller thinks he or she should buy.)

DUE DILIGENCE

Due diligence is the name given to the process of checking the operational, financial, legal and environmental position of a business that is being sold. The nature and extent of due diligence will depend on the size and nature of the business concerned. The purchaser's advisers, who are usually corporate finance specialists, accountants and solicitors, undertake the due diligence work. It is usual during due diligence for unforeseen things to crop up that cause the purchaser to have concern about the business. This can lead either to a decision not to proceed with the sale, or to reduce the offer price. It is also thought that some advisers use the due diligence process to manufacture bogus concerns about a business to put pressure on the seller to reduce his or her price.

Whatever the truth of the matter, due diligence is a stressful time for the seller, both because of the difficulty of negotiating with purchasers and their professional advisers and because it distracts him or her from running the business. It is important, therefore, to be prepared for due diligence. The way this can be done is, as discussed above, to have your own advisers conduct a due diligence on the business before you put it up for sale. This not only ensures that the business is professionally presented, but that things that will need fixing will be uncovered (perhaps your factory does not comply with the health and safety regulations or your agency agreements are not current) and can be attended to in your own time. Just as important, you will not be at a disadvantage in the final negotiating process through worrying what might come up next.

Preparing for due diligence is one of the major advantages of a properly planned exit strategy.

FINAL NEGOTIATIONS

The role of sales negotiator does not suit all business owners. You might feel more comfortable if someone else handles the face-to-face element of this while you sit in the background and make the final decisions. This could also be a reason why you choose to use an agent or accountant to assist you in selling your business. Conversely, being personally involved in negotiations means you are on hand immediately to deal with problems in the negotiations and you are not risking that someone else mishandles the situation. These decisions are usually a matter of personal choice, but it is reasonable to assume that a third party, experienced and skilled in negotiating sales, could be of great help to you in the sales process. Having been through all the hard work you do not want the sale to fall through just because, for example, you do not like the buyer.

HEADS OF AGREEMENT

We advise that you approach the drawing up of the sales contract in two stages. As a first step, draw up a commercial 'heads of agreement' with the buyer. By this we mean that you write down in clear non-legal business terms the commercial understanding of what is being sold and for what price. This heads of agreement will be on the basis that it is 'subject to contract' (that is, not binding until a contract is signed), but that you will ask your solicitor to draw up a formal agreement based on the commercial terms of the agreement.

The key issues that should be included in the heads of agreement are:

- what is being sold
- purchase price, deposit to be paid, and balance of purchase price
- settlement date
- terms of payment: is vendor finance being offered
- handover and tuition
- transfer of goodwill

- whether there are any bills of sale or other charges over the business or its assets
- if there are any requirements for warranties and indemnities
- what the post-sale arrangements are between buyer and seller
- restraint of trade (non-competition) clauses.

THE SALES CONTRACT

There are, broadly, two kinds of business sale agreements (or sale and purchase agreements) namely:

- in smaller businesses those drawn up by the owners or their accountants
- in most other cases, sales contracts drawn up by solicitors.

We strongly recommend that you use a solicitor to draw up your sales contract unless your business is very small.

To assist you, a summary of the usual contents of a business sales contract is given in Figure A8.2.

Clauses
1 Definitions
2 Sale and Purchase of the Business
3 Excluded Assets and Liabilities
4 VAT
5 Apportionment/Prepayments
6 Conduct of the Business
7 Risk/Insurance
8 Completion
9 Stocks and Cash Float
10 Employees/Pensions
11 Collection of Book Debts
12 The Properties
13 Contracts
14 Leased Plant and Equipment
15 Creditors and Liabilities
16 Statement to Customers
17 Inspection of Documents
18 Complaints by Customers
19 Warranties
20 Restrictions on Vendor
21 Interest
22 Costs/Stamp Duty
23 Further Assurance
24 Assignment
25 Announcements
26 Miscellaneous
27 Relevant Law
28 Notices

Schedules
1st Particulars of Contracts
2nd Employees
3rd Particulars of Equipment
4th Excluded Assets
5th Properties
6th Industrial Property Rights
7th Leased Plant and Equipment
8th Plant and Machinery
9th Warranties
10th Particulars of Insurance Policies
11th Limitations on Warranties
12th Pensions

Figure A8.2 Contents of Business Sale Agreement

SOME FINAL CONSIDERATIONS

There are some issues that you should consider before the details of your sale are finalized. These are:

VENDOR FINANCE (THAT IS, AGREEING TO BE PAID ON TERMS)

In a trade sale of smaller business in particular, the seller's willingness to lend the purchaser part of the purchase price is an extremely useful tool in ensuring that the seller achieves the price he or she is looking for. It is our experience that not many owners take this option, largely because they are concerned about not getting paid or because they need the full proceeds of the sale for some other business purpose or to retire.

Vendor finance can be particularly useful where the potential buyer shows strong interest in the business and says he or she would pay the full asking price if he or she could raise the money, but is short by a specified amount (say £100,000). If this £100,000 is icing on the cake and you do not need it immediately, it could be worthwhile to consider lending the money to the purchaser.

But before you make a decision to provide vendor finance, you should consider the following:

- Is the sale to my advantage and on terms that are attractive to me?
- Is the fact that the buyer cannot raise the funds likely to scupper the deal (and is there likely to be another buyer who will pay full price without requiring vendor finance)?

- Is the buyer unable to obtain the shortfall from conventional lending sources?
- Can I, for the time being, do without the extra capital I need to lend to the purchaser, or how do I intend to invest this extra sum?
- Is the interest I can get from the buyer equal to, or better than, the return I can get elsewhere?
- What is my risk in lending this money? (This can usually be answered by asking what security you are being offered.)
- Am I remaining in the business in some capacity and will this enable me to monitor the business's progress and, hence, my risk?

RETENTION OF PART OF THE PURCHASE PRICE

Retention of part of the purchase price usually arises in the sale of those businesses or professional practices where there is a concern by the buyer that he or she will not retain certain key clients or customers (or not retain an agreed overall annual sales value of clients) and that this will consequently reduce the business's profitability.

For example, the purchaser could agree to buy the business subject to retention of a part of the purchase price for a minimum of 12 months, with the funds to be held in trust by his solicitor for this period. These monies would be released to the seller if sales (or turnover) targets are achieved, or released pro rata if they are partly achieved.

As a seller you must think carefully before agreeing to a retention. Some of the questions you should ask yourself are:

- Is agreement to the retention necessary to complete the sale?
- Is this the best deal I can get? In other words, could I do an equivalent deal with another buyer, who does not require retention?
- Is it reasonable to calculate the value of my business based on gross turnover and, therefore, retention of the clients?
- Would it be fairer to base retention on the overall level of maintainable sales rather than specific key clients, because new clients could compensate for the loss of key clients during the year?
- How likely is it that the business will lose clients and is agreeing to retention a risk worth taking?

DEFERRED PAYMENTS

Deferred payment, or payment on terms, could be advantageous for the seller for all sorts of reasons, although it is likely that taxation will be the main reason why a seller could consider it. The potential taxation advantages of being paid over time need to be compared with the risks involved of not being paid and the pros and cons could be very similar to those for vendor finance. You would need expert advice before you made any firm decisions.

Loan notes are a way of delaying the receipt of consideration, but their terms have to be correctly worded if they are to have taxation advantages. The issues you need to consider are the date of redemption, whether the payment is guaranteed (and the strength of the guarantee), and the rate and frequency of interest payments. This is a complex area and you would need expert advice before you would agree to receiving payment in this way in whole or in part.

RECEIVING SHARES AS CONSIDERATION

With a sale to a plc it is not unusual to be offered some of the consideration in shares of the purchasing company. Accepting the shares could mean receiving a higher notional price (that is, the price on the day the agreement is reached based on the share value on that day), but the big question is what will the shares be worth when you come to sell them? Of course, you hope that they will be worth more, and they might well be, but they could be worth less, and even less than the cash amount you could have received if you had insisted on cash.

You can research a plc to discover such things as the volatility of the share price and the liquidity of the shares. With a private company these questions are just as important, but harder to find out, except that you can be sure liquidity will be a problem with private company shares. The question of what rights attach to the shares being issued to you and how these can be varied will not be too much of a problem with a listed company, but could be crucial with shares in a private company.

EARN-OUTS

This matter has been covered in Chapter 4, but it is worth repeating that where you are selling a business with low asset backing, or one which is predicting strong growth (and whose asking price is based on this growth), an earn out request from a purchaser is not unusual, and acceptance by you might be the only way to achieve a sale at the price you are looking for.

WARRANTIES AND INDEMNITIES

A warranty is an undertaking from a vendor to a purchaser that statements made in the sales contract are correct (usually subject to a 'disclosure undertaking' – see below). An example of this could be that all litigation with the vendor company has been settled. If these undertakings turn out to be incorrect within a specified time, a penalty will be imposed on the vendor. This penalty is usually a financial one. Warranties can be limited individually and in total.

An indemnity is usually a specific recompense matching a financial loss. For example, if an amount stated to be due to the vendor business is not paid within, say, 24 months then the vendor will pay the amount to the purchaser.

A 'disclosure undertaking' is a document that clarifies a general warranty statement. For example it could state that 'the litigation with Smith and Son, who are claiming a refund on damaged goods of £15,000, has yet to be settled'.

COMPLETION ACCOUNTS

A business's net financial position changes every day, so where the purchase consideration is based partly on the net asset position there has to be a 'cut off' date. It is usual for accounts to be drawn up on that date (which are known as 'completion accounts') to finalize the purchase price.

STAYING ON (SERVICE CONTRACTS)

Many business vendors reaching retirement age do not wish to retire completely. They consider that a sale of their business coupled with a part-time job with the new owner is a perfect way to 'phase themselves out' of business life. Others will feel they cannot afford to retire (until perhaps they reach a certain age), while others will be bound to stay on under the sales contract. You might be staying on, for example, to keep an eye on the business because you have lent money to the new owners.

In some cases a puchaser will wish the vendor to stay on and will offer him or her a service contract. This will sometimes be the case where the purchaser is a large organization which does not have the resources to manage the business.

In the case of an extended handover from one owner/manager to another, you should be aware that the relationship between a vendor who stays on and the purchaser is seldom a happy one. Few of these relationships last long and both parties are usually delighted when they are brought to a premature end. If a handover after sale is necessary, it is advisable to keep it as short as possible.

SUMMARY OF STEPS TO PLAN FOR A TRADE SALE

With proper planning for a trade sale you should expect to complete the following steps (see Figure A8.3):

1. All businesses are, on the face of it, suitable for a trade sale, but you need to decide whether a trade sale *is* the optimum exit option as far as your business is concerned.
2. Now decide when you will sell, what is being sold (assets or shares?) and whether you are selling 100 per cent or less of the business.
3. Establish the market value of the business and set a reasonable selling price.
4. Obtain taxation advice on the implications of your plans and your ownership structure as well as addressing your business continuity planning.
5. Update, or produce a new business plan; identify impediments to sale.
6. Groom the business for sale: implement the business plan, improve profitability and remove impediments to sale.
7. Prepare for the sales process, including:
   - (a) Undertaking own due diligence.
   - (b) Preparing memorandum of offer document.
   - (c) Marketing the business.
   - (d) Negotiating final terms.
8. Prepare for the sale itself, which will include:
   - (a) Drawing up heads of agreement (including price, terms of payment, cash or shares as consideration, warranties, etc.).
   - (b) Purchaser's due diligence.
   - (c) Final agreement (including decisions on whether, and for how long, to stay on).

EXCHANGE AND SETTLEMENT

Having completed all the steps above and received your money, the time has come to pay all fees and commissions due and book your holiday to the Bahamas!

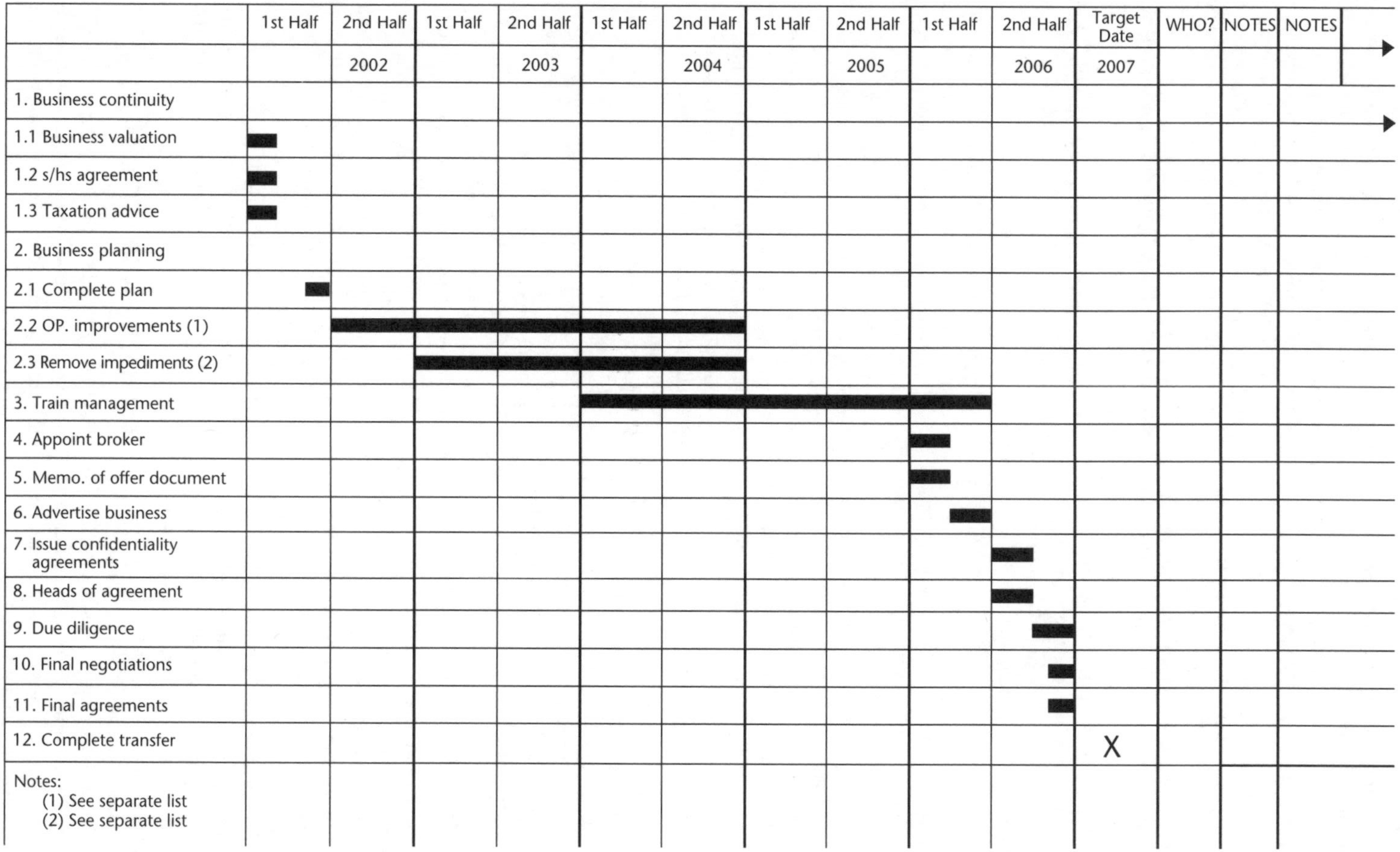

	1st Half	2nd Half	1st Half	2nd Half	1st Half	2nd Half	1st Half	2nd Half	1st Half	2nd Half	Target Date	WHO?	NOTES	NOTES
		2002		2003		2004		2005		2006	2007			
1. Business continuity														
1.1 Business valuation														
1.2 s/hs agreement														
1.3 Taxation advice														
2. Business planning														
2.1 Complete plan														
2.2 OP. improvements (1)														
2.3 Remove impediments (2)														
3. Train management														
4. Appoint broker														
5. Memo. of offer document														
6. Advertise business														
7. Issue confidentiality agreements														
8. Heads of agreement														
9. Due diligence														
10. Final negotiations														
11. Final agreements														
12. Complete transfer											X			
Notes: (1) See separate list (2) See separate list														

Figure A8.3 Master Exit Strategy Plan: Trade Sale

APPENDIX 9

THE SOLE TRADER MERGER

In this appendix we will examine the reasons why a sole trader merger could be a useful exit option for sole traders either in business or in professional practice. (*Note*: by 'sole trader' we do not necessarily mean someone who is the only person in a business, rather we refer to those businesses in which there is only one owner–manager.)

We will look at why sole trader businesses are not usually easy to sell; we consider the ingredients of a successful sole trader merger and the steps involved in planning a successful merger, including drawing up suitable merger and business continuity agreements. Finally, we will alert you to some structural and taxation issues that could be of special relevance to you.

WHY SOLE TRADER BUSINESSES ARE NOT EASY TO SELL

Most sole traders find it difficult to sell their businesses because purchasers are uncertain whether there will be any maintainable income (that is, profit) after the owner leaves. Another way of expressing these fears is to say that purchasers consider sole trader businesses as having no underlying income stream other than that which is generated by the owner's personal exertions. Even larger private companies owned by a single dominant shareholder that employ considerable numbers of support staff may sometimes find it difficult to convince buyers that their businesses have a value other than the value of their net tangible assets.

In particular, the problems sole traders have to overcome when trying to sell their businesses are as follows:

- The owner *is* the business, and there is often little specialized business knowledge, or industry expertise left in the business when he or she leaves.
- There is no middle (or executive) management in the company necessary to assist the purchasers after they have taken over. This is particularly important when the purchasers are from outside the industry and lack industry knowledge.
- The businesses are usually too small to interest professional investors.
- Potential purchasers from the same industry, who could be interested in smaller businesses, are not willing to pay going concern value (or goodwill value) for the business and would prefer to see it close down, so they can pick up the customers and, perhaps, pick up some useful assets at fire sale prices as well.

THE INGREDIENTS OF A SUCCESSFUL SOLE TRADER MERGER

If you are a sole trader and hope to exit in, say, four to six years, one exit option worth examining is a merger with another business like your own. This process, which we call a sole trader merger, is the first stage in a two-stage exit strategy, the second stage of which will see you sell your equity (or the balance of your equity) to your merger partner.

The ingredients for a successful sole trader merger include the following:

- A sole trader in any industry or profession who is planning to exit his or her business within, say, six years, who we will call the 'retiring owner' (although he or she might wish to exit the business for reasons other than retirement).
- A second sole trader from the same industry, or profession who is at least five to 10 years younger than the retiring owner, who we will call the 'acquiring owner'.
- The owners should be personally compatible and have a similar philosophy in the way they do business.
- The acquiring owner must be planning to grow his or her business, and must believe that acquisition through a merger is a viable growth option.
- Both owners must have a realistic opinion of the fair market value of their businesses.
- The retiring owner's business should be of a similar size to, or bigger than, the acquiring owner's business. (Where the retiring owner's business is considerably smaller than the

acquiring owner's business, a straight trade sale might be a simpler option for both parties.)
- Both owners must be confident of the mutual long-term benefits of the proposed merger.

THE STEPS INVOLVED IN PLANNING A MERGER

To plan for a sole trader merger you need to take the following steps (see also Figure A9.1):

- Step 1: find a potential merger partner.
- Step 2: hold initial meetings with the potential merger partner.
- Step 3: establish the ground rules.
- Step 4: enter into agreements, namely:
  - a merger agreement
  - a business continuity agreement.
- Step 5: complete first transfer (and payment for your initial equity, if applicable).
- Step 6: devise your operational strategy.
- Step 7: sell your interests.
- Step 8: implement your exit strategy.

We will now look at these steps in some detail.

STEP 1: FIND A POTENTIAL MERGER PARTNER

As the retiring owner wishing to arrange a sole trader merger, the first thing you need to do is to locate younger owners in the same industry (or profession) who are interested in growth through acquisition. Company brokers, your accountant, or your business advisers, could be a good source of this information, especially if they specialize in your industry.

STEP 2: HOLD INITIAL MEETINGS

Once you have found suitable candidates, you should hold an initial meeting with each of them to explore the possibilities of a merger. These meetings should be informal, although formal undertakings of confidentiality should be exchanged. You should be open about your plans to merge and exchange enough business information to enable both parties to form an initial opinion on the possibilities and opportunities a merger might present. To establish your respective strengths and weaknesses, an informal SWOT analysis of the two businesses should be undertaken. (See Chapter 7 for information on SWOT analysis.)

STEP 3: ESTABLISH THE GROUND RULES

If your initial meeting with any particular potential merger partner has gone well, you should now move on to the next stage, that is, of establishing the ground rules for the merger with this potential partner. The important ground rules are as follows:

Establishing the respective values of the businesses

As the respective valuations of the two businesses can often be a sticking point, it is important to get this issue settled before you go too far down the negotiation path.

The two merging entities will need to be formally valued. As the businesses should be similar in terms of type and industry sector, the same valuation method can be used for both (for example, a price earnings ratio method). The challenge is to agree on what capitalization rate, or 'multiple', should be used for each business. If the businesses were more or less the same size, it would be logical to use the same capitalization rate for both. However, it could be argued that a bigger multiple should be applied to the larger business.

(These valuation issues are fully addressed in Appendix 2 on valuation of private businesses.)

The structure of the merged entity, that is, partnership or company?

You need to decide whether you wish to trade as a partnership, a limited partnership or a limited company. There are many issues here, the most important of which are to limit your personal liability and taxation, and you need to take expert advice on these matters.

The general issue of having the right business structure in exit strategy planning is covered in Chapter 2, while the impact of taxation on disposals is covered in Appendix 1. We will look at some of the particular structural and taxation issues relating to mergers later in this appendix.

The proposed shareholding in the merged entity

There are at least two ways of approaching this. The first is to allocate shares strictly on the basis of the respective value of the two businesses. For example, assuming the merged business is a company, if business A is valued at £200,000 and business B is valued at £400,000, the total value of the merged company is £600,000 and A's owner will

	1st Half	2nd Half	1st Half	2nd Half	1st Half	2nd Half						Target Date		NOTES
		2002		2003		2004	2005	2006	2007	2008	2009	2010		
1. Business continuity														
1.1 Business valuation														
1.2 Taxation advice														
2. Complete business plan														
2.1 OP. improvements (1)														
2.2 Remove impediments (2)														
3. Search for partner														
4. Hold meetings														
5. Heads of agreement														
6. Value both businesses														
7 Decide structure														
8. Merger agreement														
9. Complete 1st payment														
10. Develop business (3)														
11. Complete 2nd payment														
12. Complete final payment														
13. Retire														
Notes: (1) See separate list (2) See separate list (3) See separate business plan												X		

Figure A9.1 Master Exit Strategy Plan: Sole Trader Merger

be allocated one-third of the shares in the merged company and B's owner will be allocated two-thirds of the shares in the merged company.

The other possibility is that the owners will wish to be equal shareholders from the beginning. This will only work where the acquiring partner has the smaller business, because the retiring partner will not wish to expend cash and increase his or her business equity relatively close to retirement. The acquiring partner will pay the retiring partner the amount necessary to bring their shareholding to 50 per cent each. This payment is known as the 'equity balancing payment' and, when made, represents the first stage of the retiring partner's exit strategy plan.

In both cases you can see that agreeing to a fair market value of the business is very important to both parties.

STEP 4: ENTERING INTO AGREEMENTS

Once you have agreed to the ground rules in principle, the next step is to draw up a merger agreement, and a shareholders' (or partnership) agreement, which can also be called a business continuity agreement. It is possible to combine the merger and shareholder agreements into one.

The merger agreement

The merger agreement will address the commercial aspects of the merger, including:

- What assets from each business are being merged?
- What sort of business entity, that is partnership or company?
- What is the value of these assets?
- What will be the shareholding in the merged entity?
- If shareholding is to be 50:50, and if the respective business assets are not equal in value, how and when will the equity balancing amount be paid?
- What duties for what monetary return, (for example, salaries, commission splits, dividends will the principals undertake?
- What is the company's policy to be on such things as motor vehicles, business expenses, entertainment, and so on?

The business continuity agreement

For retiring owners, the business continuity agreement covers the second stage of their exit strategy plan, namely, agreement to buy the balance of their equity. However, looked at more broadly from the perspective of both owners, the agreement should govern the circumstances that might lead to the termination of the arrangements between the co-owners and/or the break-up of the merged business, and what will happen to the ownership of the shares or interests in these circumstances. These circumstances will include retirement of the retiring owner, the death or disability of either owner, or merely a falling out between co-owners leading to a desire to split up. The desired result of any of these circumstances is that there will be a purchase of the interests of one owner by the other at a pre-agreed price and that funding will have been put in place to cover the purchase price. The agreement could also include provisions that compel the minority shareholder to sell his or her interests to a bona fide purchaser of the business at fair market value if the majority shareholder wishes to sell his or her interests.

(A detailed discussion of business continuity agreements is to be found in Chapter 2, which you should consult.)

Matters of particular interest in business continuity agreements for sole trader mergers are the following:

1. For retiring owners, the agreement to purchase their interests on retirement is the culmination of their exit strategy plan. Arrangements should be as watertight as possible and solid commercial grounds should exist for believing that the acquiring owner will be able to complete the purchase.
2. The question of how to treat the potential growth in value of the business while it is a merged entity managed by both owners can be a difficult issue. The matters to be considered are as follows:
   (a) The continuity agreement will usually contain a valuation formula (such as an agreed multiple for capitalization of after-tax profits) by which the business is to be valued at various times, or on the happening of various events. Should the profitability of the business grow, its value will also grow.
   (b) In the normal course, business owners strive for growth in profitability, because this leads to larger dividend payouts and higher value for their equity. For retiring owners in the merged entity, any growth

in value of the business should result in a higher price being paid for the balance of their interests in the businesses.

(c) But, acquiring owners have a dilemma: where a valuation formula is included in the agreement, the harder they work to build the merged business's profitability and value, the more they will have to pay the retiring owners for their shares (although, of course, the acquiring owners' shares will also increase in value proportionally).

There are various ways of approaching this problem. Assuming for the sake of the examples below that projected annual after-tax profits of the merged company are in the order of £150,000 to £200,000. Assume also that the aim of the agreed valuation formula is to establish a true market value for the business, by capitalizing future after-tax profits by a factor of six. There are now three ways of looking at the issue, namely:

(i) use the agreed valuation formula to calculate future value, but cap (or limit) the value at an agreed maximum amount of, say, £1.2 million, or

(ii) use the agreed formula only until an agreed value is reached and then use a lesser one. For example, apply a multiple of six on profits of up to £200,000 per annum (which would give the value of £1.2 million), and then apply a multiple of four on profits over £200,000. This retains an incentive for both owners: the acquiring owner can still build the business comfortable in the knowledge that the amount he or she has to pay out on retirement of the retiring owner is less than market value, while his or her own shares have increased by market value, or

(iii) set a fixed value for the retiring agent's shares in advance, regardless of future profits. This arrangement has a large element of risk for each party, depending on what value is set and what the realistic growth prospects of the business are. It could also be seen as giving the retiring owner no incentive to help in building the value of the merged business.

3. The co-owners in the merged entity will, in most cases, not know each other particularly well and there will be concerns about whether they will be compatible. Because of this it might be wise to include some form of trial period in the agreement, while it is certainly prudent to include provisions that facilitate an easy split of the business in the early stages.

STEP 5: COMPLETE THE FIRST TRANSFER (AND PAYMENT FOR YOUR INITIAL EQUITY, IF APPLICABLE)

You should now receive payment for the initial transfer of equity to the acquiring owner, if a transfer is to take place at this stage – see step 7, below for expansion on this.

STEP 6: DEVISE YOUR OPERATIONAL STRATEGY

You are now in a position to turn your attention to how the business is going to run, so your next step is to prepare an operational strategy or business plan for the merged business.

(*Note*: some owners might wish to address strategy issues before they sign the final merger agreements. Others might prefer to wait so that they do not waste too much time on business strategies and business plans before they have a firm agreement on the merger. We believe it is a matter of degree: there should be general agreement on strategy before you enter into agreements, but you do not want to spend too much time on the detail until you are certain that the deal is going ahead.)

The business continuity agreement would have covered the buy/sell arrangements between the co-owners and the merger agreement should cover the business arrangements, responsibilities and rewards between owners, including such things as who will undertake which tasks, salaries and dividends to be paid, motor vehicles, business expenses, entertainment and so on, but would not usually address operational planning.

During your initial meetings when you were considering the merits of the proposed merger (and when you should have conducted SWOT analyses of the respective businesses) you should have considered in general terms the broad strategy of the merged business. Your planning now concerns both the strategy for the proposed merged entity and the detailed planning issues or 'things to do' of an in-depth business plan. You should consider such things as staffing, marketing, premises requirements, financing and operating systems in your plan. The plan should also look beyond the purchase of the retiring partner's shares to the acquiring partners own exit strategy plan.

(The basic approach to strategic and business planning is explained in Chapter 7 to which you should refer.)

STEP 7: SALE OF YOUR INTERESTS

This step involves the sale of your interests to the acquiring owner. Usually, it is accomplished in two stages as follows:

The initial purchase

Sometimes, there will be no initial purchase (either because both businesses have the same value, or because the owners are happy to be in an unequal shareholding). Or there will be an initial purchase to arrive at an equal shareholding: where this is so, it would constitute step 5.

Although the initial purchase will usually be made at the time of the merger, payment for the shares or interests can, by agreement, be made at any time. Indeed, there could be a series of payments over a long period from the acquiring owner to the retiring owner, enabling the retiring owner to progressively quit his or her equity, and thus easing the financial burden on the acquiring owner.

The final purchase

This envisages, at the time of retirement, the sale of the balance of the retiring owner's interests to the acquiring owner, thus completing the retiring owner's exit strategy plan under the business continuity agreement. Again, payment terms can be negotiated to suit both parties.

In the case of the death or disability of retiring owners before the planned retirement date, the agreement could provide for an immediate transfer of the remaining equity to the acquiring owners and either an immediate payment to the retiring owners or their estates (particularly if it had been possible to adequately insure the retiring owner for death or disability); where, perhaps, no funding for the particular contingency is in place.

STEP 8: IMPLEMENT YOUR EXIT STRATEGY

With agreement to purchase their interests (and, hopefully, funding for most contingencies in place), retiring owners have an almost watertight exit strategy plan in place, while acquiring owners have the ability to plan for their acquisition with some certainty. Both parties must realize, however, that there is still a possibility that the plan will not work out entirely as planned.

The practical problems that can occur in these sorts of arrangements include the two owners not working well together in business or not getting on personally. It is as well to recognize that it may be necessary to unwind the merger and return to the status quo.

The prime intention of the merger and the continuity agreements is to bring certainty to the exit of retiring owners although, of course, it could achieve the same result for acquiring owners should they die or become disabled during the time the merged business is co-owned.

STRUCTURAL AND TAXATION ISSUES

The issues that are particularly important from the point of view of CGT include how assets are owned (that is, personally or by a company); for how long the assets have been owned; and the nature of the business (that is, is it a trading or investment business?). Income tax considerations include the respective rates of tax on salaries and wages compared with dividends and, indeed, whether to distribute accumulated profits as capital or income? These can be complex matters, and expert advice that takes account of your personal circumstances and your overall retirement planning should be sought.

The structure of the merged business could also be important from the point of view of personal liability. As you will be entering into a new arrangement with a co-owner, you will probably wish to protect yourself from your co-owner's and the business's liabilities. A limited company, or a limited partnership will achieve this aim, whereas there might be administrative and compliance reasons for considering a traditional partnership. Once more, you should take expert advice on these issues.

STAYING ON

The advantage of a merger is that it provides flexibility for the retiring partner in such areas as how to receive payment and how long to stay in the business. Even after the final sale of equity, the retiring partner could stay on as an employee of the business if this was mutually agreed (and this would depend on how the partners had got on together) and if the retiring partner so wished. There are many ways that this could be handled in the agreement, but the best practical way is to leave it open and see how the partners find working together and how the health and drive of the retiring partner holds out.

ABILITY TO OPT OUT

The strategy for sole trader mergers is simple enough: it is the implementation that presents practical difficulties. The major problem for the retiring owner is to find a suitable merger partner. Having found a potential merger candidate, it is then necessary to overcome the difficulties that can arise with a business marriage where different people have different views on how things should be done. The main differences that arise in most mergers and the ones that need to be overcome if you are to have a successful merged business are probably the following:

- different business strategies
- different working styles
- different business cultures
- different attitudes to owners' salaries and benefits
- different views on business values.

It is worth perservering to overcome these problems, because the sole trader merger might be the only way you are going to realize a goodwill value for your business, as your alternative exit options could be very limited. However, you must be realistic about the potential problems in mergers and ensure that your agreement has provision for a split up if things do not work to plan. One way is to have an option in the agreement that allows the acquiring partner to buy out the retiring partner before the date originally contemplated.

SOLE TRADER MERGER: THE ONLY WAY OUT?

By following the information in this appendix and the steps which are summarized in the earlier section, you should be able first, to, decide whether your business is suitable for a sole trader merger and, second, plan effectively for this form of exit. In some businesses a sole trader merger will be the best exit option, while in others it might be the only one. Small businesses that rely on the personal expertise of one person are notoriously difficult to sell, but a sole trader merger can overcome this obstacle and for some business owners provides the optimum exit strategy.

APPENDIX 10

CEASING TO TRADE

A DISCLAIMER

This appendix considers the circumstances in which solvent businesses might choose cessation of trade as an exit option in preference to the other options discussed in this book and provides an example of an MESP for ceasing to trade (Figure A10.1). For completeness, it looks briefly at the question of insolvency of companies, sole traders and partnerships, but it does not purport to give any legal advice about the many complex issues that revolve around the question of company insolvency and sole trader (or partnership) bankruptcy. For advice in this important aspect of business, owners and directors should consult a licensed insolvency practitioner.

IMPORTANT DISTINCTIONS

The important distinctions that must be understood by owners and directors are, first, those between companies and unincorporated businesses (that is, sole traders and partnerships) and, second, those between solvent businesses and insolvent ones.

COMPANIES AND UNINCORPORATED BUSINESSES

The law on company insolvency is derived from the Insolvency Act 1986 (as amended), and the Company Directors Disqualification Act 1986 (as amended) which deal with, among many other things, the responsibilities of directors in insolvency situations.

A company is a separate legal entity from its shareholders (also known as 'members') and its directors, whose assets are, in theory, free from creditor claims when a company becomes insolvent. In practice, however, particularly in small businesses, because of the securities and guarantees required by lenders, many company owners and directors find themselves in severe financial difficulties when their companies are put into liquidation. In this sector of the market the theory that the 'corporate veil' provides directors and shareholders with protection is becoming more and more of a theory and less and less of a reality.

The law concerning insolvency of individuals and partnerships in business is also derived from the 1986 legislation. There is no distinction in the legislation between a sole trader's business assets and his or her non-business assets because a sole trader business is legally indistinguishable from the person who owns it. With sole traders and partnerships there is no 'corporate veil', even in theory, to shield an individual from his or her business disasters.

SOLVENT OR INSOLVENT?

If the directors of a company believe it is insolvent they have an obligation to either recapitalize the company; or to enter into a voluntary arrangement with creditors (see below); or to cease to incur further credit (which effectively means ceasing to trade); or to wind it up. In these circumstances the question of selling assets before ceasing to trade, which is discussed in this appendix, does not apply. We will look at how directors might reach the conclusion that a company is insolvent later in this appendix.

Where sole traders decide that their businesses are insolvent, there is no legal obligation on them to cease trading, although one would expect that, for their own economic well-being and peace of mind, they would take every step possible to reduce their deficit through returning to profitability or ceasing their business.

CEASING TO TRADE: A LAST RESORT?

Choosing to close down a business after an orderly sale of its assets only (and not attempting to reap any going concern or goodwill value for the business) might seem to be a failure of planning: a failure by the owner to maximize a business's exit value. In most cases where this happens we believe this is true, but there are circumstances in which ceasing to trade could be a positive exit strategy, or at least a strategy no worse than any other. This appendix will examine these circumstances.

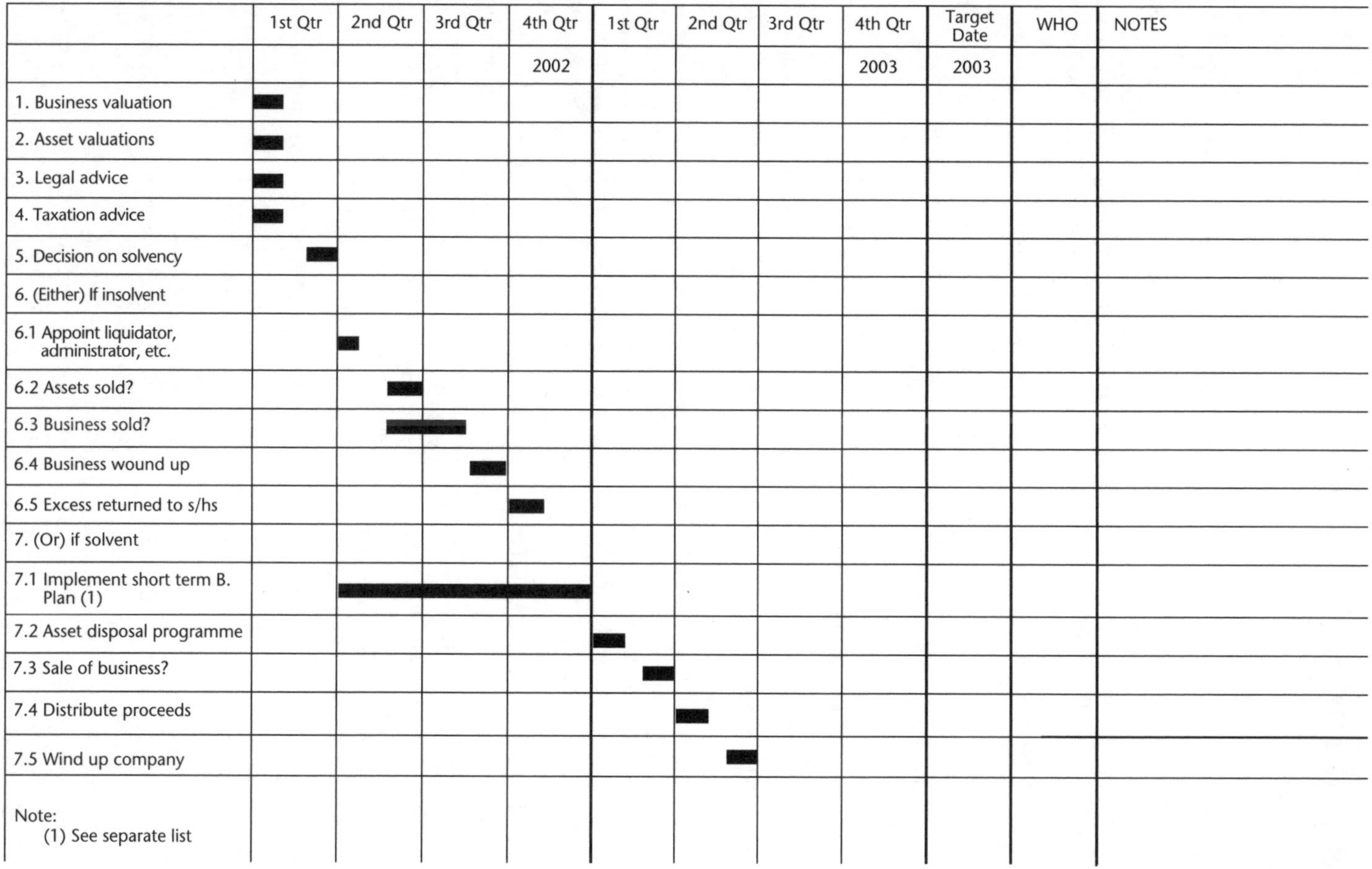

	1st Qtr	2nd Qtr	3rd Qtr	4th Qtr	1st Qtr	2nd Qtr	3rd Qtr	4th Qtr	Target Date	WHO	NOTES
				2002				2003	2003		
1. Business valuation											
2. Asset valuations											
3. Legal advice											
4. Taxation advice											
5. Decision on solvency											
6. (Either) If insolvent											
6.1 Appoint liquidator, administrator, etc.											
6.2 Assets sold?											
6.3 Business sold?											
6.4 Business wound up											
6.5 Excess returned to s/hs											
7. (Or) if solvent											
7.1 Implement short term B. Plan (1)											
7.2 Asset disposal programme											
7.3 Sale of business?											
7.4 Distribute proceeds											
7.5 Wind up company											
Note: (1) See separate list											

Figure A10.1 Master Exit Strategy Plan: Ceasing to Trade

It is important to note that where a solvent company chooses a close-down as an exit option, it is preferable to dispose of the assets before liquidating the company, rather than liquidating the company before the assets are sold. The fact that a business is under some form of official appointment (or has ceased to trade) never helps the sale value of its assets.

DIRECTORS' RESPONSIBILITIES

If the directors of a company believe that the company is insolvent and they continue to trade while taking none of the remedial actions mentioned in 'Solvent or insolvent?' above, they could be guilty of wrongful trading. There are several issues, some of which overlap, to be taken into account by directors in deciding whether their company is insolvent but, unfortunately, there is no legal definition of insolvency.

One issue to consider is whether a company is able to pay its debts as and when they fall due, or able to reach agreement on their payment or to provide acceptable security for them and, if not, whether directors knew or concluded that there was no reasonable prospect that this situation would improve in the near future.

Another consideration is whether the value of a company's liabilities exceeds the value of its assets. On a pure net asset test a company might be technically insolvent, but it can continue to trade quite legally if has the finance available to pay its current debts, or has made suitable arrangements with its creditors for payment, and has good reason to believe that its prospects will improve. The converse is also true; some businesses could appear to have strong net assets (perhaps because of overvaluation of such things as intangibles or intercompany receivables) but still fall into cash flow difficulties and, as a result, be wound up. The sad fact that many business owners discover is that assets are not cash, and without cash (or access to finance) you sometimes cannot continue to trade.

The decision that directors need to make regarding solvency is important for at least two reasons. First, the onus is on directors to make a determination on solvency on a continuing basis (and to take the remedial action described above, if necessary) so as to avoid any possible legal action for wrongful trading. Second, the way in which a company is wound up is dependent, among other things, on whether or not it is solvent.

Before we consider the circumstances in which an owner might in a solvent company choose to cease trading and then liquidate a company as an exit strategy, we will look briefly at the ways in which companies are placed under various forms of official legal appointment.

LEGAL APPOINTMENTS

COMPANIES

There are broadly two types of business creditors: secured or unsecured. Their nature depends on whether or not the creditor has security over the assets of the business to support its debt. Actions by unsecured creditors of a company can lead to the appointment of a liquidator (usually following a legal default by the debtor), while action by secured creditors can lead to the appointment of a Receiver or an Administrative Receiver. We will look at these appointments in more detail below.

Voluntary arrangements

Where the directors of an insolvent company feel there may be a prospect of a viable future but need time, capital and the support of creditors to enable this to be effected, they can try to avoid liquidation or receivership by attempting to reach a compromise with creditors through a company voluntary arrangement (CVA). This procedure is laid down in the Insolvency Act 1986. Such a scheme may be preceded by an administration order of the court where protection against initially hostile creditors is sought. New legislation coming into force in 2002 will allow a short moratorium against all creditors so that time is available to prepare the compromise proposal to put to creditors. Directors in this position should seek the assistance of a licensed insolvency practitioner.

Receivership appointments and administration orders

Under the Law of Property Act (LPA), the holder of a fixed charge over an asset can appoint an LPA receiver over that asset. The receiver's duty will usually be to secure and sell the asset to pay off the charge holder. If there is a surplus after costs it will be paid back to the company.

If a fixed and floating charge exists over the whole or substantially the whole of the company's property then, in the event of a default on the terms of the charge, an 'administrative receiver' (usually just known as the receiver) can be appointed at the behest of the debenture holder. The procedure is set out in the Insolvency Act 1986. Like the LPA receiver, the administrative receiver's duty is to the debenture holder, but the administrative receiver can carry on the business with a view to selling it as a going concern. Unsecured creditors cannot stop this and they will eventually have to make a claim in the subsequent liquidation of the company.

The law is changing and the administrative receiver will soon become a thing of the past. It seems likely that sometime soon the administrative receivership process will be replaced by a court-driven formal administration order, but its effect will be similar to the administrative receivership process as the financial rights of secure creditors will not be compromised.

Liquidation

There are three forms of company liquidation, namely a members' voluntary liquidation (MVL), creditors' voluntary liquidation (CVL) and compulsory liquidation.

An MVL is only appropriate where the company is solvent. The directors of the company, who have to swear a declaration of solvency, initiate the liquidation process. A liquidator of the directors' choice is appointed and the directors have a strong influence on the whole process, although the liquidator is legally in charge. The liquidator's task is to realize the company's assets, pay all creditors within 12 months and return the surplus to shareholders.

If the directors consider the company to be insolvent and unable to be rescued by one of the actions mentioned above, they should contact a licensed insolvency practitioner who will advise them on the statutory steps to be taken to put the company into creditors' voluntary liquidation. This involves the calling of meetings of both members and creditors. The members themselves initially put the company into liquidation and appoint a liquidator, but the meeting of creditors, which usually follows immediately after the members' meeting, has the final say as to who shall be the liquidator.

Compulsory liquidation comes about when a creditor petitions the court to make an order that the company be wound up compulsorily. A petition would not normally be heard until after a statutory demand had been issued and remained unsatisfied for 21 days. If the order is made the effect is immediate and initial control of the company, now in liquidation, passes to the official receiver. At a later date a private sector liquidator is likely to be appointed either by a meeting of creditors called by the official receiver, or by direct appointment by the Secretary of State.

In both cases of insolvent liquidation the liquidator acts for all the creditors, trying to obtain the best return for them from the disposal of the company's assets. Any surplus after payment of the liquidator's costs and expenses and the creditors claims is returned to the company's shareholders.

SOLE TRADERS AND PARTNERSHIPS

An individual is declared bankrupt rather than going into liquidation. An LPA receiver can be appointed over an asset of sole traders or partnerships.

Individuals can try to avoid bankruptcy by reaching compromises with their creditors. These compromises include an individual voluntary arrangement (IVA) and a partnership voluntary arrangement (PVA). As with companies, these procedures have a statutory general framework within the insolvency legislation and, if you have any concerns about your situation, you should seek expert advice from a licensed insolvency practitioner.

SOME IMPORTANT PRINCIPLES

There are some important principles that business owners need to understand when considering cessation of trade as a possible preferred exit option.

THE DISTINCTION BETWEEN SELLING A COMPANY AND SELLING ITS ASSETS

A business can either be sold as a whole (that is, with all its assets, business name, staff, undertakings and so on, being transferred to the buyer), or a business can sell specific assets only (sometimes together with specified liabilities also being transferred to the purchaser).

An example of a complete sale is where shareholders sell all of the company's shares, effectively transferring ownership of the whole business to the purchaser of the shares. In these circumstances ownership of all the company's assets and liabilities is transferred. Where a purchaser does not wish to acquire certain company assets or liabilities, the company will need either to dispose of or settle these before the sale is completed.

The second example comes about where a business or company sells only specific assets that it owns (and in a company's case no shares in the company itself change hands). Such a sale might not represent the sale of the business itself (which might continue to trade under the original owner), or could represent a sale of the business (which will now trade under new ownership).

GOODWILL IN CLOSE DOWNS

In Appendix 2, we explained that where a business has a value in excess of its net asset value, this value is usually goodwill. Goodwill value can sometimes be seen as the extra value that attaches to a business due to the business's ability to generate profits over and above the income represented by a reasonable salary for its owners. These profits are sometimes known as 'super profits'. A business cannot generate a profit if it is closed down and, consequently, goodwill only attaches to a business when it is a going concern. When going concern status is lost, goodwill value is also lost.

THE VALUE OF ASSETS IN LIQUIDATION

The value of tangible assets (such as plant and machinery) working together as a group in a business that is still trading is likely to be considerably higher than the value of the same assets sold individually at auction (or under 'fire sale' conditions) after the business has ceased to trade. The fact that a company is in liquidation seems to diminish the value of the assets even further.

CHOOSING AN ORDERLY WIND-DOWN AS AN EXIT OPTION

In view of the usual effect that closing down a business has on its goodwill and asset values, it would seem that, all other things being equal, this would be the last exit option any business owner would choose. But there are exceptions.

Sometimes owners might decide that continuing a business, or trying to sell it for a capital sum, is not worth the bother and, consequently, close it down. This could occur where a business is marginally profitable and the owners no longer have the will to battle on because, perhaps, they are unable to agree on how the business is to be run or are unable to work together for personal reasons.

Sometimes, because they have not planned for an exit, the directors of a solvent company might decide that an orderly sale of business assets followed by a winding-up of the company itself is no worse than any other exit strategy available to them (and may be simpler in execution than any other), and may, indeed, have taxation advantages.

Finally, some business owners might decide that, because they do not have time for a long-term exit strategy to solve the business's exit problems (that is, to remove the major impediments to sale), a close-down is their optimum exit option, and they will implement a short-term exit strategy around this option. These circumstances could include the following:

1. Where the value of the business as a going concern is less than the value of its assets (should these assets be sold separately from the business).

   The best way to explain this is to give an example. Let us assume that an earth-moving business makes an after-tax profit of £500,000 and the industry standard is to value it by applying a p/e ratio of 6. Let us assume also that the plant and equipment on its books have a written-down value of £4.5 million (and this reflects reasonable market value) and other assets and liabilities cancel each other out, thus giving the business a total net asset value of £4.5 million. The business is likely to sell for a price of £3 million (£500,000 ×6), while its net asset value is £4.5 million. Another way of expressing this is to say that the business has negative goodwill of £1.5 million. Negative goodwill is not uncommon in 'asset top heavy' businesses, and is the cause of a great deal of concern for many business owners as they approach exit.

   Assuming that the owners do not have sufficient time to build business profitability before exiting, they could approach this dilemma in one of two ways.

   (a) Where some of the assets are not necessary for the production of the business's income, these surplus assets could be sold separately from the business in an attempt to achieve the £4.5 million price.
   (b) Where the business does require all its assets to generate its income, the assets only could be sold and the business closed down. This latter approach is, of course, classic 'asset stripping'.

2. Where the value of the business is no greater than the value of the assets. Examples of this include the following:
   (a) Where a business's ability to earn an income is totally reliant on the owner's personal skills and experience, so that when he or she leaves the business it has no going concern (or goodwill) value over and above what can be realized for its assets.
   (b) The business is in an industry that has no economic future, because of such things as changes to laws or regulations, or other macroeconomic circumstances and, consequently, it has no value as a business *per se*.
   (c) Regardless of all the owner's attempts, the business cannot be disposed of and the owner is forced to sell the assets.

SELLING TO AVOID INSOLVENCY

Where directors have any concerns over insolvency they should seek immediate legal advice (or the advice of a licensed insolvency practitioner) concerning their possible liabilities should the company continue to trade. If, after receiving the advice, they form the opinion that the company is insolvent and there are no immediate prospects of reversing this situation, they are under a legal obligation not to incur further debt. In practice this means they have the choice of entering into an arrangement, recapitalizing the company, or liquidating it.

Where directors have formed the opinion that the company might be insolvent and they still attempt to sell its assets, the important thing is to ensure that the proceeds of the sale exceed the company liabilities (or, put another way, that the net proceeds are positive.) If this happens the company will not have been insolvent after all. But you will need to proceed with caution, because a company teetering on the edge of insolvency is unlikely to command much goodwill value (particularly if its insolvency has arisen because of trading losses) and hence the chance of the sale proceeds meeting all its liabilities could be small. The usual result of the sale of companies on the brink of insolvency is that their assets are sold at 'fire-sale' prices, which will effectively be a liquidation sale in everything but name.

CLOSE DOWN: ONLY A SHORT-TERM PLAN

Where a business owner recognizes that his business as a whole is worth less than its asset value, the first course of action he should consider is a plan to rectify the problems that cause this to be so. It is only when the business owner finds it impossible to embark on a recovery plan (either long term or short term) that the option of accepting liquidation as the optimum exit strategy should be explored.

If directors decide on an MVL, it is important that they stay closely involved in the process, bearing in mind always that the liquidator is legally in charge. Asset disposals should be undertaken in an orderly a way as possible to avoid 'fire sale' discounts.

Expert advice must be taken before you go down this route.

STEPS INVOLVED IN COMPANIES CEASING TO TRADE

If you are considering ceasing to trade we suggest you take the following steps:

1. Directors should obtain expert advice on the solvency of the company and whether it can legally continue to trade while you plan your short-term exit strategy through an orderly sell-off of assets and a close-down. Directors also need to check their position regarding any potential personal liability. (If the advice is that your company is insolvent, you need to take one of the remedial actions described above.)
2. If your expert's advice is that you are not breaking the law by continuing to trade, establish whether the company currently has a goodwill value and, if not, what needs to be done to make it saleable as a going concern to restore or create goodwill value.
3. If you decide that goodwill value can be created, consider how long this will take and whether you have the time available to do it. (If you have enough time, you should embark on a long-term plan to groom your business for exit through the optimum exit route.)
4. If there is no hope of creating goodwill value by improving your company's trading position or by removing its impediments to sale, or if you do not have enough time necessary for this, you will be left with the options of a short-term exit plan, or an orderly close-down strategy.
5. Contact those who specialize in disposal of the particular kind of assets that your company owns (usually, auctioneers and valuers) and ask them to value the assets on both a 'fire sale'

and going concern basis. This will enable you to decide what needs to be sold (and the likely basis of the sale) and, therefore, to gauge whether the sale proceeds will meet all the company's liabilities.

6. Get advice from a licensed insolvency practitioner as to whether the act of selling the assets before you close down the company is likely to have caused a breach of the law concerning wrongful trading, or whether the sale could be interpreted as a transaction at under value, or subsequently treated as a preference.
7. If you are assured that you will not be breaking the law, you can now embark on an orderly disposal of the company's assets and a probable subsequent liquidation of the company. You should ensure that you have expert legal, taxation, accounting and insolvency advice during the whole process.

SUMMARY

An owner-managed sell-off of business assets followed by a close-down would usually be the least preferred of the exit options discussed in this book. However, in some cases an owner-managed sell-off might be the best option (for example, when asset values exceed business value), or as good as any other option (for example, where going concern status is irrelevant to value) and you are advised to take such a course rather than allowing inaction to lead you to potential insolvency, a winding-up and a fire sale.

Where a company or business is solvent, the disposal of assets after close-down or liquidation should be avoided if at all possible, because of the detrimental effect this is likely to have on all asset values.

Where a business is insolvent and the owners are unwilling or unable to put new capital into it, or unable to reach an arrangement with creditors, or are unable to return the company to solvency in the short term, the practical effect is that the company will need to be wound up immediately and any chance of managing the exit to extract maximum value for shareholders will be lost.

USEFUL WEB SITES

The following web sites contain a wealth of information of use to the private business owner:

EXIT STRATEGY PLANNING

www.exitstrategyplanning.com
The web site of Exit Strategies Limited of whom the author is a director, which provides articles, case studies, opinions and associated information on exit strategy planning.
www.fambiz.com
An American site devoted to family business issues, including family succession planning.
www.bizroadmap.com
An excellent American small business site covering topics from start-ups to exit planning.
www.zedbc.co.uk
Useful site for start-ups, business sales and exit strategy planning.

EXIT OPTIONS

www.british-franchise.org.uk
The web site for the British Franchise Association containing information for both intending franchisors and franchisees.
www.londonstockexchange.com
The LSE provides comprehensive information on listing on both the Main Board and the AIM. It also provides an excellent CD on the listing process.
www.ofex.com
Information on how to join OFEX.
www.fsa.gov.uk/ukla
The UK Listing Authority's site.

LISTS

www.etrex.com
This site provides a list of the web addresses of various associations, groups, government bodies, and so on.
www.scitsc.wlv.ac.uk/ukinfo/ ac/working.alpha
This site provides a list of UK universities and colleges.

BUSINESS ORGANISATIONS

www.iod.com
The Institute of Directors' web site.
www.cbi.org.uk
The Confederation Of British Industry's site. Comprehensive and has an excellent business links page.
www.inst.mgt.org.uk
The Institute of Management's web site.
www.fsb.org.uk
The web site for the Federation of Small Business.
www.britishchambers.org.uk
The British Chambers of Commerce web site provides you with contact information for your local Chamber.

GOVERNMENT

www.dti.gov.uk
Home page for Department of Trade and Industry.
www.sbs.gov.uk
The government's Small Business Service web site.
www.businesslink.org
Businesslink site and linked to regional sites throughout England.
For Scotland go to: **www.sbgateway.com**
For Wales go to: **www.businessconnect.org. uk**
For Ireland go to: **www.ednet-ni.com**
www.onlineforbusiness.gov.uk
Have a look and decide for yourself what this is all about! Includes information on grants.
www.inlandrevenue.gov.uk/index/htm
The Inland Revenue web site provides a comprehensive source of information on all taxation issues, most of which can be downloaded free from the site.
www.companies-house.gov.uk
The web site for Companies House, which provides services and regulates UK companies.
www.open.gov.uk
The easy way to find government information and services online.
www.oft.gov.uk
The Office of Fair Trading's site.
www.tec.co.uk
The Training and Enterprise Council's site.

MISCELLANEOUS

www.igpcorporate.co.uk
An excellent on-line facility for incorporating new companies.
www.nfea.com
The National Federation of Enterprise Agencies provides support for business start-ups.

FINANCE AND VENTURE CAPITAL

www.bvca.co.uk
The web site of the British Venture Capital Association.
www.venture-finance.co.uk and
www.nationalbusinessangels.co.uk
Information on private funding.
www.ukishelp.co.uk
A starting point for discovering what funding is available from the European Union.
www.dti.gov.uk/europe/structural
This section of the DTI's site gives you information on the structural funds that are available to SMEs in depressed areas.
www.dti.gov.uk/enterprisegrant
Information from the DTI on enterprise grants.
www. businessangels-london.co.uk
Provides comprehensive information on how to raise venture capital.
www.factors.org.uk
Provides a full list of companies offering factoring.

ELECTRONIC NEWSPAPERS

www.ft.com
An excellent newspaper site provided by the *Financial Times*.
www.enterprisenetwork.co.uk
The web site for *The Sunday Times* Enterprise Network.
www.economist.com
The Economist magazine's web site.
www.telegraph.co.uk
The electronic *Telegraph*.

Index